Manual Labour

IN

S. THOMÉ AND PRINCIPE.

BY

FRANCIS MANTERO.

Translated from the Portuguese.

NEGRO UNIVERSITIES PRESS

NEW YORK

Originally published in 1910: Lisbon

Reprinted 1969 by
Negro Universities Press
A DIVISION OF GREENWOOD PUBLISHING CORP.
NEW YORK

SBN 8371-2035-7

PRINTED IN UNITED STATES OF AMERICA

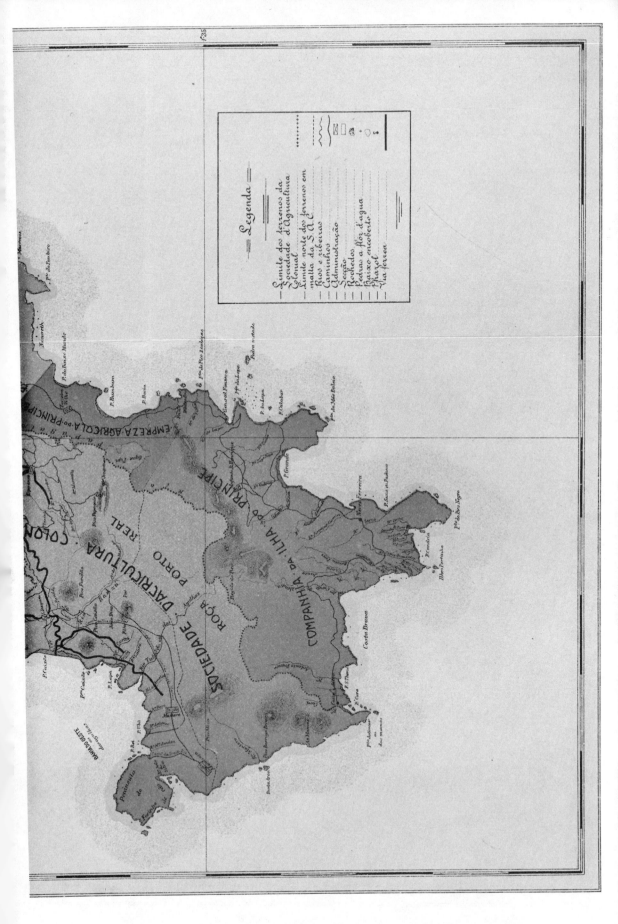

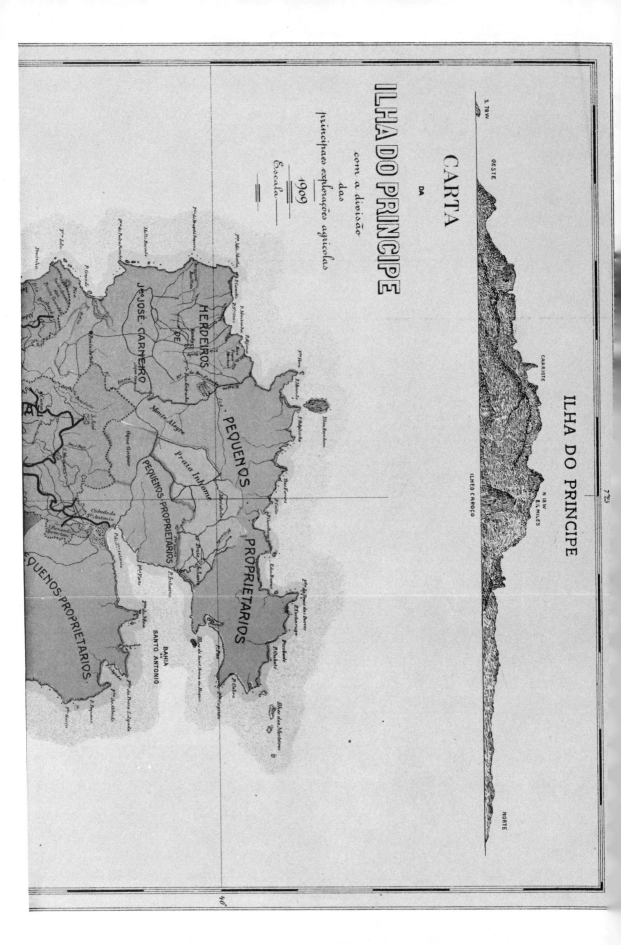

H. R. H. The Crown Prince Louis Philip

Who visited the Island of S. Thomé in July 1907

Lisbon, 20th February 1910.

To His Excellency, Conselheiro Francisco Felisberto Dias Costa.

Dear Sir

Your Excellency honoured me by suggesting my appointment as member of the Sub-Committee entrusted with replying to the series of questions regarding Colonial manual labour, and further expressed the particular wish that I should undertake the part specially relating to the Province of S. Thomé and Principe.

At the meeting held on the 9th November ult., my esteemed colleagues in the Sub-Committee expressed the same desire.

Therefore, notwithstanding my incompetency, I had no option but to accept this honourable task and endeavour to fulfil it to the best of my abilities.

After studying the questions, a vast and interesting collection of information, I decided to satisfy, as far as possible, their varied exigencies.

In my opinion, however, the special question of manual labour in S. Thomé, which the vexatious campaigns of some Englishmen, either unfriendly, or unacquainted with our nation, have raised to the category of a question of universal interest, requires more elucidation than can be contained in a work intended for a special purpose, and, therefore, the moment is opportune for making some statement in defence of the most Portuguese, as well as the most progressive of our Colonies.

This reasoning gave rise to the idea, which I at once put into practice, of writing some notes prefaced by this letter, constituting a separate work, to which, duly sanctioned, is joined the series of questions referred to, together with their respective answers. The work has no merit beyond the good will employed in its compilation, nor any further aspiration than that of rendering some service to the nation, and contributing to enlighten national and foreign opinion on a subject of vital interest to our economic prosperity at home, and to the good name of our beloved country abroad.

For more than ten years Your Excellency, as Director-general of the Colonial Department, has accompanied the economic development of the Province of S. Thomé and Principe; for more than ten years, we, the planters of that Pro-

vince, have received from Your Excellency encouragement for our work, protection for our rights, and justice for our cause; for more than ten years the noble spirit, enlightened intelligence, austere character and patriotic action of Your Excellency have made themselves beneficially felt in our, to-day, wealthy Province of S. Thomé and Principe.

Allow me, therefore, dear Friend, as the humblest assistant in the erection of that magnificent monument of civilisation constructed by Portuguese labour in Africa, which exists for the glory of those who built it, and which will continue to exist for the perpetuation amongst future generations of the good name, ever humanitarian and honourable, of our dear old Portugal, allow me, I repeat, publicly to manifest the great appreciation and high esteem in which I hold Your Excellency and your most valuable services rendered to the progress of S. Thomé, by requesting Your Excellency to accept the dedication of this unpretentious work.

By so doing, Your Excellency will add one more claim to the gratitude of

Your most devoted, grateful and affectionate Friend

Francisco Mantero.

Conselheiro Francisco Dias Costa

Head of the Colonial Department (1899 to 1910), under whose auspices was initiated
the emigration of labourers from Cape Verde and Mozambique to S. Thomé.
Minister of Marine and the Colonies, 1897 to 1898, and actually Minister of the Interior

CHAPTER I.

Brief Historical and Agricultural Notes.

The Province of S. Thomé and Principe, to which formerly belonged the Islands of Fernando Pó and Anno Bom, (discovered by Portuguese navigators in 1778 and handed over to His Catholic Majesty's Government) consists of the Island of S. Thomé and circumjacent islets, the Island of Principe, also surrounded by some rocks or uninhabitable islets, and the fortress of S. João Baptista d'Ajudá, built in the territory of the ancient Kingdom of Dahomey. Each of these groups of Islands forms an administrative district, and the fortress of Ajudá a military station.

The Province has its seat of government in S. Thomé, and is ruled by a Provincial Governor; the Island of Principe is under the charge of a District Governor, who is under the immediate jurisdiction of the Provincial Government.

These groups of Islands off the West Coast of Africa in the Gulf of Guinea, in the torrid zone almost under the Equator, separated by a distance of 81 miles from each other, and probably of the same cosmic origin, are very similar in their orography and hydrography, as well as their fauna, flora and climatic conditions. And, having been always under one administration, at first established in the Island of S. Thomé until 1753, afterwards in the Island of Principe until 1852, when it was re-established in S. Thomé, they have shared the same fate, whether prosperous or adverse, due to causes internal and external, some arising from the turbulence of the natives and ancient customs, others from the ambition of foreigners and calamitous material losses, of which we will give a short description.

According to ancient chronicles, the Island of S. Thomé appears to have been discovered by João de Santarem and Pedro d'Escobar on the 21st December in the year 1471, the day dedicated to the apostle St. Thomé.

Ancient chronicles also state that the Island of Principe was discovered by the same navigators, a few days before the discovery of the Island of S. Thomé.

The Islands only began to be colonized by the Portuguese many years later, in 1493, owing to unfavourable reports of the climate, or perhaps in consequence of great difficulties in the Capital; the colonists at first settled in S. Thomé, in the place where they landed, called Agua-Ambó near Ponta-figo, now parish of Neves. Then they built various tents and also cultivated some ground. Afterwards they removed to the Bay of Anna de Chaves, where the city of S. Thomé now stands, and there built a small town, opening up the neighbouring ground for cultivation.

Owing to favourable reports received about the fertility of the Island soil, «the Sovereign generously to help the inhabitants» — according to the chronicle of Cunha Mattos — «sent them numerous convicts, artisans, and other colonists, granted them land, and gave them slaves to cultivate it.

With this important and valuable assistance, the inhabitants increased in number; and, consequently, the Island was brought under cultivation, farmsteads were built, sugar mills set up, as well as saw-mills, cattle rearing was introduced, and important exports were effected.»

After the discovery, our navigators only rarely visited the islands which by the regal munificence of King John II had been presented to Crown donees as a recompense for their services, according to the custom of the age, with all the privileges inherent to such gifts, and remained under their jurisdiction until they were incorporated in the Crown Dominions by a contract made with the same donees — the Island of S. Thomé in 1558, and that of Principe in 1753.

In 1512, the only town existing in S. Thomé was totally destroyed by fire; the disorder and poverty suffered by the inhabitants in consequence, caused a famine, the forerunner of the war that was to break out in 1517 between the blacks and half-castes, causing incalculable losses to the nascent agriculture, and consequently retarding the moral and material progress of the Province. In 1585, a violent cyclone almost completely destroyed the buildings of the Island of S. Thomé, and, about the middle of the XVIII century, the greater part of the Island of Principe was burnt down, and the Islanders reduced to the greatest misery.

The «Angolares», a half savage tribe, castaways from a slave ship wrecked on the coast in 1550, settled in the Island of S. Thomé. These tribes, having left Angola for an unknown destination, trusting to the weakness of the incipient social organization of the Islanders, and giving vent to their turbulent and ambitious propensities, attacked and murdered many proprietors and male colonists, captured women, pillaged and destroyed the farms. Many inhabitants, terrified at such a calamitous anarchy, emigrated to Brazil, attracted thither by the progress of that country, also by the hope of finding there peace and safety non-existent in S. Thomé.

The «Angolares» colony, increasing in number, spread over the south of the Island, building various hamlets, and they might have been a valuable element of labour, had their warlike tendencies been subdued, and their robust qualities and special conditions of enduring the climate been taken advantage of; but, owing to the want of sufficient and regularly organized forces to repress their provocative and fearless nature, as they increased in numbers, so also did they increase in daring and in ambitious designs.

In 1574, a new incursion of these barbarians resulted in the burning of several sugar mills; the city of S. Thomé was attacked and destroyed, its inhabitants again robbed, and many women captured. In 1693, the military forces already more efficiently organized, attacked them, destroyed their villages, and took many prisoners, to punish them for their new incursion to capture women and destroy property.

The inhabitants, harassed by internal dissensions, had likewise to cope with the numerous raids made on the Island by foreigners.

In 1567, the Island of S. Thomé was pillaged and devastated by French pirates, and although they encountered death, where they expected to find fortune,

Marshal Raymundo José da Cunha Mattos

Chronicler of the Islands of S. Thomé and Principe, and Governor
of the Province in 1815

the damage and disorder arising thereby were so great, that they caused a most pernicious effect on the precarious state of the social economic government of the Province.

Twice, in less than 50 years, the moral and material progress of the Province was greatly impeded by the effects of raids made by the Dutch, with the object of rapine and destruction. In 1600, the sailors of a fleet, commanded by Wan-der Don, sacked and devastated the city, and, although they abandoned it at once, the state of internal affairs rendered this raid specially ruinous. The native rebellion (now at its height) was led by the terrible negro Amador, who preached class-hatred and aimed at taking possession of the Island, arrogating to himself the pompous title of King of S. Thomé. The more timid of the planters, seeing their labour paralyzed, and their lives and property in danger in the midst of the general anarchy produced by the invaders, by internal strife, and by the irregular misrule of the authorities, abandoning their houses and goods to the insatiable greed of the invaders, fled to Brazil.

The second occasion was in 1641, when a fleet, manned by a large crew, again invaded the Island and took possession of the fortress of S. Sebastião, which protected the Bay of Anna Chaves,and which capitulated owing to its badly organized defenders.

Under the inauspicious influence of the invaders, agriculture and commerce were almost stopped, until in 1644, in exchange for important sums of money, it is said, or, possibly, on account of the presence in the Bay of forces from Portugal and Brazil, the Dutch abandoned the Island, and Portuguese dominion was re-established.

In 1706, the French landed in the Island of Principe, and left it, after having sacked it; in 1709, they compelled the fortress, defending the Bay of Anna Chaves in S. Thomé, to surrender, and pillaged the provincial treasury and set fire to the city.

The results arising from internal disturbances were not less disastrous; the rebellion of the «negros-minas» — the revolt, shortly after 1735, of the rural police force, an irregularly organized body, commanded by «Capitães de Serra» leagued against the Governor and authorities — and in 1744, the mutiny of the regiment of orderlies, were a pretext for putting into practice every kind of violence, the disastrous effects of which were reflected on agriculture, the basis of all the wealth of the Province.

In 1753, at the request of the Governor, the capital of the Province was transferred to the Island of Principe, which was considered more healthy; and in 1799, this same Island was again invaded by the French, who effected their entry through the city of S. Antonio, then the headquarters of the government.

Four hundred men of the naval division under Admiral Lendolph, encountering no resistance, took possession of the city and the fortress which was without arms or ammunition, or garrison to defend it; only a few unarmed officers and men resided there. The authorities, deserted by the people who fled to the forests with the majority of the soldiers, surrendered the Province.

According to the chroniclers, this invasion did not assume the proportions of such destructive anarchy as the former ones; the invaders, after extorting from the community large sums of gold as a war indemnity, in exchange for which and a commercial treaty, framed according to their own convenience, of which circumstances obliged the acceptance, left the Island and restored the Province to the Portuguese authorities, sparing the lives of the inhabitants.

But this event, although it did not lead to acts of violence, increased the existing complications, the want of security for persons and property became more and more evident, and greatly reduced the resources for promoting the agricultural and commercial development of the Province. However, against every obstacle struggled the undaunted tenacity of our colonists whose efforts, nullified by so many and such great reverses, increased as soon as the great fury of the storm began to abate. Agricultural labourers daily became scarcer; the natives, descendants of various African races, inclined by nature to indolence and vice, preferred idleness to work; vagrants ran riot, threatening life and property. The authorities wanted the means to suppress abuses, so that only by the greatest prudence and heroic sacrifice could the proprietors exact obedience from their dependants, and carry on, though under difficulties, the cultivation of their farms.

The continual progress of the civilization of Brazil, supported by the tranquillity enjoyed by its inhabitants in the diverse provinces, the social status of which being organized with great regularity, attracted the attention of all the Portuguese desirous of emigrating.

The removal of the Portuguese Court to Rio de Janeiro, due to the French invasion of Portugal, and the neglect with which the government of the metropolis had treated African possessions, paying attention almost exclusively to Brazil, caused the currents of emigration to converge to the latter Colony. A large number of the nobility and the wealthier classes accompanied the Court to Brazil, and were followed by many literary men and artists in a voluntary exodus, so to say, this fact encouraging in the mind of popular classes, who furnished the greater part of the emigrants, the hope of finding there a way of profitably employing their time and money.

The navigation for S. Thomé had decreased amazingly. Desirable Portuguese emigrants landed only in a limited number in the Islands, and these were only enticed thither by the fearless colonizers who struggled on, and resisted every reverse, kindling in their tenacity and patriotism the ardent faith of future prosperity which they foresaw.

In the meanwhile, circumstances seemed to modify in terms to permit the study of the problem under a more auspicious aspect, but the treaty negotiated with England in 1842, in which reciprocal rights were recognized, increased afresh the deplorable embarrassments of the past, by permitting the ships of that nation to inspect the traffic of slaves carried on by Portuguese vessels. Until then rural labourers were carried to the Islands, either voluntarily or by compulsion, according to the customs of the time and the existing laws, in fairly large numbers, although insufficient to cope with the work of agriculture; but, thenceforward under the pretext of non-compliance with the treaty, the hostilities of the English against the engagement of labourers and their conveyance to the Island estates, were of such a nature, that the obstacles raised against immigration were insuperable, causing losses of every description to the colonists, and agriculture, to which the planters trusted for their future prosperity, was at a standstill, if not retrograde, owing to the want of workpeople, and the indispensable resources for cultivating the soil.

The English impeded, or raised difficulties against, the shipment of Angola ne-

Fortress of St. Sebastian situated at the entrance of Anna Chaves Bay, in the Island of S. Thomé

groes to S. Thomé, even when these were recruited or engaged according to the terms of the laws in force, all formalities and guarantees being observed in strict conformity with the treaty. They protested to the Home Government, as well as to the colonial authorities, and threatened to seize the vessels employed in this service.

These protests, founded on facts relative to the slave-trade, which the English officials exaggerated at their own pleasure, were continuous, and the difficulties placed in the way of conveying labourers to the Islands continually increased. The Portuguese authorities strictly complied with the law and the rules of the treaties; it was proved that the emigration of blacks from Angola to S. Thomé, was carried out under the existing laws and established formalities, and that the means employed for the engagement and conveyance of the blacks, were *identical* with those used for natives proceeding to the English Colonies, and even for white labourers, when they found themselves in similar circumstances in different parts of the Globe. Vain efforts! as our allies did not cease their demands.

Unfortunately, the power, exercised by those whose humanitarian motto covered the most cruel offence to the justice of our cause, destroyed the right on which our weakness rested, for the pressure of English demands reached the length of completely preventing the landing at S. Thomé of emigrants from Angola.

The words of energetic and bitter protest against the injustifiable claims of the English Government, as to the observance of the treaty of 1842, with which the illustrious Minister of Marine in 1863, Mendes Leal, concluded the information given to his colleague at the Foreign Office, regarding the measures taken on the matter, which we transcribe below, clearly and eloquently define the unreasonableness of those demands.

«Our loyalty in carrying out the treaty of 1842, has cost us the most bitter sacrifices, even to the point of receiving insults, for which we obtained no redress owing to the abandonment by our allies (1). It is necessary, it is indispensable that we should regulate the conditions of free colonization, so that we, like all other nations, may be permitted to obtain labourers to work where they are wanted. If these just demands be not attended to, if the vexations continue, expressing myself with the liberty and frankness, which patriotism and justice inspire, I consider that we ought to resume the long history of our wrongs, and, together with the full and evident proofs we possess, resolutely present them to the arbitration of Europe, that will decide as to the justice of our complaints. England herself, together with her enlightened Government, on re-reading these dark pages, will often be filled with indignation at many acts practised by the manifest abuse of her great and generous name.»

Vexatious oppressions were inflicted on a friendly and allied nation, in the name of liberty and humanity, and impediments placed against the progress of a Portuguese Colony, the prosperity of which depended chiefly on the emigration from another Colony of the same nation.

Both the authorities of Angola and those of S. Thomé and Principe, and all the planters of the latter Province made the greatest efforts to fulfil the injunctions

---

(1) Capture of the French barque *Charles & Georges.*

and cause the formalities and guarantees stipulated by law, to be observed, thc terms of the treaty of 1842 being carried out to the point of exaggeration.

Many planters even offered conditions of still greater freedom to their labourers than the law required, it is certain that «as they could not convey blacks in the condition of slaves or freedmen (according to law) they engaged, on onerous terms, free men, and even bought slaves or redeemed the service of the freedmen, giving liberty to all, conveying them as free people, which they had now become, to S. Thomé, and ran the risk of their forgetting the favour of their liberty and contracting work which should remunerate them better.» (Official letter dated 5th December 1861, from the Governor-general of Angola, Calheiros Menezes to the Minister of Marine, Report page 235).

But notwithstanding all, for many years all our efforts against the demands of the English were of no avail.

Discouragement, caused by such a state of things, would have been fully justified in people less pertinacious and experienced, in the struggle for the progress and civilization of the African territory. The Portuguese colonists in S. Thomé were not disheartened; on the contrary they knew how to give incontestable proof of a rare energy and after a stubborn resistance, finally overcame the many rude obstacles opposed to their activity.

In 1825, the independence of Brazil was recognized. That vast empire having been separated from the Portuguese dominion, the Home Government could pay more attention to the African Colonies. The internal government of S. Thomé benefited by that circumstance; the intestine struggles ceased; authority was exercised with more regularity; the maintenance of public order, and the guarding of life and property were entrusted to a first class force, regularly organized; as the supervision from the metropolis became more and more efficacious, confidence was gradually restored. At the commencement of the second half of the xix century, the Portuguese Government completed their measures for facilitating the most ample European emigration to the two Islands in the Gulf of Guinea, in absolutely normal conditions, by contracting with the «Real Companhia União Mercantil» the establishment of a line of Portuguese steamers between Lisbon and the West Coast of Africa, calling at S. Thomé and Principe.

This patriotic appeal was not in vain, as agriculture, to the great progress of which the Province of S. Thomé and Principe owes its actual prosperity, soon recommenced under far more favourable circumstances.

This renewal of the prosperity of the Colony may be divided into two periods: 1855 to 1875 and 1876 to 1909.

First period: 1855 to 1875.

In this first period it is meet to inscribe, with special mention, four names as those of true apostles, of the first four pioneers who initiated the crusade of modern progress, and of the economic and civilizing development of the Islands of S. Thomé and Principe:

They are

Conselheiro José Maria da Silva Mendes Leal
Minister of Marine and the Colonies in 1861 and 1862

Francisco d'Assis Bélard;
Conselheiro João Maria de Sousa e Almeida, 1.º Barão d'Agua-Izé;
Manuel da Costa Pedreira;
José Maria de Freitas.

During those hard times experienced in the first years of this period, these four meritorious men began their important cultivations, the first, together with Manuel Joaquim Teixeira, laid the foundation of the plantations named Santa-Margarida, Monte-Macaco, and Maianço, the second, Agua-Izé, the third, Monte-Café, and the fourth, Bella-Vista, Santarem, and Ilheu das Rôlas.

But these early efforts were rendered almost futile by a new fatality which devastated the Colony, in the shape of a small-pox epidemic, the germs of which had been imported from Angola. It spread through the Province, causing fearful havoc and carrying off by death, the greater part of the working population.

This disaster momentarily disheartened those brave men, but redoubling their efforts, they finally succeeded in overcoming every difficulty.

But, before we proceed, it is only just to render homage to Sebastião Lopes Calheiros e Menezes, (who acted as Governor-general, of the Province of Angola from 7th February 1861 to 17th July 1862), a man of great moral, intellectual, and patriotic qualities, in a word, a true Portuguese. If gratitude were the motto of humanity, this name so deserving of the nation's respect and admiration, ought long ago to have been inscribed on the pedestal of a monument in the principal square in the city of S. Thomé, as it is already inscribed in the pages of our colonial history.

It was due to that patriot, who in addition to his enlightened spirit, possessed an energetic temperament, that the efforts of the initiators of this new era of prosperity in S. Thomé were not in vain, and that the country had not to wait indefinitely for the brilliant results arising therefrom.

Governor Calheiros gave the greatest facilities, during the 17 months of his Government, for the conveyance of thousands of labourers from the Province under his jurisdiction to that of S. Thomé and Principe, in the hope of remedying the chief evil caused by the epidemic.

In order to succeed in his efforts, he had to sustain an heroic struggle, unique in our modern Colonial history, against the impositions of the English officials stationed in the Province of Angola.

We will select three documents from the voluminous correspondence then exchanged between those officials, which indicate the nature of the controversy, and show the difficulties besetting the cultivation of land in S. Thomé, at a comparatively recent date.

From the Governor-general of Angola to the Minister of Marine and the Colonies — Lisbon — (Report from Governor Calheiros, page 233.)

«Having received the visit of Commander Edmondstone, chief of the English naval station on this coast, who was accompanied by the British Commissary M.ʳ Edmund Gabriel, in the course of our conversation, the topic of the shipment of blacks from this Port to the Island of S. Thomé was discussed, and as the subject seemed to me of importance, I think it my duty to communicate the same to Your Excellency.

«The British officials expressed their disapproval regarding the conveyance of blacks to the Province of S. Thomé in sailing vessels, and especially so in the «Companhia União Mercantil» steamers, averring that slave-trading could be carried on in them, and endeavoured to persuade me to put a stop to this practice.

«I proved to them that those blacks were shipped in strict accordance with the Portuguese laws and the treaty of 3rd July 1842; notwithstanding, they renewed their importunities, and as my reply was, I could not do so, as I had not the right, the Commander of the Station declared that he would submit this subject to the consideration of H. B. M. Government.

«As it is possible, that some claim may be made in England or Lisbon, it is my duty to state clearly what takes place in connection with the blacks sailing from here to S. Thomé.

«No vessel leaving Loanda for S. Thomé receives more than ten black slaves or freedmen, therefore the terms of the treaty of 3rd July are carried out to the point of exaggeration, as freedmen are not, nor could they be, included therein. — Both carry out the conditions expressed in the respective laws.

«In the case of free blacks, only those sail who, as such, take out legal passports, and also satisfy the following regulations imposed by me, with the object of verifying their condition. When, as free blacks, they petition for their passports for S. Thomé, surety must be given proving their identity, and the petitions for passports must also be accompanied by a document, given by the administration of the District, stating their free condition, all these transactions being registered, — in addition to which, I also send, in my official capacity, to the Governor of S. Thomé a nominal list of the free blacks, and another of the slaves and freedmen shipped in each vessel.

«Therefore, it would be an abuse of authority and an offence against the State's fundamental laws, to prevent the departure of negroes, seeing, that they are only shipped for S. Thomé, under the strictest observance of all legal formalities. So I replied to the before mentioned English functionaries, that I could not refuse passports to Portuguese subjects placed in such circumstances.

«I regret to see the insistence employed by the English Agents on this coast, to prevent the emigration of blacks to S. Thomé; it appears to me that such insistence is not inspired by sentiments of humanity, as the blacks leave here according to the terms of the treaty, and run no risk of having their freedom attacked, nor is there any danger of their being sold as slaves and thus taking another destination, either on the voyage, or after their arrival in the Province.

«The Province of S. Thomé now attracts universal attention; the coffee industry promises a bright future; numerous enterprising individuals find their way thither, and as there is a great want of labourers, great sacrifices are made to obtain them.

«I will not go to the length of affirming, that the English Agents wish to impede the development of the prosperity of that rich Colony; it is not just, however, to give way to all their demands, for, to do so would necessarily offend general law and individual rights, and sacrifice the interests of the country.

«It is necessary to state in order that Your Excellency may appreciate the sacrifices forced on the planters of S. Thomé, owing to the want of labourers, that as the former cannot convey the blacks in condition of slaves or freedmen, they have to contract free people under onerous terms, even going the length of buying

General Sebastião Lopes de Calheiros e Menezes
Governor-General of Angola in the years 1861 and 1862

slaves or redeeming the service of freedmen, all of whom receive their liberty and are taken to S. Thomé, where the proprietors run the risk of the men forgetting the favour received in Angola, and accepting more remunerative work from other employers.

«I have stated to Your Excellency, what I consider sufficient for the enlightenment of His Majesty's Government on so important a matter.

«I will only add that I would not prevent, even if I could do so, the conveyance of blacks to S. Thomé in a condition of freedom, as it would be against the legal interests of the nation.

«As these Islands require labourers, I feel the greatest regret that it is indirectly forbidden to me to allow them to go as freedmen, for the latter having been forced to work for some years and learn certain habits of civilization, are more suitable than free blacks who soon give themselves over to indolence and vice, owing to the fact of their never having acquired working habits and the necessities arising therefrom.

«Your Excellency will find three petition-forms enclosed, similar to those used by blacks when starting for S. Thomé, and which remain in the archives of the General Government.

God preserve Your Excellency.

Loanda, the 5th of December, 1861.

«Official letter from Messrs. Edmund Gabriel and H. W. Huntley, British Commissaries in Loanda, to the Governor-general of Angola. (Report from Governor Calheiros. Pages 273 and 274.)

«Loanda, the 11th of April 1862.

Your Excellency — We had the honour of receiving Your Excellency's reply to our communication of the 5th inst, relative to the conveyance of blacks from this Province to S. Thomé.

«We will hasten to forward the above mentioned reply to H. M. Government, and in the meanwhile, we may be permitted to make some observations regarding certain points.

«Once Your Excellency distinctly admitted, that the treaty of 3rd July 1842 authorizes H. M. officers to examine Portuguese vessels, to ascertain if they carry slaves, we consider any reflections on this point to be superfluous; and the more so, since article the first of annexe B of the aforesaid treaty is sufficiently clear and explicit in this case, as it states that the commander of any ship belonging to the Royal British or Portuguese navies, after receiving precise information, has the right to visit, examine, and detain, unless it be in the exceptional case of article 2 of the treaty, any British or Portuguese ship, which actually is employed, or suspected of being employed in «the conveyance of blacks or others for the purpose of slavery.» We consider it unnecessary therefore, to insist that, in virtue of the same treaty, H. M. officers have the right to ascertain if the blacks on board Portuguese vessels, be or be not intended for slavery, and when it is proved that they are, to take the necessary steps for putting an end to this abuse and to secure to the mentioned blacks, the final and complete emancipation to which the same treaty entitles them.

«Your Excellency expressing the hope that H. M. officers will not have recourse to such measures, adds that such procedure would present to the World a notable difference in their treatment of Portuguese vessels, as compared with the French ones, the latter, according to Your Excellency, having lately conveyed from Congo tens of thousands of blacks, without any opposition whatever on the part of England; besides, these negroes, not being French subjects going from one province to another of the same nation, were not in the same circumstances as these leaving here for S. Thomé.

«As to what Your Excellency states regarding the difference in the treatment of the British officers towards Portuguese vessels as compared with the French, we beg leave to say that the position in which the vessels of the two nations stand is in no way analogous and, therefore, no comparison whatever can be made.

«There is no treaty between Great Britain and France that states that the conveyance of African natives by sea, for the purpose of reducing them to slavery, be considered a great crime in their respective dominions and for the subjects of the two countries, or concedes the mutual right to visit vessels actually carrying, or suspected of carrying blacks and others to slavery.

«But there does exist a treaty of this nature between Great Britain and Portugal; and, consequently, no parallel can be drawn between Portuguese and French vessels, as to acts of trafficking in slaves and their pursuit.

. . . .

«Official letter dated the 14th of April 1862 from the Secretary-general of Angola to the British Commissaries in Loanda, (Governor Calheiros' Report). Pages 276 and following.)

«Dear Sirs

«According to the communication addressed to you on the 7th inst., His Excellency the Governor-general of the Province commands me to return to you the letter addressed to him and dated the 11th idem, which please find enclosed.

«I am likewise instructed to let you know that His Excellency owing to information by him received, has every reason to make an unfavourable comparison between the treatment accorded to vessels carrying passengers from Loanda to S. Thomé, and the mode of procedure, up to the present date, regarding French vessels leaving the Zaire with blacks.

«The treaty existing between Portugal and Great Britain cannot possibly include the pretension now brought forward, according to your letter, of English officers boarding Portuguese vessels carrying passengers from Loanda to S. Thomé, to ascertain if these passengers go voluntarily.

«These ships only sail after due inspection by the respective employees and all legal formalities have been complied with; they convey free passengers, all supplied with passports given them by the superior authorities of the Province; therefore, they are not ships which carry, or can be suspected of carrying blacks to S. Thomé for the purpose of being reduced to slavery; and, consequently, the English officials can only board them to see if the list of the crew, and the number of passports correspond to the people on board.

Francisco d'Assis Belard

One of the four pioneers of the present great agriculture of S. Thomé

«The investigation indicated, if carried out, besides being illegal would be an insult to the authorities of Angola and S. Thomé.

«Therefore, the pretension brought forward cannot be justified by the treaty of 3rd July 1842, as the case in question is that of Portuguese going from one Portuguese province to another. The country presenting such a demand to Portugal might, and with much more right, more reasonably protest against the purchase by France of human beings from the tribes of Africa, taking them against their will from the Zaire to her Colonies.

«France would not admit such a pretension, because she is a free and independent country, and for the same reason His Excellency in his own name, and in that of the Portuguese nation, protests and continues to protest against the claim brought forward. And His Excellency does so with all the more reason, as there is no doubt that if Portugal, with more foundation, presented a similar claim to Great Britain, the latter would ignore it.

«Portugal can declare that the blacks captured by English cruisers from slave-dealers in ships of no definite nationality, taken to English Colonies and there employed by planters, are compelled to do this, and go therefore, very much against their will; and England cannot allege a shadow of right to dispose of those blacks, unless it be the right of the stronger.

«As this is manifest, it is impossible to prove the contrary; nor even can it be alleged that a happier lot awaits those negroes in the English Colonies, because Portugal has an example at home, that shows the fate which awaits the labourers imported; it is that of the colonists engaged some years ago in Santo Antão de Cabo Verde.

«These blacks were so barbarously treated in Guiana, that their cries of anguish were heard across the Atlantic from Demerara to Lisbon; and the Portuguese Government had to send a ship there, to deliver them from the martyrdom they were undergoing.

«And can it be maintained that a happier lot awaits those savage blacks from the wilds of Africa, and left there without the least protection?

«If then we admit, that English crews may board Portuguese vessels to ascertain whether the free Portuguese going from here to S. Thomé, with their passports quite in order, do so voluntarily or not, and can detain the said ships, if any of the passengers should think of declaring they are coerced, with how much more right may the Portuguese detain English ships conveying the blacks above mentioned, when it is positively known they are not English subjects, and have been violently torn from their homes and constrained to go to a foreign land?

«His Excellency, therefore, orders me to inform you that the comparison which he has made is quite correct, that the treaty lately carried out between England and France does not alter the question in the least, and that, in the same way as the right to prevent the conveyance of blacks from the Zaire by the French is denied you, and that you also do not permit the Portuguese to detain English vessels in identical circumstances, therefore, much less can you interfere, in the way you propose, with vessels employed in the lawful conveyance of free Portuguese from here to S. Thomé.

«His Excellency also commands me to inform you, that in the same way as you state that you will continue communicating to him any information received, tending to further the end which the Portuguese and English Governments have in view, according to the treaty of 3rd July 1842, likewise will he continue to return you your letters addressed to him; not that he wishes to end the correspondence on this subject, but it is not with you that he should maintain it.

«His Excellency desires to receive all information on the matter, so that he may be enabled to do everything his duty points out, but as H. B, M. Consul is the only person in a position to give it to him officially, you must approach him for that purpose.

«In conclusion, His Excellency also declares that the British officials will be held responsible, if any unfavourable results arise from the non-reception of the said communications, if they refuse to act according to rules generally followed by nations and the special terms agreed upon by the Portuguese and English Governments.»

. . . .

The portions quoted from these three official documents and from the Report of the Minister Mendes Leal, already transcribed in these pages, give an idea of the tenacious and energetic struggle, which it was necessary to sustain against the pretensions of England.

The defence of Portuguese interests could not have been more brilliant, nor more consistent with the interests and the honour of the country, but our rights so nobly upheld, were of no avail; in the end, England prevailed, for after seventeen months of a model administration, not only honourable for his own name, but also of utility for the nation, General Calheiros was recalled from the governorship of Angola; emigration, reduced at first to ten emigrants per each ship, was at last completely suppressed!

Nevertheless, the very valuable assistance, rendered by the Governor of Angola, stimulated afresh S. Thomé planters, and thus, the second part of this first period was signalized by new and important enterprises, started and carried out with their own resources, or under the protection of some of their four great pioneers, of Lisbon capitalists, and of the «Banco Nacional Ultramarino», an institution of credit, founded in 1867 and subsidized by the Government.

In 1870, a violent fire completely destroyed the building where the Town Hall and Law Courts were established, the city archives, including all the books and documents of the Orphan Fund, being almost entirely reduced to ashes.

And finally, the most notable event of the epoch closed the period 1855 to 1875, which, although at the time it caused serious apprehension to the planters, their courage once more being put to the proof, was really the happy forerunner of the great prosperity in store for them.

The law of 29th April 1875 determined that on the same date, a year later, slavery should be abolished in all the Portuguese Crown dominions; a sentiment of disinterestedness, carried to excess, led the authorities of S. Thomé to anticipate that date, resulting, at once, in the exodus of labourers of all conditions, from the plantations for the city.

That was an anxious moment for the Colony, because the small force at (1)

---

(1) The only forces at the disposal of the Province were the battalion of rifles n.° 2, a body of 60 police, and the gunboat *Rio Minho*. According to its organization, that battalion

Conselheiro João Maria de Sousa e Almeida, first Baron of Agua Izé
One of the four pioneers of the present great agriculture of S. Thomé

NOTE

One conto of réis is egual to £ 222.4.4 at the rate of Réis 4:500 per £, calculated at par exchange viz: 53 $^1/_3$ d. per 1:000 réis.

the disposal of the Government, composed mainly of Angola blacks, was insufficient to cope with such a number of men and women, that for many days crowded the streets of the city, notwithstanding the strict discipline maintained by its never-to-be forgotten commander Major Antonio Joaquim da Fonseca, afterwards Visconde de Santa Margarida; and moreover the local government had no legal instructions for suppressing disorder, as the special regulations now under discussion in the metropolis had not yet arrived.

That imprudent measure resulted in the loss for agriculture of thousands of workers, and the increase of the legion of loafers, some of whom still exist and are known as «fórros gregorianos».

The resignation with which the planters suffered this reverse, their prudence, their coolness in facing the situation, as well as, it is only just to say, the kindness with which, as a rule, they had treated their labourers, both free and bondmen, prevented acts of violence being committed.

Notwithstanding the abnormal circumstances, this transition was effected without the shedding of one drop of blood, a single case of incendiarism, or any wilful act of destruction.

The first period of the new era of prosperity ends here.

Second Period: 1876 to the present Day.

The first years of this period are characterized by the great efforts of the planters to raise capital for the cultivation of their properties, and to obtain labourers, as substitutes for those who had left the plantations in 1875.

The abandonment of the plantations on the eve of the coffee harvest, at that time the most important culture of the Island, caused in the year 1876 the loss of the crop, and damaged considerably that of 1877, for the plants could not blossom as the fruit of the preceding year had been left ungathered.

The loss of these two harvests considerably increased the financial struggles of the planters, (at a time when they required large sums to engage fresh labourers), and the uncertainty of the results of the new regulations about to be adopted made it most difficult to obtain credit.

The pioneers of the first period had to face in the early years all these difficulties, as well as the mortiferous small-pox epidemic of 1877, and overcoming them with admirable constancy they gave at the same time, on an occasion when they were struggling against such grave financial embarrassments, a proof of great

---

should have consisted of four companies, each composed of one hundred privates: the first being of white and the other three of black soldiers, but part of these had been detached to the districts of Ajudá and Principe. At the moment the crisis broke out, there existed in S. Thomé 50 white and 200 black soldiers, the latter natives of Angola; Commander Fonseca faced the many difficulties of those anxious days, maintaining order and obedience to the authorities, without bloodshed, with this small and admirably disciplined force, the guarding of the Fortress and Governor's Palace having been entrusted to sailors, landed from the «Rio Minho».

disinterestedness by refusing to accept the indemnity, which the emancipation law decreed should be paid by the State to the proprietors.

The free emigration of labourers from Angola was finally regulated, as the official difficulties brought forward by England against the ingress of Africans into the Islands had now ceased, for that opposition could no longer be based on the treaty of 1842, as the inhabitants of S. Thomé and Principe and other Portuguese Colonies were now all free people; and, as the convict settlement of S. Thomé was suppressed in 1881 by the Home Government, at the suggestion of the distinguished Governor Pindella, the Colony commenced to have the reputation of being a country suitable for emigration, its customs became more moral, and thus it entered fully into the period of its great social and economic development.

English hostility, though under other aspects, did not cease to make itself felt when occasions arose. As manual labour, for cultivating its soil, was always the principal agricultural problem of S. Thomé, immediately the abolition of forced labour allowed emigration from all sources, the planters endeavoured to obtain these indispensable auxiliaries in different parts of Africa, including the Republic of Liberia and Accra, where they engaged, in the years 1875 and 1876, about 2500 labourers, who were shipped to S. Thomé in steamers of the English Company, which traded on the West Coast of Africa; but, as soon as the current of emigration began to increase, owing to the favourable information regarding the treatment received in S. Thomé and Principe, taken by the first «Krumànos» on their return home, the English Navigation Company refused to convey new emigrants, the report being, that this resolution was taken owing to the pressure of English merchants, who threatened, as was then said, to stop their shipments by those steamers, if the conveyance of labourers from our Colonies continued.

To remedy this new difficulty, as we had no direct shipping communication with the coast of Kroo, the S. Thomé planters determined to obtain a vessel for that purpose, and, with this intent, they chartered the brig *Ovarense,* belonging to the well-known Lisbon shipowners, Fernando d'Oliveira Bello and Manuel Rodrigues Formigal.

After all the necessary regulations had been complied with, the captain obtained his certificate from the Governor of the Province, allowing him to call at Liberia and Sierra Leone, and ship up to 400 labourers for S. Thomé. (1)

The contracting agent, Francisco Ferreira de Moraes, (2) and a military Hospital attendant at (3) S. Thomé also sailed.

Therefore, after all legal formalities had been carried out, and, taking as a further guarantee, the personages who were to accompany the vessel on her outward voyage, and the labourers on the return, the *Ovarense* sailed from S. Thomé on the 26th of September 1876 (4) for Liberia, calling at Cape Coast and Cape Palmas, to land passengers and the contractor Moraes, who there stayed to engage emigrants, while the captain sailed for the port of Sierra Leone, the capital of the

---

(1) Official Bulletin of S. Thomé — N.o 40, of 1876.
(2) Official Bulletin of S. Thomé — N.o 39, of 1876.
(3) Official Bulletin of S. Thomé — N.o 40, of 1876.
(4) Official Bulletin of S. Thomé — N.o 43, of 1876.

Manoel da Costa Pedreira
One of the four pioneers of the present great agriculture of S. Thomé

neighbouring English Colony of Senegambia, to take in supplies and prepare for the reception of the emigrants, under the supervision of the English authorities, and also to communicate to them the mission entrusted to him, and to present the legal documents passed by the Portuguese officials with which he was furnished.

The answer of the English authorities to this act of loyalty and good faith on the part of the captain, was the seizure of the vessel in the Bay of Sierra Leone, as suspected of being employed in the slave-trade!

The ship's documents were of no avail, the capture was maintained, and an action was brought against the owners of the vessel, and begun in the London Civil Court, a year after the capture, (1) and only concluded on the 9th of August 1880, judgment being given in favour of the defendants. Although it is certain that the English Courts condemned the authorities that seized the ship, and through them, the Colony, where the act of violence was committed, the damages for the shipowners Bello and Formigal were assessed at £ 8000, and for the owners of the cargo £ 1000, besides legal costs which were about another £ 1000, it is not less certain, that a decisive blow was intentionally aimed at the emigration of «Kroomans» for S. Thomé.

After the capture of the *Ovarense,* the current of emigration from Liberia to S. Thomé ceased; since then, only occasionally and exceptionally, have any of those excellent labourers gone there.

In later times, English hostility has manifested itself by articles in the Press, and in meetings, the sorry honour of libelling us to the public, belonging to Nevinson, Pienaar, Burtt, and other English persons, forming themselves into «Societies for protecting the aborigines of Africa»; and finally, since we initiated the emigration of labourers from our Province of Mozambique, a little more than a year ago, to prevent these blacks going to S. Thomé, those interested in emigration for Transvaal have endeavoured to fill their heads with all sorts of ideas, from the everlasting story of slavery, and the spectre of the stormy seas they have to cross, where ships founder and all lives are lost, to the mutilations of noses, ears, legs and arms, which totally transform those foolish enough to go to our Island!

The English campaign against S. Thomé, has lasted more than half a century.

Firstly, under the pretext that forced labour still existed in the Portuguese African dominion, they professed to consider as slavery, the immigration of Portuguese natives of Angola, whether composed of freedmen, or of persons moving their residence from this Province to that of S. Thomé.

Afterwards, the law of the 29th of April 1875 having abolished forced labour, the planters endeavoured to engage free labourers then numerous in Liberia, and their proposal was favourably accepted without encountering any opposition from the U. S. of America, the free Republic of Liberia having been, since its foundation, under the latter country's protectorate. England's hostility, for impeding our efforts to obtain workers, was again manifested by the arbitrary capture of the *Ovarense,* resulting in the discredit of the emigration for S. Thomé, which this proceeding spread amongst all the inhabitants of Kroo and the Gold Coast.

---

(1) The 9th November 1877, *The Independent* N.ºs 108 to 110 of Freetown, and *Jornal do Commercio* N.º 7732 of Lisbon the 20th April 1878.

Then comes the campaign of Nevinson and Company against the modern form of labour. The Angola blacks working at S. Thomé, are considered slaves because the majority of them prefer remaining there to returning home.

And finally, when we go to Mozambique to engage labour on much more liberal and humane conditions than those prevailing in Transvaal, the champions of the interests of the latter English Colony discharge a torrent of abuse and calumny against us, filling the minds of the labourers with the fear of running great risks, and suffering the most cruel punishments if they go to S. Thomé.

Since S. Thomé started in earnest its modern agricultural work, hitherto it has been the English, and only the English, that, employing different forms of pressure have impeded the progress of the Colony; they have always been vanquished by the pertinacity of the Portuguese colonists, but nevertheless, determined as they are, they do not desist or lose hope, — they powerful and rich — of destroying our efforts, which poor and weak though they be, are based only on right and justice.

We must now mention an event which took place early in this period, and influenced enormously the future of the Island of S. Thomé; namely, the effectual occupation of the region populated by the «Angolares». It was to the renowned Africanist Doctor Matheus Augusto Ribeiro de Sampaio, that the Province and the Country owe that great service.

These tribes had lived a savage and independent existence for more than three centuries, concealed in the mysterious and thick forests, which covered the mountainous and southern zone of the Island, never acknowledging the sovereignty of the country. The attempt to conquer that region, for the purposes of civilization, had always failed, and nobody ever thought of renewing it with the slender resources at the command of the local Government. But Matheus Sampaio was not of the same opinion as others, and refused to give up, without a struggle, the possession of a large tract of land which he had bought, and was occupied by the «Angolares». This man, without other resources than his faith in the result of his attempt, a firm intention of conquering, and with the small means a private individual can dispose of for such undertakings, accompanied by some friends, as fearless as he, landed in the Bay of S. João, taking immediate possession of part of the territory which he had bought; he settled there with his companions, built dwelling houses, tilled lands, made plantations, opened roads, and with the occupation effected the sovereignty of our country over that part of the Island, where it had never before been acknowledged, and, in the course of time, and with the civilizing contact promoted by Sampaio, those indomitable savages were transformed into the present docile and valuable auxiliaries of the agriculturists, settled in the southern part of the Island of S. Thomé.

This courageous and patriotic act of Matheus Sampaio, crowned by such a brilliant result, did away with the secular legend regarding the invulnerability of the Angolares; the southern part of the Island was no longer the mysterious region, where nobody valuing his life durst venture; in a short time, the solitary wilds were cultivated, and those unknown territories transformed into vast fields of pacific labour, where the febrile activity of the planter produces a most important part of the cocoa industry, which S. Thomé exports annually to the different markets, without the least outlay or sacrifice on the part of the nation.

It does not appear that the modest originator of this great national service has

José Maria de Freitas

Died in 1868

One of the four pioneers of the present great agriculture of S. Thomé

even been praised by his country, but the badge, which, in our nation represents valour, loyalty, and merit, would worthily decorate the breast of that true Portuguese.

We will not conclude this historic memoir without mentioning another event, much spoken of at the time, and which signalized the forethought and patriotism of the illustrious official, who governed S. Thomé in the years 1885 and 1886.

On the 5th of August 1885, a mixed treaty of sovereignty and protectorate was signed in the Auguanzum Palace, district of Gebé in the Kingdom of Dahomey, between Doctor Bernardino Meyrelles Leite, Envoy of the Governor of S. Thomé, representing the Portuguese Nation, and Prince Conhondú, (afterwards King Behanzim) who represented the Kingdom of Dahomey, by which the suburb of Zomai, forming the extension of the Port of Adra to the fortress of S. João Baptista, and the Port of Adra itself, were put under Portuguese dominion, and our protectorate established over all the remaining seaboard of the Dahomey Kingdom.

On the 2nd of September, in the same year, the Governor of the Province, Custodio Miguel Borja, with his wife and the forces requisite for the occupation, embarked in the gunboat *Sado,* commanded by Lieutenant Commander Schultz.

Some days later, the *Sado* arrived at the Port of Adra, and on the 8th of September, Governor Borja, in the name of Portugal, occupied the territories and Port given over to our sovereignty by the treaty alluded to; then, the protectorate of the seaboard was proclaimed, the chief points occupied and fortified, and everything being concluded in five days, he returned to S. Thomé, where he landed on the 19th, making immediate official communication to the Foreign Powers, through their respective Consuls, according to article 34, Chapter VI, of the final act of the Berlin Conference, held on the 26th of February, 1885.

This opportune measure of the far-seeing Governor Borja at once opened a new source of emigration, and during the 27 months that our dominion and protectorate of Dahomey lasted, S. Thomé received from there 716 labourers.

But this courageous act of Governor Borja, fully sanctioned by Pinheiro Chagas and the Government of which this notable statesman was a member (Decree of the 29th of December 1885), was not fated to have a prolonged existence.

That minister fell, Henrique de Macedo, afterwards Conde de Macedo, being appointed Minister of Marine and the Colonies, and by the Decree of the 19th December, 1887 signed by him, the treaty of Aguanzum was set aside, and thus, all the advantages gained by this treaty, were lost to Portugal and the Province of S. Thomé. Shortly afterwards, France, without hindrance, conquered Dahomey, and incorporated into her Colonial possessions what we had abandoned, our Fortress of S. João Baptista d'Ajudá lying within the bounds of French territory!

It is just to say that, whilst our serviceable planters were dedicating themselves to the construction of that great work of Portuguese Colonizing genius, some of the Home Governments, with notable forethought, followed and protected the work of the colonists and labourers, although slowly and with intermittance, decreeing adequate laws, destined to guarantee the rights of both, and facilitate the progress of the community.

We have already mentioned the opening of communications with the metropolis in 1858, by means of a monthly line of steamers, the establishment of the «Banco Nacional Ultramarino» in 1867, destined to exercise great influence in the material prosperity of the Province, and the suppression of the convict settlement, a most powerful source of native demoralisation, and a discredit to the Province. Other measures, tending to the same purpose, were successively adopted.

The general labour regulations of the 20th November, 1875 issued by Andrade Corvo, those of the 21st November, 1878 by Thomaz Ribeiro, those of the 29th January, 1903 by Teixeira de Sousa, the latter serving as the pattern by which later reforms have been modelled, those of the 23rd April, 1908 by Augusto Castilho, those of the 31st December in the same year by Antonio Cabral, and those of the 17th July, 1909 by Terra Vianna, the provincial regulations of the 29th April, 1876 of the Governor Gregorio José Ribeiro, and those of the 17th August 1880 of the Visconde de S. Januario, and many other measures scattered in the books of Colonial legislation throughout the evolution of years, succeeded in resolving the labour problems, assuring and guaranteeing the rights of the labourer and planter, and maintaining the most complete harmony between those two great factors of agricultural life and progress.

Andrade Corvo's organization of the Colonial Public works, entrusting the important duties of this branch of the Public service in S. Thomé, to a technical Department duly furnished with professional and material resources; the different alterations in the shipping contracts, thus obtaining three voyages per month; the great reduction in freights; the great improvement in the plant employed by the companies; the increased velocity of steamers, connecting the East and West Coasts of Africa; the telegraphic communication established between the two Islands and the submarine cable, contracted by the Minister Pinheiro Chagas, and the alterations in the original contract tending to make the service cheaper; the gratuitous passage, in Government vessels, of African labourers for the plantations of S. Thomé decreed by the same minister, as well as, that of Chinese labourers shipped from Macau to S. Thomé and Principe, also in Government vessels, by order of the Ministers Neves Ferreira and Ferreira d'Almeida; the establishment of the telephone in S. Thomé, under the direct administration of the Government; the navigation round the coast of the Island of S. Thomé, the erection of light-houses in the Port; the building of bridges and quays, the Trindade-Magdalena railway in course of construction; the founding of the Ultramarine Building Society which is of such great benefit to the Colony; the starting of labour emigration, from all the Portuguese Colonies to the plantations of S. Thomé and Principe; all these measures and others of less importance of daily occurrence, and lastly the visit of the ill-fated Crown Prince D. Luiz Filippe and the Minister of Marine, Ayres de Ornellas, with their suites, to the plantations of S. Thomé, at the time when the English defamation campaign, against the agrarian regime of the Province, was at its height (July, 1907) marking a celebrated date, which history and tradition will perpetuate in the memory of the future agricultural generations of S. Thomé; demonstrate the solicitude and interest, with which the higher representatives of the Nation, beginning with the Royal Family itself, have assisted, appreciated and encouraged the efforts of private enterprise.

The S. Thomé planters complain that the Government has done little or nothing of what they could and ought to do to improve ordinary traffic, and the inhabitants of the city likewise state that sanitary arrangements, public hygiene and the Port services, leave much to be desired.

Major Antonio Joaquim da Fonseca

Commander of the battalion of Rifles n.º 2, stationed at S. Thomé,
in the year 1875

All have some reason for their complaints, but between such a statement and the affirmation which sometimes is made, that the Government has done nothing, there is a vast difference, as is clearly proved by this explanation we have given above.

And to conclude this chapter, we will reproduce Mr. W. A. Cadbury's notification of the boycottage of our cocoa and our reply to him.

«Bourneville, Near Birmingham — March 15th 1909.

«Francisco Mantero, Esq. — Lisbon.

Dear Sir

«I have now returned from Africa and propose to publish a full account of my journey in connection with the labour question on the cocoa estates of S. Thomé and Principe. During my visit in Angola the first 15 men were repatriated from the Island, only one of these having any money from the Repatriation Fund on arrival in Angola.

«The Governor General of Angola told me that no alteration had been made in the system of recruiting. I had the pleasure of meeting Commander Paula Cid, who, I was glad to learn, intended to suggest some reforms to his own Government.

«My firm, in conjunction with the others who have supported us, feel that they have now no alternative but to withdraw for the present from the purchase of S. Thomé cocoa. The enclosed circular will show you that they will be glad at any time to find that the necessary reforms have actually taken place.

«Yours truly

«(Signed) *William A. Cadbury.*»

«*Circular.* — Labour on the Cocoa Plantations of S. Thomé and Principe.

«Mr. William A. Cadbury returned to England last week from a journey extending over five months, to the Portuguese Islands of S. Thomé and Principe, and to the mainland of Angola, in which he was accompaned by Mr. Joseph Burtt.

«The object of his visit was to ascertain to what extent the promises of reform made to him at Lisbon in December 1907, by the Portuguese Government had been carried out. These promises were the result of the presentation to the Government and the Estate Proprietors of the report of Mr. Joseph Burtt and Dr. W. Claude Horton. It will be remembered that these gentlemen were sent out in 1905 by the three principal English cocoa firms and a leading German firm to investigate the conditions of indentured labour in S. Thomé and Principe, and the methods by which, it was recruited in Angola, and that their inquiry lasted nearly two years.

«Mr. Cadbury has found that no adequate steps have yet been taken to remedy the evils proved to exist. He intends very shortly to publish a full narrative of his investigations.

«His report has been carefully considered by the three firms on whose behalf he went out: — Messrs Cadbury Bros, Ltd, Bourneville, Messrs J. S. Fry & Sons, Ltd, Bristol, and Messrs. Rowntree & C.º, Ltd, York. These firms have come to the conclusion that the time has now arrived when they must mark, by definite action, their disappointment at the failure of the Portuguese Government to fulfil the pledges of reform, on the strength of which they agreed for a time to continue commercial relations with the Islands.

«They have therefore decided not to make any further purchases of the cocoa produced in the Islands of S. Thomé and Principe.

«They will watch with sympathetic interest any efforts which may be made by the Portuguese Government or by the Estate Proprietors to remedy the evils of the existing system.

«They will be prepared to reconsider their decision as to purchase, when they are satisfied that such reforms have been carried out as to secure to the indentured labourers from Angola, not merely on paper but in actual fact, freedom in entering into the contract of service and full opportunity of returning to their homes when the contract expires.»

«Lisbon, 22nd March, 1909.

«William A. Cadbury, Esq. — Birmingham.

Dear Sir

«I acknowledge the receipt of your letter of the 15th inst., and note, your return to England from your journey to our African Provinces on the West Coast; your intention to publish a report of that journey; that during your stay in Angola, 15 repatriated labourers returned, but one only brought money from the Repatriation Fund; that the Governor for Angola stated that no reforms had been effected, and that Commander Cid was going to propose them; and that your firm, together with others accompanying you, regret being compelled to give up purchasing our cocoa for the present, but will be very pleased to learn that reforms are being carried out, etc., etc.

«Thanking you for the kindness of your communication, I beg to congratulate you on your return to your home and family.

«The law of the 29th January, 1903 establishing the Repatriation Fund and bonus has no retroactive effect, this being the case with all Portuguese legislation.

«Its terms are applicable to the immigration which took, or will take place after the law came into force. The immigration previous to that date is regulated by the legislation then existing.

«Owing to this, only labourers arriving after the law of the 29th January 1903 came into force, deposit part of their earnings in the Repatriation Fund, but those who came to the Islands before that date have no share in it, since their wages were paid them in full, and they did not contribute in any way towards its maintenance. Regarding the 15 repatriated labourers mentioned by you, 14 belonged to the second category and one to the first, hence the reason why only the latter received a bonus.

Dr. Matheus Augusto Ribeiro de Sampaio
Who effected the pacific occupation of the Angolares region

«I am not in a position to make any statement as to the opinions and projects of Conselheiro Cid, nor as to the intentions of our Government. Both will doubtless do their utmost to forward the interests of the Nation.

«Part of the English public do not approve of the manner in which our country is governed, and consider the time taken by the Government excessive to find out whether reforms are necessary and what form they should take, and on this account, the chocolate makers are forced to give up the consumption of Portuguese cocoa until our processes of administration are modified, according to the taste of that fraction of the English public.

«If the Portuguese way of thinking and mode of proceeding were identical, as in this country there is a portion of the public that does not sympathize with certain methods of Government employed in England, that public would force those Portuguese who buy English goods to suspend their imports, shippers and passengers not to make use of English steamers, the natives of Mozambique not to emigrate to Transvaal, etc., etc., until England should resolve to govern according to the way of thinking of that portion of the Portuguese public.

«But our way of thinking is very different.

«We understand that each country should govern itself as it thinks fit.

«This, however, is merely an expression of opinion between two countries, because as regards cocoa, the Portuguese planters do not attempt to force their produce on anyone.

«Only those who require and desire it, need buy.

«Wishing you much prosperity

I remain, dear Sir

Yours truly

«(Signed) *Francisco Mantero*».

Conselheiro Manoel Pinheiro Chagas

Minister of Marine and the Colonies in 1885. Signed the Decree sanctioning the treaty of a Protectorate
and sovereignty in Dahomey,
and ordered the free transport of labourers from Ajudá to S. Thomé, in Government ships

CHAPTER II.

Conditions of Production and Labour at the present Day.

As we have remarked, ever since slavery, the principal element of agricultural work in the Islands, ceased, owing to the legislative measures adopted by Parliament in 1875, the pretext no longer existed for the English Government to hinder the immigration of African hands; and those measures having contributed, though insufficiently, to facilitate the introduction of agricultural labourers to be employed in tilling the soil, in the culture of trees, and the gathering of the harvests, a new period of prosperity opened for the energy and colonizing capacity of the Portuguese, making, within a few years, the Island of S. Thomé the richest of our possessions, the model colony, par excellence. In its plantations, the colonists of other nations served their apprenticeship, there acquiring the knowledge, experience, perseverance, and prudence inspired by example, which afterwards served to initiate the development and prosperity in their own Colonies, which they now enjoy.

The modern labour conditions in S. Thomé and Principe can be, and have been seen and studied by Portuguese and foreigners, when they visit the different plantations of the Islands. The contracting of work is public, a week's notice being given, and anybody so wishing may be present.

The hospitality on the plantations is proverbial and is denied to no one, and anybody can stay for a length of time with the planter; nothing takes place there secretly, or that may not be seen, and — excepting some English visitors who have unfavourably criticized everything, or almost everything, — there is not one person, French, German, Belgian, and even some English, that does not agree that the labourer in S. Thomé and Principe, enjoys an exceptionally favourable treatment, having his welfare so assured as to cause the envy of many workmen in Europe.

The crisis of manual labour, determined by the transition from slavery to freedom, and the natural desire of the planters to increase their cultivations, caused them, in the first period of expansion, to seek the assistance of labourers from various sources.

It was due to this, that the immigration of black labourers, from the opposite coast, was commenced and maintained for some time. Numerous natives from

Liberia, Accra, and the Cameroons, came to work in S. Thomé and Principe, and stayed there for some years. Later on, when repatriated, they took back, together with agricultural knowledge, habits of order, work, and thrift, the seeds of the plants they had cultivated in our Islands, founding future plantations which were to enrich their country.

The plantations of Monte-Café, S. Nicolau, Saudade, Nova-Móka, Santa-Margarida, Monte-Macaco, Rio d'Oiro, Boa-Entrada, Agua-Izé, Porto-Real, Sundy, etc. etc., were all schools of agriculture and civilizing colonization, for the half savage hordes sent to us by the English and German Colonies of Accra and the Cameroons.

Portugal has this further share of glory in the European nations which have worked for the civilization and progress of Africa. We do not educate only our own labourers in S. Thomé and Principe, but those of other nations as well; we not only created the emporium of cocoa in S. Thomé, but also that of England on the Gold Coast, and that of Germany in Biafra Bay.

On the 1st of February, 1876, the first labourers from Accra arrived at S. Thomé on board the English steamer *Congo,* and on the 19th of September 1875 by the same steamer, the first batch from the Cameroons. At that time, the cultivation of cocoa was unknown in those countries, and the production in the Province of S. Thomé was 1.000:000 kilogrammes.

In the year 1909, the exportation from the Colonies was:

S. Thomé and Principe	30.261:000 kilos.	(1)
Accra	18.913:649 »	(2)
Cameroons	3.000:000 »	(3)

. . . .

These eloquent figures render other considerations needless regarding the civilizing influence exercised by S. Thomé over the population and territories of those Colonies.

If the fertility of the soil of our islands is unrivalled in any part of the Globe, so also are the Portuguese planters unsurpassed by any other nation's African colonists in their efforts to adapt themselves to the exigencies of so inhospitable a climate, in their agricultural skill, and in the humane treatment of their labourers.

Hence the reason why, in the space of half a century, great tracts of land have been cleared for agricultural purposes, plantations of rich tropical products multiplied, and dwellings built for labourers, managers, and the remaining European personnel; roads have been opened, and Decauville railways laid down in most of the plantations, thus lessening the difficulties of the carriage of produce; by the improvement in the sanitary conditions of the cultivated districts, and also by the

---

(1) Calculation based on the imports into Lisbon and Funchal, from 1st January to 31st December, 1909. (504:350 bags of 60 kilos.)

(2) Statistics of the agricultural year from 1st October, 1908 to 30th September, 1909 l. b. s. 41. 206,297 (Martin Weinstein & Ct.ª

(3) Approximate calculation, as no complete statistics are to hand (ditto).

Conselheiro Custodio Miguel de Borja
Governor of the Province of S. Thomé and Principe,
who ordered
the negotiations for the Protectorate over Dahomey

teaching of hygiene to the natives, the conditions of health have been modified; and as production has been perfected, and conditions of labour so regulated, as to make them easily supportable to all, nothing remains of the roughness and anarchy of former times beyond the disagreeable recollection that we all are anxious to forget.

General Conditions of the Labourer's Welfare. — All our remarks refer to properties exploited by Europeans or intelligent natives, or by their descendants and successors, who have continued the improved methods initiated by their antecessors; as the «forros» and small native plantations are cultivated, in a rudimentary manner, by the owners themselves assisted by their families, they are being gradually absorbed into the larger estates, which are worked by more modern methods, so it is needless to take them into consideration.

We must now state that no important industries exist in either of the Islands, but merely unimportant manufactures, inherent to small centres of population.

Agriculture is the main-spring of all the commercial movement in the two Islands. United under the same political and administrative management, each constitutes a small Colony divided into numerous individual enterprises. As labourers from the Tropics more easily overcome the trying effects of the climate, both Islands offer them conditions of life superior to those enjoyed in their own countries.

The climate is no doubt unhealthy for Europeans, but for Africans, owing to the sanitary conditions, coupled with many comforts, it is vastly superior to that of the hinterland of Angola, whence come the majority of labourers imported into S. Thomé. Here they are not exposed to the five great scourges which cruelly decimate the continental populations of Equatorial Africa, — sleeping sickness, (1) small-pox, (2) venereal diseases, alcoholisms and wars.·

The hygienic resources and medical attendance, the well-supplied pharmacies and comfortable infirmaries established in all the working centres guarantee, from a sanitary point of view, the care indispensable for the preservation of health and the nursing of the sick.

The labourers occupied by day in moderate work, fed with good and abundant food, living in healthy dwellings, spending their holidays in amusements and dances according to their native customs, with no family cares, as these are undertaken by the proprietors, lead a tranquil and even a happy life in the compounds with their fellow countrymen.

They acquire habits of civilization and thrift, can form family ties and look forward to a happier future than if they had remained in the savage regions of their native countries.

Form of Work. — As we have already mentioned, large tracts of land suitable for agriculture have already been cleared in the two islands of S. Thomé and Prin-

(1) In our Islands, sleeping-sickness only exists in the north of Principe, where it is being energetically combated with excellent results, by the destruction of the tzé-tzé. This fly only exists in that region, but is now rarely seen, and owing to the isolation of those bitten, the hope is entertained, that this scourge will shortly be extinguished.

(2) Since vaccination was made compulsory, small-pox epidemics have ceased in the Islands, and when any case appears it is generally sporadic and very slight.

cipe. Besides cocoa the principal product of the Islands, coffee, sugar, rubber, quinine, palm, bananas, bread-fruit and other fruits for local consumption are cultivated.

However, there is still a large quantity of virgin soil, and generally, the plantations are increased every year by new tracts of land. Cultivation is preceded by cutting down the gigantic brushwood, which grows wild in all uncultivated districts.

As a rule this work, one of the hardest demanded by agriculture, is not performed by the ordinary labourers in many plantations. Generally, the «Angolares», strong men but averse to salaried labour, and descendants of the Angola blacks already alluded to, who settled in S. Thomé when a ship carrying slaves was wrecked in 1540, undertake to cut down the forests by piecework, as, jealous of their nomadic habits, they prefer occasional work to the methodical and permanent work of the ordinary labourer, and do the jobs when they feel disposed. When the ordinary labourers are employed in this work, the more robust are always chosen.

The ground is prepared for the plants, the plantations are laid out, and periodically, the young plants are pruned and the ground weeded; afterwards the fruit is gathered, laid out to dry, prepared, and conveyed to the port for shipment.

Carriers have been practically done away with in most of the plantations. Decauville railways, either of animal or steam traction, aerial lines and vehicles, drawn by oxen or mules are used to assist in the execution of this heavy and important work on the estates, and thence to the shipping ports. Transport by sea is also largely made use of, there being a coasting steamer of 300 tons register, which runs round S. Thomé four times monthly, and several private tug-boats used for towing the numerous barges occupied in this service. By private landing-stages in each plantation, the maritime arrangements are completed, and labourers are not obliged to go into the water or carry heavy burdens.

Conditions of the Present and Future Prosperity of the Province. — Notwithstanding the heavy cost of manual labour arising from the permanent difficulty of the contracting of labourers, and the heavy rates charged by the Government and the Municipality, the actual conditions of prosperity in the Province may be considered satisfactory.

But, if the situation may be considered favourable from a general point of view, the same cannot be said regarding a great number of enterprises.

The owners of the old estates, who started the plantations in the first period of the agricultural revival in the Colony, and those who followed, commenced their business at a time when general charges were much smaller, and have already repaid the capital lent them, a large part of their plantations having reached maturity; therefore, the cost of their explorations is proportionately less, and an income considerably larger is obtained. The condition of those planters is prosperous.

But such is not the case with those who began later.

Land, which formerly was very cheap, became very dear, and all agricultural expenses increased fabulously.

Nearly all the plantations having been acquired with borrowed capital, the cost of land and houses being very great, and there being a long delay in the development and maturity of the cocoa, the modern estates, the most numerous, are undergoing financial difficulties, increased by the actual low price of cocoa, which, if prolonged,

Conselheiro João Antonio de Brissac das Neves Ferreira

Minister of Marine and the Colonies, who ordered the transport of Chinese labourers to S. Thomé and Principe, in Government ships

will compel the State to lower the rates to avoid the ruin of the planters, and the serious consequences of such a disaster for the latter and for the Treasury.

However, history has taught us during the last 3o years, that the fluctuations of the cocoa market are periodical, and that low prices are generally succeded by high ones, and so forth.

These fluctuations, helping to overcome the critical period of their primary difficulties, constitute the chief hope of modern agriculturists in S. Thomé and Principe. As there is no reason to suppose that such fluctuations will not be repeated, the hope is well founded that a brilliant future is reserved for our Islands, due to the unrivalled fertility of their soil and the planters' indefatigable efforts to hasten results, plantations are annually extended, those of former years grow and flourish abundantly, the production increases from year to year, and the quality is constantly improving.

The last measures, decreed by the Government of the metropolis, tend to facilitate and regulate the engagement of labourers, by which it is confidently expected that the supply of hands will be increased, and consequently, the conditions of manual labour improve, and attenuate the difficulties of many planters and assure the increasing prosperity of the Colony.

It is certain that, as we have already had occasion to mention, following the example of the Portuguese planters, so unjustly criticized of late, owing to the envy caused by their flourishing agriculture, centres of similar produce have been established in the Colonies of other countries, which ship to the different markets large quantities of products, in competition with S. Thomé and Principe, and this may, in the future, cause stagnation or a lowering of the prices, as it has already done. But at the same time, it is evident, that the world's consumption of the chief product of our Islands, cocoa, tends to increase in an extraordinary measure, as is proved by the map accompanying this work.

It appears to us that, considering the incontestable existence of a privileged soil, the evident capacity for colonizing and the enterprise of our planters, assisted by the most modern processes of labour the new rules for regulating the engagement of labour, shortly to be put into execution, the labourers being employed under a humane system, all the elements of prosperity unite to enable this Province to maintain in the future, the pre-eminent position gained amongst the most flourishing Colonies of a similar kind, if the traditional enemies of the Province of S. Thomé and Principe, the philanthropic English (sic), do not succeed in destroying, by some means, that prosperity, and if the campaign of ruin and discredit be stopped, which has recently been carried under the pretext of humanity, which neither England nor any other country practises with greater generosity than the planters of S. Thomé and Principe.

Economic Conditions of Labour — In view of the permanent scarcity of hands the cost of manual labour is very heavy, and is further increased by the reasons already mentioned, namely, the continual development of the plantations, the constant necessity of importing labourers, and the great expenses incurred with their recruitment, transport, food, clothing, medical attendance, housing and wages.

According to the latest general rules, relative to the emigration of labourers for S. Thomé and Principe, dated the 17th of July, 1909, the monthly wages for males will never be less than rs. 2⍾5oo, and rs. 1⍾8oo for females, but, as a rule, it is more, there being labourers who earn, from rs. 4$000 to rs. 9$000. Half of the wage is paid monthly to the interested parties on the first Sunday or Monday after it is due, and the balance is paid over by the employers themselves into the Repatriation Fund, established by the same rules, where it remains deposited, until it is given to the repatriated labourers on their arrival home; the payment to the Fund is effected annually, after all advances, connected with contract expenses and pensions paid to the men's families, have been deducted.

The employer, in addition to the above mentioned wages, has to bear the charges of housing the men, according to the regulations established by the authorities, and also their board, clothing, medical attendance, and return passages from the starting point. Therefore, having to incur all these expenses, and keep a stock of provisions, merchandise, various kinds of manufactures, as well as to pay doctors and medicines, it is evident, that in a Colony where everything necessary has to be imported from distant countries, excepting a very limited number of agricultural products, such as coffee, cocoa, etc., which are generally for export, that it is only by the outlay of capital, that stores and employees for work on the estates, can be obtained.

Conditions of the Labourers' Life — The life of the labourers of both sexes in the plantations passes smoothly, in the monotony of work and the sports peculiar to people in a state of imperfect civilization.

The climate, though not always suitable for Europeans, is not so unfavourable for Africans, in fact, it compares advantageously with that of some of the regions where the labourers have been recruited, the work is methodical and moderate, and the treatment — dwellings and food — is much superior on the plantations, to that in the irregular and savage life of the backwoods.

At day break a bell is rung to awaken the dwellers, who, at 6 o'clock, begin their daily task. At 8 o'clock the work is suspended for breakfast until 8.30, and again at 11.30, for dinner, and after a rest of two hours, is resumed until sunset, which, in S. Thomé and Principe, is invariably at 6 p. m. When work is over they present themselves in a body in the courtyard of the estate, to receive their evening meal, and, at a given signal, they disperse and go to their compounds, where they sup and amuse themselves in talking and dancing until the bell rings at 9 o'clock, which is the hour for going to bed. On holidays, when leave is given them to retire later, they generally amuse themselves by getting up war dances, a favourite amusement, and give vent to their feelings of joy by dancing and gesticulating, singing and yelling accompanied by drums, causing a deafening clamour.

They have no trouble with regard to the support of their families, seeing all are under the charge of the employers, who, as stated, in addition to dwellings, wages and return passages to the starting points, give them three meals a day, already cooked, or raw for them to cook at their own choice, besides clothing, healthy dwelling-houses, medical attendance, medicines and dietary.

The labourers also enjoy the following advantages:

The right to leave the plantations, and lay any complaints before the authorities regarding infringements of their contracts or against bad treatment. In the actions arising from these complaints, which are summary and of rapid solution, they pay no costs and have free legal advice, and are assisted by the Curator-gene-

Rear-Admiral Augusto de Castilho

Minister of Marine and the Colonies, under whose administration the emigration from Mozambique to S. Thomé was initiated

ral in any criminal cases in which they may be involved; they are not subject to military service, nor do they pay taxes; they receive good conduct rewards from the planters, instruction in agriculture and trades, a home in old age, or when unable to work, as well as food, clothing, housing and medical attendance for their children; they are encouraged by the advice and example of their employers to give up heathenism, and, with their families, are prepared for baptism, the planters standing sponsors in these solemn acts of Christianity; the planters suppress polygamy and encourage the formation of family ties, and instil into their employees habits of temperance for the complete abandonment of drunkenness. The laws and regulations in force prohibit, even to the authorities, corporal punishment or the stoppage of food.

Owing to all these advantages and privileges, coupled with the fatherly interest always shown them, both by employers and Curators, the labourers enjoy a comparatively enviable existence, and therefore, on the termination of their contracts, as they are enjoying a position happier than they would have done in their own villages, the natives of Angola prefer to fix their residence in the Islands rather than return home, and regarding those of Cape Verde, Cabinda and Mozambique, countries of a more advanced social organization, some remain, others go and visit their families and return afterwards accompanied by their wives (1).

Provident Institutions — In the measures, adopted by all Portuguese Governments, for the emigration of labourers of S. Thomé and Principe, the foreseeing and kind spirit of the Portuguese is displayed in various ways, for ameliorating the lot of those placed by Providence under their care.

Curators are appointed, in connection with the Governmental departments, in each of the Provinces of Angola, Mozambique, S. Thomé and Principe, according to the law of the 29th of April, 1875. These officials are magistrates, and by the regulations of the 21st of November, 1878 are considered the natural protectors of the labourers and colonists. They have ample power, together with responsibility, to render the duty they have to exercise, effective.

The Curator-general, in the execution of his duties, intervenes in the effecting of contracts between employers and men, and according to the respective regulations is responsible for the inclusion of those conditions in all contracts, as stipulated by the laws and regulations; he refuses to sanction them, if he find reasons for so doing; he observes on his own account, and on that of his subordinates, if the terms of the engagements are faithfully complied with, and carries out inspections directly, or through his delegates, when necessary; he receives all communications and complaints personally or through his delegates, regarding the manner in which laws and regulations are carried out; finally, he has to do everything necessary for the protection of those engaged, and also, to compel the latter to fulfil their part of the contract.

The Curator-general, for the speedy removal of any obstacles which may arise,

---

(1) Many labourers of Quillimane (Mozambique) recently repatriated, have already returned to the Agua-Izé plantation, taking their wives back with them. The emigration, from Mozambique to S. Thomé, was started about a year and a half ago.

and to have a free hand for the execution of his duties, is in direct communication with the Minister of Marine and the Colonies, all the Provincial authorities and all Provincial governors and curators. He cannot be impeded, in the exercise of his office, by any Provincial authority, all are bound to render him assistance in the fulfilment of his duty, and the administrative authorities of each district, as well as the Government agents, must also give him every assistance, and execute his orders.

It is strictly forbidden to employ labourers in any work that forces them to cross rivers or walk in water above the knee, and adequate measures are also established for the protection of women in the critical period of maternity; and also for minors and children, and to assure medical attendance to all the labourers and families.

Every employer of more than fifty labourers is obliged to establish separate infirmaries for each sex, to be gratuitously attended by a proper nursing staff and provided with the necessary ambulance service, in cases of illness, if there is no hospital within five kilometres distance from the patients' place of abode or habitual occupation. If the labourers go into hospital, expenses are borne by the employers.

The Island of S. Thomé is divided into fourteen sanitary districts, and the Island of Principe into two, each district having a doctor who must be a licentiate of any of the medical schools of Lisbon, Porto, or Coimbra, who is paid by the estate owners residing in each district, and the remuneration he is to receive is determined by the local Board of labour and emigration.

The doctors are obliged to reside in the districts where they have to exercise their profession or in the neighbourhood; they visit daily the plantations where one thousand or more labourers are employed, bi-weekly where there are six hundred or more, and at least weekly, all the other estates, in addition, they are obliged to pay extra visits in urgent cases. They are the sanitary inspectors of the plantations, and, in that capacity, they can examine all the personnel, order any restrictions even to complete cessation of work; these orders are compulsory, and are registered, as well as any other medical occurrences, by the doctor himself, in a book furnished by the employer, the leaves being numbered and initialed by the Curator or his delegate.

Women labourers have leave thirty days previous to the probable date of their confinement, and thirty days after, without loss of wages; during the first six months of nursing, they may only be employed in light tasks, whether indoor or outdoor.

The work of felling trees and gathering coffee may only be performed by males over 16 years of age; minors, aged from 11 to 14 years, must only be employed in picking fruit, tenting fields, looking after poultry, and in any domestic work suited to their age.

In each plantation or establishment where there are children under 7 years of age, whatever their number may be, belonging to labourers or colonials, a crèche exists where they are looked after, whilst their mothers are at work.

The Council presided over by the Governor of the Province, after consulting the local Board of labour and emigration, determines the requisite rules for the regulating of infirmaries or hospitals, crèches, dwellings or compounds for the habitation of labourers, as well as their hygienic conditions, system of cleanliness and everything conducive to the welfare of the labourers.

If the planters do not carry out the rules established by the Governor, they

Conselheiro Antonio Teixeira de Sousa

Minister of Marine and the Colonies, author of the Regulation Decree of 29th January 1903,
which has served as a model for all subsequent legislation relating to manual labour
in S. Thomé and Principe

are subject to heavy fines, ranging from Réis 5o$000 to Réis 1:200$000, (1) which are paid into the labour and emigration Fund.

The regulations in force establish provident measures, tending to protect the present and future necessities of the labourers and their families.

According to the regulations, a Fund styled «Labour and Repatriation», is established in S. Thomé for the exclusive benefit of the labourers. (2) The employers deposit annually half of the labourers' wages in this Fund, which amount is reserved as a repatriation bonus and credited to each of the interested parties, and is paid to them, on the termination of their contracts, by the Government agents accompanying them on board, on arrival at the ports of destination. The money is paid in the presence of the Curator and the local emigration agent.

Should the labourers renew their contracts, they are paid in full, and the sum, which had previously been deducted as a bonus, continues deposited until their repatriation.

The Local Board of Labour and Emigration furnishes each repatriated labourer, before leaving S. Thomé and Principe, with an authentic document stating the exact sum he has to receive on arrival at the port of destination.

On accepting contracts, labourers are permitted to receive two months wages in advance, and pensions, of the fifth part of the same wages, may also be paid to their families.

These pensions are forwarded direct by the employer to the respective emigration agents, and the latter send to the Curator's office at S. Thomé a receipt in duplicate, viséd by the curator of the locality where the payment is effected. The amount of the advances and pensions is deducted from the balance of the wages deposited annually, by the employers in the Labour and Repatriation Fund.

In cases of death, the sum deposited belonging to foreigners and to natives of Angola, will immediately be transferred to the Provincial Treasury department for payment to the heirs, and that belonging to labourers of other Portuguese Colonies, forwarded to the families through the local emigration agent, in presence of the respective Curator, documents being made in triplicate and witnessed by two trustworthy persons, one copy is sent to the local Board at S. Thomé, another to the Government office, and the third to the agency which carries out the transaction.

All the measures stated are to be found in the official diplomas in force, which also determine the heavy fines imposed on all that do not comply with the same.

In conclusion, a local Board of Labour and Emigration meets in the Island of S. Thomé under the presidency of the Curator-general, its members being the chief sanitary officer, a surveyor, a manager of the «Banco Ultramarino», and three proprietors or estate managers. There is also another Board in the Island of Principe, under the presidency of the district Governor, consisting of the Curator's delegate and one planter.

The duties of these Boards are to supervise, without interfering with the attri-

---

(1) £ 10 to £ 240.
(2) On the 28th January, 1910, the sum deposited in the Labour and Repatriation Fund, amounted to Reis 445:762$157 (about £ 89:000).

butes of the Curator or his delegate, everything that concerns labour in the Province of S. Thomé and Principe, to draw up plans and instructions, after due consultation with the local authorities and Government of the metropolis. They have amongst other attributes, the right of supervising the Labour and Repatriation Fund, without encroaching upon the duties of the Treasury Inspector, and of seeing that the terms of the contracts are faithfully carried out, especially with regard to dwellings, medical attendance, nursing the sick, repatriation, renewal of contracts, etc. etc.

Laboratory in the hospital, Porto-Real Plantation (East). Island of Principe

CHAPTER III.

Centres whence the Labourers come.

The places, whence labourers emigrate to the Province of S. Thomé and Principe, are chiefly those we are about to indicate, according to the number of emigrants attributed to each: Hinterland of Angola, Cabinda, North Coast of this Province, Mozambique, Cape Verde, and Guinea.

Angola.

The hinterland of Angola, to which we had occasion to allude in another part of this work, consists of vast regions in which predominate mountain ranges and table-lands, covered with thickets and forests, situated on the West Coast of the African Continent.

Various rivers of secondary importance rise in these table-lands, while others, of greater length, cross the Province and flow into the Atlantic Ocean. As it is situated hundreds of kilometres from the Ocean, without roads or railways, excepting the Ambaca line which serves the East of that Province, and that of Lobito, begun a few years ago, the reflections of a still backward civilization are but faintly felt. The best known signs of civilization in the regions of the hinterland, are fire-arms and the respective ammunition, cotton stuffs with which some of the natives partly clothe themselves and brandy.

The climate, less unhealthy than that of the coast, is subject to the general conditions of the tropics.

The natives of these regions live in a savage state, forming many independent tribes. They are children of nature, without ideas of morality, or of obedience to any principles. They are born, they grow and multiply, living in a promiscuousness of sexes, in primitive nakedness favoured by the climate, impelled by their animal instincts and merely restrained by the fanatical superstitions of gross fetichism.

They generally inhabit filthy huts or wig-wams, roughly put together, the construction of which is rapid and easy, as is suitable to the primitive nature of the inhabitants, the huts are grouped together into compounds and are abandoned in case of a quarrel with neighbouring tribes, or if they resolve to migrate to another locality.

Polygamy is recognized by tradition and custom in the union of sexes. One of the chief ambitions of the males, on attaining manhood, is to obtain means so as to support various wives. With this end in view, the natives decide to procure some remunerative labour, approaching the points inhabited by Europeans, or the roads leading to the coast, engaging themselves generally as carriers of merchandise, some also doing business on their own account.

Having acquired some means, they return to their tribes, get wives and endeavour to obtain cattle and other property, chiefly agricultural, the women tilling the land.

Individual property is unknown. Agriculture is scarce and uncertain, each one cultivating, as a rule, what is necessary for his own needs and, in some cases, for sale in the local markets.

As we have already stated, agriculture is worked by women, hap-hazard and unmethodically without much expense of labour; the younger boys watch the flocks; the men, principally those who have wives to work for them, go hunting, or remain in the compounds, giving way to their natural indolence, sleeping or smoking pipes.

The climate, nearly always warm and damp, invites quietude, and the complete absence of methodical work, the complete ignorance of the rights or duties of mankind ruled by definite social laws, the polygamy and promiscuousness of sexes, the war dances and spirits stimulating the senses, involving the race in an exhausting atmosphere, gives them a character of lassitude and negligence which overcomes their physical energy and natural robustness, making them averse to any methodical labour. Idleness and repugnance for work often force them to plunder provisions and cattle.

In fine, without any instruction or ideal of progress, without other necessities, except those arising from animal existence and from vices and passions inherent to rude and uncultured natures, the fertility of the soil permits them to pass their existence in almost permanent idleness.

Their favourite amusement is the war dance which takes place almost daily, a real orgy of dancing, singing, barbarous music and drunkenness, the neighbouring tribes also taking part in large numbers.

The war dances and other savage festivals solemnizing the burials of chiefs, which last three or four months, according to the rank of the deceased, plunder, and the conquest of wives give rise generally to quarrels, which often are the origin of wars between one tribe and another.

Dominated exclusively by barbarous traditional customs in which fetichism predominates, unlimited authority is exercised by the «regulos» or «sobas», chiefs of the tribes, who either inherit this position or conquer it by force, having absolute power over the life, liberty, and property of the tribesmen whom they rule, which right they exercise by proxy, substituting rational justice by cruel punishments, founded on supernatural proofs, invented by professional wizards in the service of these tyrants.

The existence of these people, compared with European civilization, can well be termed moral and social wretchedness, in which animalism triumphs by the right of the stronger. Polygamy, in both sexes, renders the formation of family ties impossible, whilst the despotic exercise of authority, which gives no regular guarantee for the security of persons and property, as well as other circumstances

Conselheiro Alfredo A. Freire d'Andrade

Governor-General of Mozambique, under whose administration the emigration of labourers
from that Province to S. Thomé was initiated

already mentioned, are so many agents for causing evil passions and dissolute customs.

To all this, must be added the propagation of syphilis, prevalent through all the interior, further aggravated by sleeping-sickness and frequent small-pox epidemics, and the actual effects of the economic, agricultural and commercial crisis, which the Province of Angola has felt for many years, causing the increase of misery from the coast to the confines of the hinterland.

Cabinda.

In Cabinda the social circumstances which from a remote era have surrounded the natives, have advanced, under many aspects, their state of civilization. Cabinda, a dependency of the general Government of Angola and administrated by a district Governor, is the Capital of the Congo district, the region being further divided into circumscriptions under European officials.

From the fact of this district being nearly all situated on the coast, or on the banks of the great estuary of the river Zaire, the natives, since the time when our navigators first landed there, have been in permanent communication with the Portuguese, and for centuries have considered them as the only white people worthy of the name, which, amongst them, signifies a superior race, and whose prestige was enough to subdue them, without recourse to violent means. The Portuguese occupation dates from centuries, at first under the rule of native chiefs acknowledging our sovereignity, and later under the regularly organized administration and authority of Europeans, and being exercised by officials from the metropolis, civilization was, consequently, more effectively spread.

A beginning of European colonization has been made in the district, in the shape of two companies, one commercial, and the other agricultural.

Domestic habits, as well as religious superstitions, native dwellings, villages and other traditional usages and vices, constituting the hereditary source of the negro race, still prevail amongst the natives, but these characteristics are now much attenuated. They already appreciate the benefits of progress, subordination, discipline, order and the advantages gained by working peacefully in the different occupations in which they are employed. European civilization scattered on the coast, especially in Cabinda, and the navigation to the latter and Zaire ports, give some impulse to the industries and trades which reach to the confines of the district, and thus, the natives become more civilized by being in contact with the traders.

The climate is essentially the same as that of the remainder of the Province of Angola, the seasons of the year being also identical, individual property is recognized, the soil is fertile, and in many places, agricultural products for use of the inhabitants are cultivated, as well as palm trees for the production of oil and cocoanut, and some plantations of cocoa, rubber, etc. exist.

The people have also appreciable qualities and aptitudes. The Cabindos are robust, well-proportioned, and their features are pleasanter than those of the majority of Africans in other regions.

Notwithstanding their violent language and their abuse of strong drinks, they are generally inoffensive, endowed with a good temper and rather intelligent, employing themselves in various occupations. There are amongst them skilful blacksmiths, locksmiths, weavers, cabinet-makers and carpenters who construct rowing and sailing boats, etc.

Born and bred on or near the coast, they have great vocation for the sea, many being employed on board vessels plying between the Gulf of Guinea and Mossamedes, as well as on the small craft used for cargo in the ports, and also as domestic servants.

In the steamers running between S. Thomé and Tiger Bay, many Cabindos are employed as stewards, etc.

The Cabinda district is therefore a region conquered by civilization, and shows its progress by different manifestations in the social life of its inhabitants, and constitutes a centre for the supply of labourers, who, although not very numerous, are very much appreciated, owing to their good qualities.

The natives emigrate freely to the Islands of S. Thomé and Principe, where they obtain a more advantageous wage for their services, and with the savings acquired, they buy ornaments for their wives on their return home.

In these Islands there are many Cabindos who are employed in various occupations, principally as sailors on the craft which load and unload the imports and exports of the Province, and also on the coasting vessels, rendering valuable assistance to the planters by conveying products for exportation from the estates to the Bay of Anna de Chaves, and from the Bay, stores and merchandise for the use of the plantations.

Mozambique.

The Province of Mozambique is situated on the eastern declivity of the African Continent bordering on the Indian Ocean, and extending from the mouth of the river Rovuma near Cape Delgado in the North to beyond Delagoa Bay in the South, having extensive but very irregular tracts of territory in the interior; its width in Zambezia from the mouths of the river Zambeze to the Nucabelle waterfall above Zumbo, is more than 800 kilometres.

The area of the Province 1.300:000 square kilometres, is inhabited by various races, such as «Landins», «Macuas», «Kaffirs», «Zulus», «Arabs», «Indians», half-castes, etc. etc.

Its chief products are rice, sugar, wax, Indian corn, cotton, tobacco, castor oil, jalap, senna, salsaparrilla, rubber, ivory, gum-copal, orchilla-weed, vegetable grease (mafurra from Inhambane), pepper, kidney beans, manioc, cocoanut, sesame, fruits, vegetables, magnificent timber suitable for cabinet work, dyed goods, etc., gold, silver, and coal.

The climate is tropical, very hot and generally unhealthy in the proximity of rivers and stagnant waters.

There are two seasons in the year, the rainy one lasting from December to March, and the dry one from April to November. The rainy season is the more unhealthy.

Conselheiro Francisco de Paula Cid
Governor of Cape Verde
when the emigration of labourers from that Province to S. Thomé
and Principe, was initiated

The social status of the inhabitants of the Province varies according to the regions. In the great towns on the coast, like Lourenço Marques, Beira, Mozambique and Quelimane, the habits are European; in other parts of the coast civilization advances but slowly and diminishes as one penetrates into the interior, many regions of the hinterland being still in a savage state. This difference is naturally explained by the permanent relations which the towns of great maritime movement maintain with the civilized World, and its progress irradiates in intensity from other parts of the coast to the interior, according to the distance of the localities and the facilities and frequency of the means of communication.

We must now refer to the treaty made between the representatives of the Portuguese and Transvaal Governments on the 1st April 1909, in the part relative to the acquisition of manual labour for the mines on the Rand, by the engagement of natives from Mozambique which this Province can supply, and which acquisition no doubt constitutes one of the chief purposes of the treaty referred to.

The execution of the clauses relative to the recruitment of labourers from Mozambique for the Transvaal, if not suitably modified, will exercise a disastrous influence on the centres of population of our Province, and may shortly cause difficulties to the introduction of labourers in the Islands of S. Thomé and Principe.

By the clauses alluded to, the English, represented by the Transvaal Government are permitted to treat the natives of Mozambique destined for the mines on the Rand in a manner, which the same English, actuated — they say — by humanitarian sentiments, would absolutely condemn, if carried out by the S. Thomé and Principe planters.

That it is to say: the Portuguese of this latter Province can only engage labourers for their agricultural enterprises in other Portuguese possessions burdened by heavy obligations almost beyond their resources. The English will not allow this recruitment under more economical conditions, but forgot their vaunted humanitarian sentiments, when they made the clauses relative to the recruitment of natives of Mozambique for the Rand mines, and dispensed with all, or nearly all the obligations established for the recruitment of labourers for the Islands of S. Thomé and Principe.

And this is verified, if we examine the clauses of that treaty relative to the subject, which was negotiated at the same time as when the Portuguese Government decreed the regulation of 31st December 1908, actually substituted by that of 17th July 1909.

By both these conventions the planters of the Portuguese Colony of S. Thomé and Principe, as has been stated more than once in this work, are obliged to contract labourers from other Portuguese provinces, guaranteeing them the privileges of an exceptional situation such as:

Board and lodging until they leave the port of embarkation, a free passage and their keep during the voyage;

Healthy dwellings, food, clothing, nursing in case of illness of the labourers and their families;

Medical attendance, medicines, crèches, hospitals, everything in fact indispensable and perhaps superfluous for the welfare of even civilized beings, much more so for people who neither know nor appreciate the benefits of civilization.

And in order that they may have pecuniary means of subsistance, and may return to their homes with some savings when the contracts expire, the tutelar measure of the Repatriation Fund was established, in virtue of which the employers deposit half of their servants' wages to be handed over to them when they arrive at the home port on the occasion of their repatriation.

The authorities, the emigration Boards, and the Curator of the natives, their legal and constant protector, supervise the execution of the regulations; the natives have the right and full liberty to make complaints and seek redress from the Curator against the non-compliance of the obligations stipulated in the contracts, or against any abuses consented to by the masters, or practised to the detriment of their interests.

But in the convention with the Transvaal treating of the engagement of Portuguese labourers destined to a foreign country — to an English Colony — no clause to that effect was inserted, therefore we may conclude that the English in Transvaal can utilize the services of Mozambique natives under conditions which are not permitted to the Portuguese planters of S. Thomé and Principe.

All the clauses of the treaty tend to favour Transvaal, facilitating the recruitment of blacks in Mozambique and placing difficulties for their return.

The recruitment of blacks in unlimited numbers is allowed, in conformity with the regulations actually in force in the Province, which may contribute to depopulate the interior of Mozambique and consequently tend to ruin its agriculture, commerce, and industries.

It is established that the recruitment can only be forbidden when it is proved, through an investigation carried out conjointly by the representatives of each Government, that the employers in Transvaal do not properly fulfil the conditions of the contracts, after they have been warned so to do, then if the Government representatives do not agree with the result of the investigation, it will be settled by arbitration.

It is evident by this that neither the investigation will be carried out nor will the recruitment be forbidden, and whilst the emigration for Transvaal enjoys this enormous privilege, that for S. Thomé can be stopped by a simple governmental decision, without consulting anybody and without any indemnity whatever for the loss caused by the suspension (General Regulations of 17th July 1909).

The labourers are not allowed to make complaints or rescind their contracts, as is the case in S. Thomé, when the employers do not comply with the conditions stipulated; the cost of their return passage to the Province of Mozambique is not guaranteed, nor are they bound to save part of their earnings, so that they may be repatriated at their own cost on the termination of their contracts; obligatory repatriation is not enforced, as it appears the English wish to enforce for S. Thomé; on the contrary, everything has been calculated in such a manner that the natives cannot easily return from Transvaal but remain there, and thus lose their nationality for ever.

It is true that the liberty of returning to their homes is allowed them, but the means for so doing are not guaranteed. Instead of that sensible measure, an elusive benefit is conceded, and that is, goods bought by them in Transvaal up to a certain amount are exempt from duties, which really results in the labourers spending the money they ought to save for the cost of their return, and the profits of those transactions remain in Transvaal, causing loss to the trade of Mozambique and preventing the repatriation of the labourers at their own cost.

Outside view of the hospital, Boa Entrada Plantation. Island of S. Thomé

If on the termination of their contracts, the emigrants do not possess the means to pay their repatriation to Mozambique, as will be the case with many owing to their well known improvidence, they will be compelled to remain in Transvaal, and it is obvious that they will be forced to renew their contracts, if they do not wish to be considered clandestine emigrants, and subject themselves to the corresponding penalties.

The labourers for S. Thomé and Principe can only be recruited by a limited number of special agents, who have previously complied with certain regulations which prove their respectability, and have guaranteed the fulfilment of their duties by a deposit in money or trustworthy bail, and can be suspended by the governor of the province where they exercise their office.

For the Transvaal recruiting agents there are no restrictions, the appointments are not preceded by the guarantees necessary in S. Thomé, and once appointed they are allowed a free hand in the fulfilment of their duties, even if they should commit abuses, as has been shown.

As far as official protection is concerned the emigrants are left in Transvaal without resources of any kind. It is sufficient to state, that for the protection in a strange country of nearly 100.000 Mozambique labourers existing in Transvaal, there is only one official, the Curator, who is overburdened with the service of supervising the new contracts and other office work which prevent his giving his attention to what takes place in the compounds where the natives are lodged, and in the mines.

Besides this, the Curator, the only authority of his country charged with duties relative to the natives, according to the terms of the treaty makes no enquiries, nor does he supervise the carrying out of the obligations stipulated; he has merely the right to be informed as to the distribution of the labourers through the different mines for the purpose of registering where they are employed, the Transvaal Government having to assist him by facilitating access to the places where the Portuguese natives are living, but not to where they work!

If the force of circumstances, more powerful than the will of men and more subtle than the perfidy of their intentions, did not impose the modifications of the clauses established in the convention, the depopulation of the interior of the Province of Mozambique and consequent ruin of its sources of riches, as well as the scarcity of manual labour in S. Thomé, fatal to its agriculture, would shortly be accomplished facts. But the advantages of emigration to S. Thomé are already so manifest to the eyes of the Mozambique natives, that to their recognition of the fact is due the alteration already introduced «de facto», although «extra-officio», regarding Zambezia in the articles of that convention.

Although the rate of wages which the exceptional mining industry of the Rand can offer to the labourers is higher, because the work is much harder and more dangerous, the conditions of the recruitment included in the convention, owing to the reasons stated, are much less favourable to the natives than those established for emigration to the Islands of S. Thomé and Principe.

And this is proved by the fact that the English Press has recently mentioned, as we have read in Portuguese newspapers, that an agreement has been concluded between the «Zambezia Company» and «The West Native Association Limited», in which it is stipulated, that for the purpose of ameliorating the conditions of emigration to the Transvaal contained in the treaty, half of the wages due to the natives of Zambezia emigrating there, will be paid them at Quelimane and Tete on their repatriation, following the example of the law for S. Thomé emigrants.

Without this clause inserted in the rules for emigration for S. Thomé, this agreement in favour of Zambezia would certainly not have been realized.

Circumstances arising from the conditions of emigrants ·in S. Thomé, have, in the case of Zambezia, caused a clause to be inserted in the treaty, by which means are assured to the natives for their repatriation. It would be a matter for congratulation, if the same measures were carried out with regard to those parts of the Province of Mozambique where the Rand obtains the contingents of its labourers.

The agreement referred to is a step in the right direction, but is not sufficient for doing away with the dangers threatening the Provinces of Mozambique, S. Thomé and Principe.

It is indispensable to make an attempt to establish recruitment conditions for Transvaal, so as to prevent the Mozambique natives losing their nationality, securing their repatriation, and taking back with them a portion of their earnings.

We have not the least objection to the emigration for the Transvaal, although there is no reciprocity of proceeding towards S. Thomé on the part of the Rand, as we understand that it can co-exist without loss for either country. Emigration for S. Thomé has always been a sore subject to the employers on the Rand. The author of this work did his utmost during many years to introduce the Mozambique labourers into S. Thomé, but all his attempts up to a certain period failed owing to the reasons mentioned. We renewed our efforts in 1908, Admiral Castilho being Minister for the Colonies, and Conselheiro Freire d'Andrade Governor-general of Mozambique, and were successful in starting emigration, assisted by the decided approval of that Minister and of Conselheiro Dias Costa, Director-general of the Colonial Office, and also owing to the energetic resistance opposed by Conselheiro Freire d'Andrade to all intrigues and difficulties raised against the realization of this patriotic attempt.

On the 30th of July 1908, the first emigrants from Mozambique shipped by the steamer *Luzitania* landed at S. Thomé. They numbered 104, of these 83 were sent to the Plantation of Agua-Izé belonging to the Island of Principe Company, and 21 to the Boa-Entrada Plantation, the property of Henrique José Monteiro de Mendonça.

Since that date fresh contingents have arrived monthly, their number having already reached 2373, and of these 450 have been repatriated as can be seen by the table annexed.

The repatriations were started in July 1908, and already many of those repatriated from Agua-Izé have returned to this plantation accompanied by their wives.

The current is therefore established, and it is our firm belief that no manœuvring will now turn it aside.

We repeat then, that to the decided goodwill of Admiral Castilho and Conselheiro Dias Costa, and the energetic attitude of Conselheiro Freire d'Andrade, to the well directed policy and great patriotism of those three high and worthy officials, the nation owes one of the greatest services that can be rendered by colonial administration.

The emigration from Mozambique, now directed to S. Thomé, constitutes a

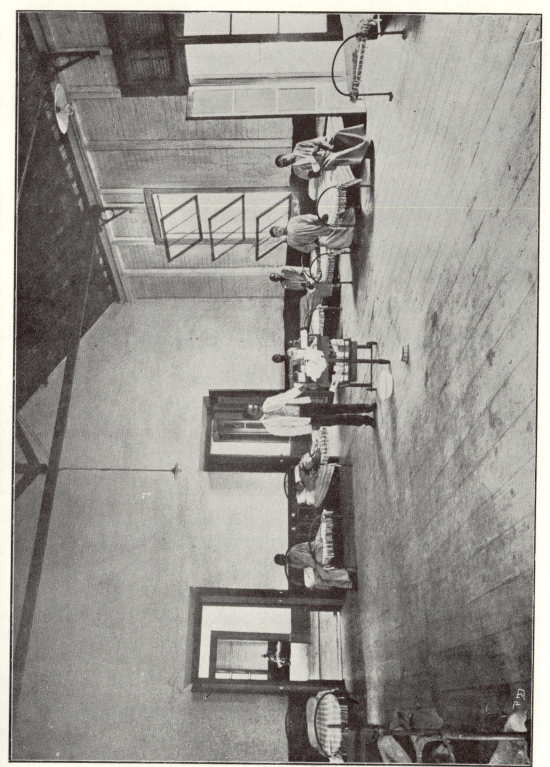

Interior of a ward in the hospital, Boa Entrada Plantation, Island of S. Thomé

new and powerful element of security, and a most valuable guarantee for the existence and prosperity of agriculture in our Colony, and was obtained at a moment when England, owing to the question of manual labour in Angola, was most violently attacking us, it having therefore besides all its other advantages, the inestimable moral and utilitarian value of having been obtained at an opportune moment.

May we be permitted by our dear friends, Admiral Castilho, Conselheiro Dias Costa, and Conselheiro Freire d'Andrade, to inscribe here our profound personal gratitude for their great and patriotic service rendered to the country, which we think deserves also the gratitude of the entire nation.

Cape Verde Islands.

The region known by this name consists of ten islands and two islets forming two distinct groups, the Windward or northern group, and the Leeward or southern group, which constitute the Archipelago of Cape Verde, situated in the Atlantic Ocean, to the west of Cape Verde, off the west coast of Africa, and having for its Capital the town of Praia in the Island of S. Thiago.

The islands are generally very mountainous, excepting Sal, Boa Vista, and Maio. In those islands where the mountain ranges are highest, namely Fogo, Santo Antão, S. Thiago, and Brava, there are some fresh water streams, in the others water is scarce and more or less brackish; and both in these mentioned and the remaining ones — S. Vicente, S. Luzia, S. Nicolau, and Branca and Raza islets — the frequent scarcity of rain makes the soil arid and sterile, notwithstanding its prolific nature in normal circumstances.

The principal island is S. Thiago, but the one enjoying most maritime movement is S. Vicente which owes its importance to the international navigation calling at its magnificent port, the best of the Archipelago, named Porto Grande, sheltered on all sides. Important deposits of coal exist there for the use of steamers navigating in the Atlantic.

The shipping trade forms the chief business of the island and furnishes elements of prosperity to the neighbouring Island of Santo Antão, which is the granary and kitchen-garden, so to say, of the Windward group and S. Nicolau. It is generally these two islands that supply stores to the steamers frequenting the port of S. Vicente.

Owing to the scarcity of rain, the islands of the Archipelago are scantily arborized, and have little vegetation and agriculture. Some of them are completely barren and arid, there is a great want of fuel where formerly dense forests existed which were destroyed by prolonged droughts, by volcanic eruptions and chiefly by the equally pernicious action of ignorant people.

The Island of S. Luzia is neither inhabited nor cultivated, it merely produces orchilla weed; Boa Vista has little cultivation, and Sal and Maio are sterile, salt being the only industry. S. Thiago, Santo Antão, S. Nicolau, Fogo, and Brava are the islands where agriculture is most developed.

The most valuable products are coffee, sugar, brandy, and castor-oil, but the production of the three first named articles is very small, castor-oil being the only important one.

The remaining products — cereals, vegetables, and fruit — have little value, the people cultivating them for their own use; the want of water and the scarcity of rains do not permit agricultural enterprise on an extensive scale or of a more remunerative nature.

Consequently the lower classes, which constitute the chief part of the population of the islands, live as a general rule in poor circumstances depending on the scanty cultivation, some trade, chiefly in castor-oil, on fishing and services rendered to navigation.

The precarious conditions of existence in the Archipelago are sometimes increased by severe storms, accompanied by torrential rains which destroy and devastate everything, or by the droughts, which, as we have already said, render the soil unproductive. On some occasions the droughts have lasted for successive years, destroying all vegetation and producing a famine, which at times has assumed calamitous proportions.

One of these calamities devastated the Archipelago in 1863-1864, thousands of people died from want, notwithstanding the assistance rendered by the Government and private individuals.

In 1903, Conselheiro Paulo Cid being Governor of the Province, a fresh calamity devastated the Archipelago, especially the Island of S. Thiago; but on this occasion, with the double object of assuaging the misfortune of the Cape Verde people and of obtaining labourers for agricultural enterprises, the Island of Principe Company, in the month of February of that year, and later on other proprietors of the Province engaged for their plantations all the persons desirous of emigrating, 1901 labourers of both sexes and different ages having arrived at the islands in that year, 1143 in S. Thomé, and 758 in the Island of Principe.

Since then emigration from the Archipelago to this Province has never ceased.

It is only just to mention here the patriotic and valuable assistance rendered by Governor Cid, in persuading the famished inhabitants of Cape Verde to emigrate to S. Thomé, in preference to Colonies of other nations.

The climate of the Archipelago, similar to that of all inter-tropical regions, is hot and unhealthy in the low-lying parts of the coast and in the vicinity of rivers; but in the interior of the mountainous islands it is pleasant and healthy, for these being situated at a considerable distance north of the Equator, are less influenced by the rays of the tropical sun.

The social status of the inhabitants of the Archipelago presents appreciable effects of civilization.

The houses similar to those common to the people of southern Europe, are of masonry and suited to the exigencies of the climate, some of them being grouped into towns of agreeable appearance.

The inhabitants as a rule dress in the European fashion, but adapt their dress to the dominant temperature, according to the class to which they belong; they follow the Catholic religion, though they are not entirely free from fetichism imported from Guinea and family ties are constituted according to the precepts of Christianity, and ruled by the same Portuguese civil law that is applicable in the metropolis.

Labourers' dwellings on the Porto Real Plantation (West). Island of Principe

Public administration and authority are regularly organized under the same principles and by the same system as in the metropolis, the collective and individual departments being similar.

The Archipelago is the see of a bishopric; it is divided into various administrative, fiscal, judicial and religious circumscriptions, in which the respective officials maintain order, transact public business, levy rates and taxes, administer justice both in civil and criminal courts, and minister to the spiritual wants of the people.

The different administrative circumscriptions are subordinated to the general government of the Province, which has its head-quarters in the town of Praia in the Island of S. Thiago.

The public forces are constituted by two sections of artillery, each consisting of 48 privates, their barracks being in the towns of Mindello and S. Vicente, a regiment of military police of 129 men, and another civil police corps composed of a commissary, a commander, a registrar, and 58 men.

The territory in the islands is divided into private estates, there being also municipal and state properties, and their ownership is guaranteed by the law in force.

Property in Brava Island is very divided; in the other islands, however, it is less so, large properties even being numerous in the Island of S. Thiago.

Public education has received some attention; in 1874, there existed in the islands 36 schools for boys and 9 for girls for rudimentary instruction, frequented by nearly 2.000 scholars, 1.800 boys and 200 girls. In 1909 there were 50 schools for primary instruction, 39 for boys and 11 for girls and 2 schools for apprentices, one in S. Thiago and the other in S. Vicente and a Seminary-Lyceum in the Island of S. Nicolau.

There is not much traffic in the Archipelago, no railway, with the exception of a small Decauville line in Sal Island, for carrying salt from the pans to the port of embarkation. The communications on land are very deficient; plans for various roads were made, but only in the Islands of S. Thiago and Santo Antão have any works of importance been carried out; in the other islands only a few kilometres have been constructed. The remaining means of communication are limited to foot-paths which cross the steep interior elevations of the islands. The roads leading to the coast are the worst.

Due to the influence of the civilizing elements mentioned, and especially to the communication established with the exterior, which the proximity to Europe often facilitates, the social status in the Archipelago is more advanced than that of any other of our Colonies on the West Coast.

Inclination for work is not a distinguishing trait of these people; on the contrary, they suffer from the evil inbred in all tropical races — indolence. The natural necessities of life, however, force them to work, otherwise they would die of starvation, as the soil does not produce spontaneously, as is the case in the fertile land of S. Thomé. The population employs its activity in agricultural work, small trades, breeding cattle, local rudimentary industries, services in the ports, in the exercise of public functions, and fishing on the coast.

Owing to the poor results which the workers generally obtain, either from the mentioned occupations or from the cultivation of lands, due to the circumstances alluded to, after the termination of the famine, the effects of which were still painfully reflected in the Colony during all the year of 1904, many labourers from Cape Verde have continued to emigrate to the Islands of S. Thomé and Principe, where they render valuable assistance to agriculture, with beneficial results for the economy of the two Provinces, and for the welfare of both those who emigrate and those who remain in the Archipelago.

In Cape Verde many people exist who have returned from S. Thomé with savings which they invest in their native land, encouraging local trade, and thus contributing to lessen much want and misery. The example given by those who return, the news periodically received from the absent ones, and the monthly allowance which the latter send their families, stimulate the desire for emigration amongst their fellows, who thus easily resolve to go and seek the means of livelihood in S. Thomé and Principe, which the ungrateful country where they were born so often denies them.

Guinea.

Portuguese Guinea is situated on the west coast of Africa, between the Senegal on the north, and French Guinea on the south, and from the western declivity of the Futa-Dejallon plateau on the east, to the Atlantic Ocean. Different islands, opposite and near the coast, some situated in the mouths of the rivers and others within the coast line, form part of the region of the same name.

The region, therefore, is divided into two parts: the insular and the continental. The insular part is formed by the Archipelago of Bijagoz, a group of islands outside the African coast, and those situated within the coast line in the mouths of the river, surrounded by the sea on one side and on the other by the passages and creeks separating them from the mainland. The continental part includes the territories situated between the coast and the Futa-Dejallon table-land, the inland islands and peninsulas formed by the passages and estuaries of the rivers watering those territories, and marshy districts of considerable extent. Both in the islands and on the mainland there are no mountains; the soil is generally low-lying, flat and marshy, but is fertile in diverse products and rich in vegetation.

Forests and agriculture are the chief wealth of the Colony; its secular forests contain an abundance of excellent timber for building purposes and cabinet making, such as cedar, mahogany, ebony, and rosewood. The soil is propitious for plantations on a large scale, and produces Indian corn, rice, manioc, palm oil, cotton, indigo, oranges, rubber, «mancarra», yams (Indian potatoes), «kola», and gum-copal, but agriculture is in a very backward state. On the banks of Rio Grande there were formerly most extensive plantations, where both natives and foreigners carried on the cultivation of «mancarra» with great success, but owing to the unhealthiness of the climate, to the want of security caused by the constant strife between the «Beafadas» and «Fulas» inhabiting the region, and principally to the great reduction in the consumption of oleaginous products in Europe, the cultivation ceased and the plantations were abandoned.

At the present time the Colony supports itself solely by bartering natural produce, namely; rubber, mancarra, wax, hides, elastic gum, palm oil, and cattle, for European merchandise, such as brandy, wine, fire-arms and ammunition, tobacco, textile

Labourers' dwellings on the Porto Real Plantation (East). Island of Principe

goods, and cutlery, but this trade has greatly decreased in recent times on account of the wars we waged in Bissau, Geba River, and Quinaca, and it is now chiefly in the hands of the neighbouring French and English settlements.

The climate, as in all tropical regions, is very unhealthy for Europeans, chiefly on the coast and in swampy districts. Some of the islands of the Archipelago where no marshes exist, are less unhealthy; in the other islands, and on the mainland, the heat and the dampness rising from the rivers and swamps fill the atmosphere with mephitic exhalations which Europeans resist with difficulty. The meteorologic phenomena divide the year into two seasons: the rainy one, the most unhealthy, lasting from May to November, during which there are torrential rains and severe thunder-storms, the temperature being very high and subject to continual changes; and the dry one from November to April, which is less hot and unhealthy.

Portuguese Guinea, both continental and insular, forms an administrative circumscription composed of the districts of Bolama, and the military stations of Bissau, Cacheu, and Geba, being under a Provincial Governor, generally a naval or military officer, who combines military and civil functions. The seat of Government is Bolama, a city situated in the island of the same name, within the coast line, at the mouth of the Rio Grande.

The Colony is garrisoned by a force consisting of a company of native sharpshooters numbering 229, and of two sections of artillery with 62 privates, all quartered in Bolama, with detachments in Bissau, Farin, Geba, and Cacheu.

European civilization is only reflected in the chief towns of the coast and in some of the inland river districts, where Portuguese functionaries, in the exercise of their offices, provide for the wants of public administration.

In the towns above mentioned, there are six masters and three mistresses for teaching the rudiments of education, but the attendance at the schools is very small; justice is administered by an assessor from the War Councils, who is at the same time the judge of the civil and criminal courts; from the ecclesiastical point of view, the district forms a dependency of the Bishopric of Cape Verde, religious rites being ministered by missionaries residing in the different towns.

There are neither railways nor roads. European settlements hold communication with one another by means of the sea, or by canals and the estuaries of rivers; communication inland between the natives is made by primitive paths, forming labyrinths in the dense forests, and on the water by rivers and canals crossing the district in various directions, and by canoes and other crafts constructed by the natives from trunks of trees.

The development of progress in these regions is a problem which has not been resolved up to the present, therefore, a great part of the natives are in a savage state, similar to that of the inhabitants of the Angola hinterland and other countries of Central Africa, which is further increased by the warlike and turbulent nature of some of the races existing there.

In the city of Bolama, the capital, and in other towns where Portuguese officials or European settlers reside, there are some buildings where public departments are established, others being used for barracks, schools, hospitals, dwelling houses, shops, and stores.

The natives live in wig-wams and rustic huts grouped into «tabancas» in the interior as in the inland districts of Angola, fire-arms, ammunition, spirits, and cotton cloths with which they partly cover themselves are almost the only signs of civilization.

The inhabitants of the different regions form numerous tribes of diverse races, all differing greatly in their characteristics, religion, habits, and modes of government.

Some consist of veritable savages who are cruel and defiant, vagabonds, pirates, and thieves, such as the «Felupes», «Papeis», «Bijagoz», «Balantas», and «Nalus», other tribes of less barbarous tendencies, more given to peace, work, pastoral life, and trade, such as the «Mandingas», «Manjacos», «Biafadas», «Fulas-Pretos», and «Fulas-Forros», amongst whom some civilization exists, the most advanced being the «Mandingas» who have schools where their children learn to read and write Arabic, their native dialect; some tribes profess an adulterated Mahomedan belief, but the majority are fetichists; in politics the «Banhuns» and «Balantas» are democratic, and are composed of independent parties over which the head of the family rules without recognizing any other authority; the remainder, however, are governed despotically by the chiefs with traditional absolute rights over the lives and property of their vassals.

The majority of the natives of Guinea lead a precarious existence, not acknowledging any right except that of the stronger, without any idea of duties or desire for moral and material improvement resulting from a state of civilization which they repel, as it represses their savage instincts. These circumstances, coupled with their rebellious and impetuous temperament, lead some tribes into wars and rapine, in which they spend a great part of their existence. Amongst the Balantas, the most successful robber is considered the noblest individual.

As a contrast to the above, the «Mancanhas» settle in Bolama where they cultivate «mancarra» receiving goods, liquours, and money as a loan which they bind themselves to repay with their work, namely the harvest of that product, and honourably fulfil the trust reposed in them.

The «Manjacos» also migrate in large numbers to the River Casamança, employing themselves every year in cultivating «mancarra» in the plantations of the French settlers.

Polygamy is sanctioned by custom, and to have many wives is the mens' absorbing passion.

The possession of cattle, especially cows, constitutes their chief riches. There are numerous herds of cattle, goats, pigs and flocks of sheep.

Cattle breeding is carried on to an extraordinary extent in the region of Geba, the territories of Cabu, but chiefly in those of Puba.

The scanty cultivation of agriculture from which they obtain their sustenance, and the products of the soil intended for export, is, as a rule, in many tribes entrusted to women. The men in the intervals of their sensual life, the excitement caused by «battuques» and drink, as well as indolence which the climate and habits encourage, when not employed in internal warfare, which is frequent, barter natural products with Europeans, and hunt wild animals, some of which they sell, or make use of the skins for clothing themselves, and eat the flesh of those fit for food.

None of the tribes wear regular clothing; some only a cotton shirt, others straw shoulder capes and skirts of native manufacture; but generally, the largest number cover merely part of their bodies with cloths imported from civilized countries, or

Groups of native men from the hinterland of Angola, labourers on the Porto Real Plantation (West). Island of Principe

Groups of native women from the hinterland of Angola, labourers on the Porto Real Plantation. Island of Principe

with skins of goats and other animals dressed by the natives, their heads being ornamented with feathers and turbans.

Their food consists of rice, millet, fish, shell-fish, vegetables, meat, and fruits; rice which forms the staple native food, is of magnificent quality and extensive cultivation.

They are generally robust, of high stature, and more intelligent than the blacks of other regions, the characteristic traces of their features indicating a race, superior to those inhabiting the regions of Equatorial Africa, due possibly to the intermingling of the aborigines with the Arabic race.

But the turbulent life which they lead from childhood, the savage example of their associates, the natural impetuosity of race, without other necessities than the satisfying of their animal instincts, which the fertile soil furnishes almost without need of labour, the adventurous and bellicose temperament, the separation from their families and their religious superstitions, all result in unruly passion and vice which unless repressed by moral rules, either of individual or collective force, shortly overcome their energy, and destroy aptitudes and qualities which might have been put to a good use by means of civilization.

The wars in which the natives are frequently involved and the sanguinary attacks on Europeans in which the Portuguese authorities have to interfere forcibly, are as a rule caused by native indolence, the lawless and uncertain life, the rebellious temperament of the natives generally, their thirst for mastery, and the natural resistance against their oppressors who dominate and perchance take advantage of them, and the plundering instincts of some tribes; these conflicts have cost the nation, on different occasions, the loss of many lives and much money, without any special benefit for the civilization of the Province, and with enormous sacrifices to the Portuguese Treasury.

The Province of Guinea may become a mart for colonial produce, if civilization penetrate there. To obtain this end, it is necessary to change the Colony from a focus of rebellion into a centre of emigration for labour.

The most effectual way for civilizing the native population, is by the indirect means of their emigration to more or less civilized countries or colonies.

The unhealthy climate, making the region almost uninhabitable for Europeans, together with the enormous capital required by the Province for sanitary improvements, principally on the mainland, are factors which place extreme difficulties in a direct solution of the problem of civilizing these regions.

A measure of the greatest utility for Guinea, the nation, and the Islands of S. Thomé and Principe, would be the greater development of periodical emigration, regulated by the Governments of the metropolis and Guinéa, to those Islands, for their climate, being milder, does not injure the health or robustness of the natives of Guinea.

It would be advantageous for S. Thomé and Principe, because the introduction in larger quantities of the natives of Guinea would assist the planters in acquiring excellent means of labour, which are much needed, for their agricultural enterprises.

The years spent by these people in S. Thomé and Principe, and employed by them in labour and in acquiring civilized customs, which are fairly advanced there, would be sufficient for them to contract regular habits, modify their barbarous tendencies, and forget the unruly and adventurous life of the tribes to which they formerly belonged.

These settlers being converted to Christianity and forming family ties, according to our laws or even according to the local customs which forbid polygamy, having learned arts and trades, and the methodical cultivation of the soil, on their repatriation would take to their native country, together with their savings, professional instruction and acquired habits of work, suggesting, by their example, the value of civilization, and the employment of their own activity in work.

It is natural that the repatriated natives should continue their newly acquired and pacific habits, marry, and devote themselves to work, either as artisans, or as agricultural labourers; make proselytes and find imitators, that emigration should be the bearer of elements of wealth and civilizing progress, as happens to emigrants from Portugal to Brazil and the Colonies. It is also natural that these factors should influence the natives, and make them become labourers and artisans and thereby contributing to the gradual civilization of the people, finally cause them to abandon their adventurous and warlike life.

Such, in our opinion, would be the great advantage which Portuguese Guinea would obtain from emigration, if it were promoted carefully by the Home Government under normal conditions, and with reciprocal guarantees for the emigrants and contractors. The English and German Colonies of Accra and the Cameroons have increased and prospered, thanks to the lessons learned in S. Thomé and Principe by the emigrants of those Colonies.

The advantages of this measure for the metropolis are such, that we deem it unnecessary to enumerate them. Civilization would be spread through the different tribes of Guinea by the natives, with far less sacrifice of health and life than is incurred by Europeans. Elements of work and progress, introduced into the Colony, where exist enormous natural unexplored sources of wealth, requiring only skilled manual labour and peace to assure the possession of them; it would be licit to expect that little by little agriculture would naturally receive a great impetus, and the natives enjoying the fruits of peace, would become the greatest enemies of public disorder.

The warfare in which these half savage tribes are so frequently involved, and cost the metropolis valuable lives and money for their pacification, would be followed by a period of tranquillity and profitable labour, by which the State would obtain important pecuniary advantages, the people of Guinea would enjoy the benefits of peace, and the welfare arising from abundance and riches, and the Portuguese Nation would give the world another proof of its colonizing aptitude.

Types of native artisans from the Angola hinterland, educated on the Porto Real Plantation, and their teacher. Island of Principe

CHAPTER IV.

Engagement of Labourers.

The Portuguese Government maintaining the liberal traditions which, in the history of Portuguese legislation, signalize the civilizing and humanitarian work of the negro race, recently published measures tending to improve the system of the engagement of labourers, together with guarantees which cannot be illuded, in order to avoid that their execution suscitate any doubts prejudicial to the planters of S. Thomé, or to the labourers, their valuable and serviceable collaborators in enhancing in value the properties cultivated.

These measures are included in the general regulations, sanctioned by the decree of 17ᵗʰ July 1909, and it is evident that the engagement of labourers for the Islands of S. Thomé and Principe, is carried out under rules which fully recognize the rights of the natives as free citizens, and conditions of protection worthy of a civilized and humanitarian nation, which protection however, has always been accorded to the natives of our Colonies by the Portuguese Governments.

The emigration of natives, contracted in the Provinces of Angola, Guinea, Mozambique, Cape Verde, and India, to the Islands referred to, is only permitted when the labourers come from districts where emigration agents, or their delegates, are legally established; the emigration to the same Islands of Chinese rural labourers is also allowed, when agencies in identical conditions are established in Macau or any of the treaty ports of that Empire.

The engagement and contracting of labourers is effected through the above mentioned agencies of emigration and labour contracts, established in the ports of those Provinces, as well as in Macau or in the Chinese ports referred to, but these agencies are only permitted where a curator of the natives, his delegates, or judicial and administrative authorities to substitute them, exist.

These agencies are established after certain legal formalities have been carried out, and are entrusted with the promoting of emigration and the contracting of labourers for agricultural, industrial, and domestic work in the Province of S. Thomé and Principe, in accordance with the terms fixed by the regulations under the supervision of the provincial governors and curators.

A Central Committee entrusted with the study of the subjects relative to the employment and emigration of labourers engaged for the Province of S. Thomé and Principe, holding its meetings in Lisbon, and consisting of the higher officials of the

Colonial and Marine Office, and planters of the said Islands elected by their fellows, under the presidency of the Director-general of the Colonial Department, appoints the emigration agents who are to serve in the different districts, each having to give bail for Réis 2:000$000, either in money or trustworthy recognizancies for the fulfilment of the legal obligations imposed, amongst which are the following: the agents to employ the means at their disposal for preventing clandestine emigration, and impeding natives from emigrating under false declarations; to abstain from employing, either directly or indirectly, any violent or fraudulent means for engaging labourers.

In the Province of Angola the engagements are effected in zones, situated in the regions of Libolo, Ginga de Ambaca, Amboiva, Selles, Bailundo, Hambo, Sambo, Caconda, and Quillengues, previously established by an edict of the Governor of the Province, published in the official Bulletin. The engagement or recruitment of labour for agricultural work in S. Thomé and Principe, or for plantations in the Province of Angola, can only take place in the zones previously fixed, the number of natives of both sexes to be recruited annually within the limits of the zones referred to, to be also determined by edicts.

For the purpose of direct recruitment, or engagement of labourers, in the villages situated within each zone, guaranteed recruiters are appointed by the governors of the districts where the recruitments take place, on the proposal of the emigration agents established in the ports. Each recruiter has to give bail for Réis 300$000, and is furnished with a licence by the Curators in Loanda, Benguella, and Novo Redondo, stating the zone where he may exercise his calling, the presentation of the licence to all the authorities of the interior is obligatory, as recruiters are the only persons permitted to recruit labourers for the Islands of S. Thomé and Principe, or the plantations in the Province of Angola.

Before proceeding to recruit in any locality, the recruiters must seek the nearest administrative authority, and prove their legal right to exercise their office, only after this may they commence operations, in the presence of the native local chief and under the supervision of the administrative authorities referred to.

On the conclusion of the recruitment, the agent obtains a pass from the administrative authority, in which the name, parentage, and probable age of each engaged labourer are stated, as well as the names of the chief and the locality where the recruitment took place, and, for purposes of identification, the pass, together with the labourers, must be presented to the authorities, at the locality on the coast where the contracts are signed.

The law specially forbids the recruiters:

To engage infirm, aged, or other persons manifestly incapable of agricultural work;

To convey to the coast, natives who are not recruited according to legal formalities, especially without the consent and presence of the local chief, without the supervision of the administrative authority, or when it is known that they have been coerced by the chief to contract themselves;

To employ Europeans or natives in acts of recruitment who have not been legally appointed for that purpose; to dissuade natives from fulfilling their contracts, to compel them to carry their own or others' burdens, or to carry anything except their wearing apparel and their rations for their journey.

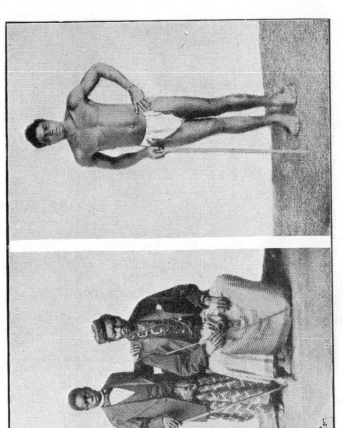

Native types of Cabinda, working in S. Thomé

To disturb or endeavour to disturb public order, to commit violent or fraudulent acts resulting in loss to the Government or the natives, or carry on the bartering of merchandise whilst they are engaged as recruiters.

Conditions of Displacement.

If we take into consideration the half savage state of natives recruited for emigration, their displacement is carried out under conditions which, far from being prejudicial, are of inestimable benefit to them.

As they live scattered about the interior, subject to the chequered existence of their tribes, unable to obtain safe dwelling places, owing to the lack of police organization for assuring security of life and property, these natives are subject to the contingencies of periodical displacements, arising from the necessities of existence and personal defence, and have no notions as to the meaning of home and family, as these words are understood amongst civilized nations, ties which render separation so painful.

Other facts influencing the naturally precarious existence of the natives, also tend to make their displacement and emigration beneficial.

For many years the Province of Angola has suffered from an economic, agricultural and commercial crisis, which has caused its impoverishment. Encircled on all sides by colonies belonging to powerful industrial nations, (England, Germany, France, and Belgium) the traders of the Province are heavily handicapped by the high prices of imports, and as they are unable to make use of certain foreign goods in bartering transactions, owing to the excessive tariffs, they are out-distanced by rivals with whom they cannot successfully compete, owing to the reasons stated, and to the annihilation of the chief agricultural product, alcohol, by the terms of the convention of Brussels, agriculture in the Province has dwindled, mercantile transactions have decreased, and commercial currents converged to the markets of powerful neighbours and competitors.

The inhabitants shared in the general impoverishment of the Colony, and thus the social conditions and the state of backward civilization of the hinterland of Angola, were increased by the misery which the ruin of agriculture and trade caused amongst the people living there.

Under these conditions emigration to a richer country, to a more advanced social centre, enjoying a more modern civilization where resources of all kinds abound, official protection is more efficacious, and social aid is complete, as happens in S. Thomé, emigration, we repeat, represents for the native of Angola a great benefit, which he recognizes and appreciates once he begins to enjoy its advantages.

The displacement of natives is regulated and protected by rules officially established.

The general regulations determine, as has been stated, the only zones where recruitment may be effected, and the Governor of the Province of Angola fixes the routes by which the emigrants have to travel, from the regions where they are contracted to the cities of Loanda, Benguella, and town of Novo Redondo, the ports of embarkation.

The recruiting agents must convey the individuals contracted by the routes previously determined, using, as much as possible, the railways on the journey to the coast; in certain localities on the route, indicated by the Governor-general of the Province, there will be dêpots established and maintained by the contracting agents in hygienic conditions, examined by sanitary inspectors or their delegates, for the emigrants to lodge comfortably, both on the outward and homeward journeys; during their sojourn in the dêpots, food, clothing, and medicine in case of sickness, are supplied to the labourers by the contracting agents, who also have to defray the expenses of the first five days, should the patient go into hospital.

The recruiting agents are also obliged:

To accompany the recruited natives on their journey to the coast, to take measures to prevent any want of food on the road; and, on arrival at the destined sea-port, they must seek the contracting agent, present and hand over to him all the natives contracted by them, as well as the passes given by the administrative authorities to prove the identity of those recruited, and a written account of all that may have occurred during the journey, and the certificates of death, given by the aforesaid authorities, of natives who may have died on the way, exceptional cases duly proved, being excluded.

The responsibility of the recruiting agents ceases, once the natives are handed over to the contracting agent; but, if they transgress the regulations relative to recruitment, they forfeit their security of Reis 300:000 which goes to the State, besides, being liable to any penalties imposed on them by common law, and losing, at once, the right to recruit labourers.

The contracting agents are obliged to have dêpots in the sea-ports, in the same conditions as those required for the dêpots on the route, where they will lodge the natives handed over to them for the purpose of being contracted; to board them at their own expense in those dêpots until after the contracts have been signed, and the natives start for the provinces where they have to fulfil them; to inscribe them in a numbered register which corresponds, so to say, to the civil register of the labourers, as their inscription number has to accompany them henceforward in all the contracts in which they may enter, and wherever they may go, until they return to their native country.

Transport of Labourers.

Labourers are conveyed to the Islands of S. Thomé and Principe by Portuguese vessels exclusively, registered for that purpose, or by foreign vessels duly authorized by the Governor of the Province of S. Thomé, or by governors of the provinces whence the emigrants start, in ports where no regular Portuguese navigation exists. The captains of these vessels bind themselves to carry out the legal regulations relative to the conditions of transport, by a written declaration which they guarantee by depositing, or giving bail for Reis 2:000♲000, all being duly authenticated in the presence of the Secretary-general of the Government and witnesses, the declaration being signed by all.

The labourers are treated as third class passengers on board, and the number

Vice-Admiral Conselheiro Francisco Joaquim Ferreira do Amaral

Author of the law for the repression of vagrancy of 21 st May 1892,
former Governor of the Province of S. Thomé and Principe, Colonial Minister in 1892,
and Premier in 1908

of emigrants which each steamer can receive, in regard to their tonnage, is fixed by the regulations of the Province of S. Thomé and Principe — one for 2 tons register, if the steamers start from any port situated on the coast between Liberia and Mossamedes, and two for 5 tons when they come from longer distances (1).

The agencies of emigration and contract and the delegations established in the ports of call of the vessels chartered for transport, ship the labourers direct to their destinations; the other agencies use the ports of most easy access, where there also are agencies or delegations established.

All the expenses incurred by the labourers on their journey are defrayed by the employers who have contracted them.

After the employers have also paid the respective passage money, the labourers go on board with their baggage, accompanied by the passes given by the administrative authorities, and duplicate lists of their names, indicating the destination of each, and all signed by the agents of emigration or their delegates.

The commander of the vessel compares the lists with the number of labourers shipped, and inspects their baggage, and if everything be in order, signs and returns one of the lists to the agents of emigration, keeping the other, and becomes responsible from that moment for the safe delivery of the labourers and their baggage at the port of destination.

Two other copies are taken of the aforesaid lists and forwarded by the emigration agents or their delegates, one to the Governor and the other to the curator or his delegate, at the port of destination.

The emigrants are separated on board, according to their sexes, in completely isolated compartments, and are forbidden to sleep on deck or return in the morning before the decks have been scrubbed. Their food consists principally of rice and different kinds of flour, small quantities of salt cod-fish, salt or fresh meat and fresh vegetables.

Each ship always conveys an interpreter well acquainted with the Portuguese and Ambundo languages, who is obliged to accompany the natives until the end of the voyage, be present at the doctors' visits, and serve as intermediary in case the natives have any complaints to make to the chief steward who is obliged to attend to them.

If any of the labourers should die during the voyage, the ship's doctor will give a written declaration of the death to the respective commander, stating the cause, and any other circumstances worthy of mention. The commander must present the declaration to the curator at the port of destination.

It is forbidden to ship aged labourers, or those suffering from rachitis, mental derangement, skin complaints, sleeping sickness, and any other diseases or deformities which unfit them for work; it is also forbidden to sell any article or spirits to the labourers, either on their voyage to S. Thomé and Principe or on their return home.

The labourers may not be placed under arrest unless they commit crimes to justify this action; in this case, on landing they are immediately handed over to the competent authorities who will take proceedings against them.

---

(1) Article 31th of Provincial Regulation of the 17th August 1880.

After the labourers have landed at the destination port, they must be vaccin-ated, unless this has already been done, or if they do not show evident signs of hav-ing had small-pox; and those on whom the vaccine does not take, must be re-vaccinated on arrival at the plantations, where a stock of lymph must be kept, and renewed periodically.

During small-pox epidemics, the labourers must be vaccinated in advance, as no contract can be effected, or shipment take place until the results of the inocula-tion are known, except it be proved that the emigrant is refractory to vaccina-tion, or shows evident signs of having had small-pox.

Government commissaries are expressly appointed to supervise periodically the form in which the legal prescriptions, established relative to the emigration and contracting of labour, are carried out on board the transport vessels and in the respective agencies. One of these commissaries has to accompany the labourers on their sea voyage, both to the port of destination in the Islands of S. Thomé and Principe, and on the return of the repatriated natives to the ports of their respect-ive countries.

These commissaries are the bearers of the bonus belonging to the repatriated labourers; they have to see that the latter only land at the ports to which they are destined, and pay them the bonus in presence of the respective Curators, a tripli-cate document of this transaction being made out and signed by the officials present and two witnesses, one copy being forwarded to the Government office at S. Tho-mé, another kept in the emigration agency at the port of destination.

The government commissaries and interpreters have free passages on the ves-sels conveying labourers; this condition is expressly mentioned in the license of the ship. The governor of the province of their destination, at the end of the voyage, gives the capitans a defeasance to prove that the latter have fulfilled their legal obligations; the ships may not make fresh voyages in the same service of labour transport unless the said defeasance is produced.

On the arrival of any vessel at S. Thomé or Principe, the respective capitain presents the emigrants to the Curator-general or his delegate, who, when their identity has been proved, questions them as to the circumstances in which they have been contracted, and if they did so uncoerced, and only ratifies the contracts if he obtain an affirmative reply, and then advises the employers to take immediate charge of the labourers they have engaged.

In previous regulations no zones had been fixed for the recruitment in the province of Angola, no routes established for the journey of the emigrants between the interior and the embarkation ports, nor had the post of recruiter been limited to duly authorized agents; the recruiting ground embraced all the Angola hinterland, the routes of the caravans were arbitrarily selected by irresponsible and anonymous recruiters, who in unlimited numbers exercised their badly supervised calling throughout the vast inland regions of the Province.

The actual regulation puts an end to all the imperfections and omissions of former laws, and the result of the rules in force, together with others contained in our special legislation, is that the recruitment, displacement, contracting, and trans-port of natives are all carried out under such conditions, that the official supervi-sion does not abandon them from the moment of their recruitment to their embarkation, during the voyage, in their sojourn at S. Thomé, up to their return home, the li-

General view of Praia Rei, head quarters of the Agua Izé Plantation. Island of S. Thomé

berty of each being recognized, and all furnished with means adequate to their condition. And as the regulations referred tó could only come into force on 1st February, 1910, the Government, by their edicts of 29th July and 22nd November of 1909, suspended the recruitment, contracting, and shipment of Angola labourers to S. Thomé and Principe until that date.

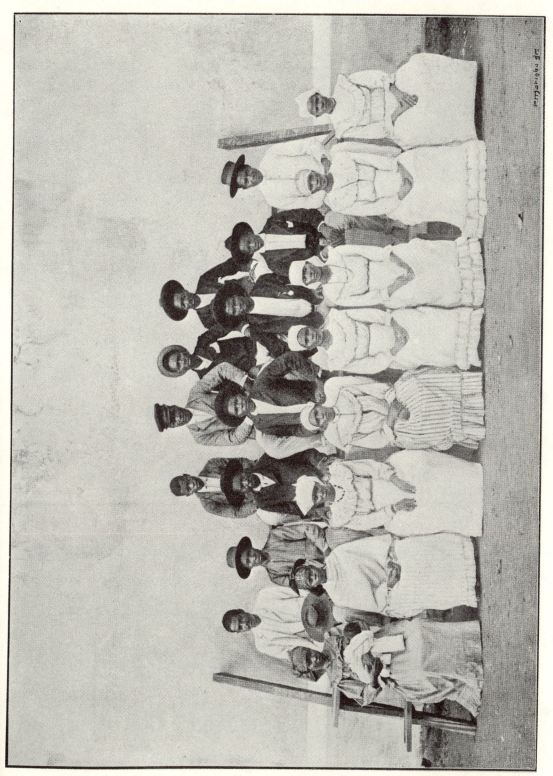

Types of labourers from Cape Verde, working on the Boa Entrada Plantation. Island of S. Thomé

CHAPTER V.

The English Campaign and the Economic Relations of S. Thomé and Principe with the Metropolis.

In the brief historical summary sketched in Chapter I of this work, of the different phases undergone by the Province of S. Thomé and Principe for centuries, from its discovery to the present day, we endeavoured to give an idea of the causes which, in the course of time, produced the periods of prosperity and decadence experienced by agriculture, until the Province completely vanquished the enormous difficulties heaped in its way, and finally reached the brilliant era of prosperity and civilization it now enjoys, which places S. Thomé and Principe on a par with the most advanced Colonies of Equatorial Africa.

Our other Colonies also contributed to the construction of that monument of our activity and colonizing aptitude, which so greatly honours Portuguese labour, capital, and administration, by supplying the greater part of the manual labour. Angola, in the first place, and afterwards Cape Verde, Mozambique, Guinea, India, and Macau, some in a greater others in a less degree, all these dominions, still of the great and vast Colonial Empire discovered and conquered by the genius and efforts of our navigators, have their share in the glory reflected on the name of Portugal; the remaining portion belongs to the native element, that also contributed its share, even if in a limited degree, to the common work.

A work of such magnitude, however, could not escape the attacks of envy and the antagonism of these who see in the brilliant result of our action in this part of Africa, an obstacle to the exclusive dominion over Southern Africa, which has long been the aim of their unscrupulous actions. The situation conquered by the success of our colonization, the methods of which are perfidiously distorted, ought to serve as a bait thrown in the teeth of all the enemies that are leagued against us, to divert the world's opinion from analogous campaigns against interests more ably defended abroad than ours have been.

We must recognize, however, that it is in the English language that we have been insulted and defamed with the epithets of being inhuman, slave-dealers, etc, and that the English are the only foreigners who treat us as such, applying all their rácial tenacity and powerful efforts to this odious and selfish war, without taking into account the money and time spent in so unjust and inglorious a task.

But in England, to the honour of the country of whom we have been friends and allies in all phases of good or ill fortune, all are not detractors of our colonizing methods, some authoritative voices, also English, like that of Colonel Wyllie, have been raised in the Press of their own land, to stygmatize the accusers of Portugal and to render us the justice due to us.

We have received most amable references from the subjects of other nations visiting S. Thomé and Principe; French and German explorers, travellers and scientific men, have stayed with our planters, and, on their return home, as ocular witnesses have rendered full justice in their narratives, to our model system of agrarian labour and to the complete liberty and welfare enjoyed by our African labourers.

We can reply to the accusations of Nevinsson, Pienaar, and Burtt, by the unsuspected and disinterested reports of Frenchmen like Dr. Auguste Chevalier (1), Dr. Charles Gravier (2), and Maurice Montet (3), and Germans like Spengler, and Strunck (4), etc.; and, to which we to-day have the honour and the pleasure of adding the testimony of Prince Alfred of Loewenstein Wertheim Freudenberg and his suite, who have just paid a lengthened visit to the plantations of our Islands, staying in the houses of those pseudo slave-dealers, where also the Crown Prince of Portugal and our Minister for the Colonies stayed two years ago, those slave dealers, of whom Cadbury himself did not disdain to be a guest, and to whom he wrote letters like the following:

(Translation).

«S. Thomé, 24th November 1908.

«To the Manager of the Porto Real Plantation — East.

«Dear Sir

«I have much pleasure in forwarding to you, as promised, the statistics of the consumption and production of the World's cocoa, copied from the German newspaper *The Guardian*. I take the opportunity to thank you once more most cordially, as well as your wife, for your kindness to me and to M.r Burtt, during our charming visit to your plantation.

«With my compliments to your household.

«I am, etc.

«(S.) *William A. Cadbury.*»

---

(1) *Bulletin de la Societé de Géographie de Paris* n.º 4, of the 15th April, 1906, Masson et Cie.
(2) *Nouvelle Archive des Missions Scientifiques,* t. xv. Imprimerie Nationale, Paris.
(3) *La Dépéche Coloniale Illustrée,* of the 15th March, 1907.
(4) *Guardian of Hamburg,* 5th October 1905 (Reproduced from *Troupeau Flauver*).

Native types from Portuguese Guinea, labourers on the Porto-Real Plantation (West). Island of Principe

«Monte Café — S. Thomé.

«To Madam Claudına de Freitas Chamiço.

«I hasten to write and thank you, in my name and in that of M.ʳ Burtt, for the kindness with which we were treated by your representative Mr. Lucas. Every attention was paid us, and we have had great pleasure in visiting this fine estate. In the report, which I will present to my firm, I shall have much to say regarding the good treatment which the labourers receive on this and on many other plantations, and it was with great satisfaction, that I learnt your good wishes for the establishment of a good repatriation system. I believe also, that your efforts to afford the benefits of religion to these people, will greatly increase their happiness I sincerely hope to hear measures have been adopted in Angola to end, once and for all, the great cruelties practised by irresponsible men, who herd people together in all parts of the interior, and also, that a more equitable system may shortly be organized, and that ancient Colony, instead of decreasing annually in population, by the loss of its inhabitants, may increase not only in wealth — but also in agricultural knowledge and habits of civilization, acquired by men and women who, after having worked in S. Thomé return home peaceably.

«Repeating, once more, my thanks.

«I am, etc.

«(S.) *William A. Cadbury*».

The above letters will show that the planters are far from being the tyrannical slave-dealers, to which certain English writers allude.

At the same time the curious obstinacy is to be noted, with which they insist that planters and labourers should act contrary to their wishes and interests; this persistence would become monomania, if we could regard it simply from its pseudo philanthropic form.

But these appearances, which illude the ingenuousness of some, are very different from the reality.

Our detractors are aware, once they say they have studied and know the subject thoroughly, that the Angola blacks, who are not repatriated, are generally natives of the Angola hinterland regions, where, as yet, no permanent European occupation exists, and where the lives and property of the inhabitants are subject to the caprice and ambition of the native savage chiefs.

The blacks who emigrate thence belong to different tribes, sometimes nomads, and speak different dialects; as a rule it is unknown, the blacks themselves do not know, where their native villages lie, and when they do know, feign ignorance, fearing that they may be compelled to return thither.

It is in S. Thomé that men and women of different countries get acquainted and marry; it is also in S. Thomé that they learn the current languages Ambundo and Portuguese, which they and their children will speak in the future.

There are, then, three nationalities in the family: those of the husband and wife, generally unknown, and that of the children, which is S. Thomé.

If both are unknown, to which of the first two named can repatriation be directed? But even, if they should be known, and the man go to the tribe where his wife came from, or the latter go to her husband's tribe, would they be repatriated? Will he be well received in a certain tribe when he belongs to another, or ought they to be separated, each one going to his or her own village?And the children, should they be divided between the father and mother? Will these young folk, who were born and bred in a fairly civilized centre, having been affectionately treated by their parents and the planter, find in the savage regions, the cradle of their parents, the same welfare they enjoyed in their birth place?

Is it humane or equitable to oblige creatures who, during five years have enjoyed the benefits of liberty and a comparative civilization, shielded by just laws, and protected by civilized authority, to return to barbarism, handing them over to the dominion and subjection of despotic chiefs, despoilers of the earnings they acquired by honest labour and saved during many years, and to sacrifice their children, dragging them into similar dangers?

The answer is clear: such an action would be neither worthy nor humane, and as the Angola black does not voluntarily return to his primitive state, nobody has the right to compel him to do so (1).

But if that imposition should be legally enforced, as some wish, the cost of the conveyance of labourers, the S. Thomé planters' chief item of expense, would at once be doubled.

This operation being repeated periodically, the new burden thus created would considerably increase the actual price of cocoa production in S. Thomé; well, this is just what above all things would suit the plantations of Trinidad and the Gold Coast, English Colonies which produce more than forty million kilos of cocoa and are capable of producing much larger quantities.

In these circumstances we may believe that the firms, boycotters of Portuguese cocoa, who insist on the forced repatriation of our labourers, would be of opinion, in case of success, that the culmination of the campaign against us had been reached, a campaign, which they wish to see ended up to a certain point, as it is also prejudicial to them.

Our sacrifice would be to the advantage of Trinidad and the Gold Coast, assuring economically a perpetual supremacy to the production of these Colonies, even if, to obtain this, it should be necessary to set aside the fundamental code of the Portuguese nation, and commit the iniquity of compelling free men to leave S. Thomé against their will, and return to their former savage life; in this way, the campaign against us would decrease in violence, and the English makers could again buy the cocoa of S. Thomé without risk.

Admirable combination to resolve difficulties in favour of English interests!

But the witnesses mentioned are not the only ones that Portugal can offer to the appreciation of the cultured World, as a proof of its correct mode of procedure.

---

(1) Mr. Cadbury, having been asked if a labourer, who receives these benefits on the termination of his contract, wishes to remain in S. Thomé should be forced to return to Angola, replied, that to wish such a thing in these circumstances, would be absurd (*Minutes of the meeting held in Lisbon*, page 14).

Portion of the interior of an infirmary for males, in the hospital of the Porto-Real Plantation (West). Island of Principe

To its English accusers, Portugal can oppose the impartial testimony of other Englishmen and of a high American official. Consul Harry Johnston (1), Colonel J. A. Wyllie (2), the American Consul John A. Parkinson (3), and L. Mc Hale, a highly esteemed merchant in Manchester (4), etc. etc., are worth something more than Pienaar, (5), Nevinsson and Burtt.

Admitting that the intensity and persistence of the English campaign against us, its extension throughout Great Britain, its irradiation to the United States and Germany, do not evidently result from the sentimentality of affectionate temperaments, the argument alleged, which many an Englishman may have perhaps believed in good faith, the selection of the labourers of S. Thomé among so many tyrannized people existing in the World for the exercise of philanthropy who, all admit, are treated with exceptional kindness, has no justification, and leaves enveloped in mystery the true causes moving that formidable and most expensive campaign, and gives rise to various conjectures.

When we think that the competition caused by thirty million kilos of cocoa which S. Thomé produces, cannot be looked upon with friendly eyes by the twenty two millions harvested in the Island of Trinidad, and by the twenty millions which Accra exports — two English Colonies in America and in Africa;

When we consider the loss caused to Englishmen interested in the speculation of the thirty three million produced in Bahia, owing to the competition of our cocoa in the World's markets;

When we study history and see the part which evangelism takes in our African Colonies, to the detriment of our credit and dominion;

When we analyse the effects of the violent campaign of discredit started in England against the administration of the Congo Free State, and witness the atmosphere of the World's disfavour in which, at a given moment, the future Bel-

---

(1) Meeting held at the London Geographical Society (Official Bulletins of S. Thomé, N.os 42, 43, 44, of 1884).

(2) *The Times* of London, of 23rd October 1909, *Evening News* of Edinburgh, of 27th September 1909, *Daily Despatch* of Birmingham of 23th October 1909, *New York Times*, 26th November 1909, *Journal of Commerce*, of New York, November 1909, and various journals of Boston, Washington and Canada of the same epoch, and correspondence published in Lisbon newspapers, which are transcribed in the appendix of this book.

(3) The journal, *Chicago Examiner* and others of the U. S. America. (This correspondence was published in November or December of 1909).

(4) Articles published in the *Manchester Guardian* of 24th and 30th October, 6th and 21st November 1908.

(5) Threatened Armed Invasion. British Intervention. General Francois Joubert Pienaar formerly a Boer leader, and now a British subject, visited Birmingham some months ago and spoke on the slave-trade in Africa making grave allegations against the Portuguese.

In furtherance of his crusade against the trafic he visited London subsequently, and later on went over to America.

Yesterday some sensational disclosures were made. General Pienaar admitted to the *Daily Telegraph's* New York correspondent that he had contemplated an armed invasion of Portuguese West Africa with the object of civilizing and evangelising Angola for Great Britain. He asserted, however, that he abandoned the idea a few months ago because of representations from the British Foreign Office, which refused to sanction his enterprise. His plan for driving out the Portuguese, included the raising a force of 500 armed men with two Maxim-Nordenfeldt

gian Colony became involved, the expropriation of that sovereign State in the name of humanity and in benefit of powerful neighbouring Colonies, appearing imminent;

When the struggles of the competition of similar industries of other countries endeavour to dominate the markets where English chocolate holds sovereign sway;

When the very struggles of English internal politics, in which the industries of that great nation certainly take part, divide the United Kindgom into two powerful rival parties;

Will it not be permissible to think that the discredit of the cocoa of S. Thomé and Principe would be profitable to the Colonies of Trinidad and Accra, so as to put out of the market an importune competitor, and cause us difficulties which would impede the increase of our production and advance the price of our manual labour?

Have not those who in England speculate in Brazilian cocoa identical interests?

Will it not be a factor of discredit, increasing the strength and predominion of the evangelical sect in Africa, as a humanitarian and civilizing South African power, — to the Catholic nation, which, after England, possesses the vastest Colonies contiguous to the English in that part of the black Continent?

Would not the Free State have great interest in drawing away from itself, the attention and the unfavourable opinion, which the English campaign has created in the World against it, and endorsing them to Portugal? (1).

---

guns and a mule train, and he believed that £ 30.000, if it could be raised, would have covered the cost.

The former Boer leader has some interesting letters relating to his project. Here is one which he received on December 18, 1897 from the British Foreign Office:

Sir

I am directed by Secretary Sir E. Grey to state that his attention has been called to the fact that articles have been published in the Press from which it would appear that you are contemplating an attack on certain Colonial possessions of Powers with which his Majesty the King is at peace. I am to draw your attention to section 2 of the Foreign Enlistment Act 1870, and to warn you of the serious penalties to which any such act would render you liable.

The «Birmingham Evening Despatch», April 30. 1908.

I am Sir,
Your most obedient, humble servant

(s.) *W. Langley.*

Section II, of the Foreign Enlistment Law of 1870 determines, that any individual breaks this law, if within the dominions of His Majesty and without his consent, he prepares or equips any naval or military expedition to attack the dominion of any friendly state. The penalties of this crime are regulated.

(1) Meeting of the African section of the Liverpool Chamber of Commerce, held 30th September 1907.

«M.[r] John Holt, Vice-President of the African Section, said that he considered it just that a Commercial Body, like theirs, should go a little out of its ordinary way, when its

Conselheiro Ayres d'Ornellas e Vasconcellos.

Minister of Marine and the Colonies, who visited the Island of S. Thomé, in July 1907

And will not foreign industries, rivals of the English have the greatest interest in influencing public opinion in England itself, to compel English manufacturers to break off relations with the Portuguese planter, to place the latter in conditions of inferiority in the markets where the raw material is acquired, and the markets themselves under the dependency of the said industries?

And would it not suit internal politics, or the rivalry between English industries, to injure, in injuring us, the great English manufacturers or their own industrial rivals, thus also doing us an injury?

Are not some of these isolated facts, many or all of them united, the principal reason of the war against us?

These are questions we cannot reply to, but which occur to the thinking mind and in themselves contain, peradventure, the solution of what is enigmatical and mysterious in the unqualified proceeding against us of a certain number of enrolled propagandists, and by part of the English Press and public; we do not accuse the English manufacturers, because we believe that, so as not to suffer greater losses by the decrease of their clients, they were forced by the unreasonable current of opinion of those consuming their manufactures, to act against their convictions and interests.

But putting aside the insidious English accusations, and leaving the sorry personalities who promote and encourage them to the judgment of their own conscience, let us analyse briefly the position which S. Thomé and Principe hold in the general economy of the country.

-----

members were touched by the sufferings of the oppressed, and make their voices heard in matters which affect the rights of man and liberty. He did not deny, or make excuses for the methods of obtaining labour for the cocoa plantations in S. Thomé, but, he asked, how was it that the members of that Chamber could present themselves to the World, as philanthropists in this case of Angola, if their President was not ashamed of exercising the function of Consul of the Congo State. We cannot, he said, present ourselves as philanthropists in Angola, or condemn the iniquities of the Portuguese, whilst we tolerate the still greater evils of the Congo State, where we have rights guaranteed by a treaty, and obligations which we can enforce, if we so wish».

(«The Labourers of S. Thomé», by William A. Cadbury, Portuguese edition).

Without taking into account for our study the value of the less important exports, and adopting as basis of our calculation, only the two great products exported by the islands — cocoa and coffee, — in the last decade, we have:

Years	Cocoa		Coffee		Total value of cocoa and coffee
	Quantity — Kilogr.	Value in reis (1)	Quantity — Kilogr.	Value in reis (1)	(1)
1900	13.935.040	4.217.672$106	2.472.440	721:952$480	4.939:624$586
1901	16.982.640	5.140.079$040	1.758.610	513:514$120	5.653:593$160
1902	17.969.000	5.438.617$333	1.931.300	563:939$600	6.002:556$933
1903	22.450.900	6.795.139$066	1.431.150	417:895$800	7.213:034$866
1904	20.526.000	6.212.536$000	1.586.620	463:293$040	6.675:829$040
1905	25.379.320	7.681.474$186	810.810	236:756$520	7.918:230$706
1906	24.477.060	7.408.390$160	1.378.760	402:627$120	7.811:017$280
1907	24.356.640	7.371.943$040	1.325.730	387:113$160	7.759:056$200
1908	28.728.000	8.695.008$000	1.610.700	470:324$400	9.165:332$400
1909	30.261.000	9.158.996$000	1.073.170	313:365$640	9.472:361$640
	225.065.600	68.119:854$931	15.379.290	4.490:781$880	72.610:636$811

OBSERVATIONS. — The calculations of the productions have for their basis the imports into Lisbon and Funchal from 1st January to 31st December of each year, 60 kilos net weight being imputed to each bag of cocoa, and 70 kilos to each bag of coffee.

The average price for the ten years is calculated on the prices realized every fortnight in the Lisbon market for the fine quality, and corresponds to Reis 4$540, for every 15 kilos of cocoa, and Reis 4$380 for the same quantity of coffee.

As can be seen by the preceding table, the Islands of S. Thomé and Principe contributed to the economy of the country during the last decade, the important sum of 72.000 contos of réis (round numbers), or an average of 7.200 contos of reis per annum.

These sums remained almost entirely in the country, and are distributed approximately in the different branches of national activity as follows:

Taxes to the State in S. Thomé and Principe in the year 1909-10, (Budget 1909-10 page 7).....................	896:956$000	
Ditto paid in the country by companies, societies and private individuals on incomes proceeding from the Province of S. Thomé, (approximately)	80:044$000	950:000$000
Stores, cattle and other products of our other African Provinces...............		276:584$960
Contracts with natives of other Colonies, and in balance of wages taken by them on repatriation..................		500:000$000
Carried forward.........		1.726:584$960

Mechanical Saw-Mill, Porto-Real Plantation (West). Island of Principe

Brought forward..........		1.726:584$960
Freights of national merchandise and passage money to the national navigation (not including passage money paid by the State)	529:550$000	
Freights of merchandise in transit........	50:000$000	579:550$000
Payment of national wines, spirits and vinegar (1)..................... .		300:733$004
Payment of other articles of national agriculture		481:926$103
Payment of articles of national industry and commerce		680:120$788
Interest on national capital lent by Banks, trade and private persons (according to information given by the interested parties).		450:000$000
In payments in the country to the families of private employees transferred to various destinations on account of the same (according to information given by the respective employers) (2).........		300:000$000
Municipal rates in the Province of S. Thomé and Principe		79:462$793
Dividends to shareholders of the agricultural companies		503:000$000
Agricultural, industrial, and commercial enterprises, urban buildings in the country, scrip and the support of the planters and families who reside in the metropolis		898:622$352
		6.000:000$000
Foreign merchandise, in transit via Lisbon, imported into S. Thomé under the Portuguese Flag, (*Official Bulletin of S. Thomé, n.° 30 of 1909*)	823:971$886	
Less 50 contos of freights belonging to national navigation	50:000$000	
	773:971$886	
Foreign merchandise imported direct, including the freights in foreign steamers (Ditto)	327:579$540	
Voyages of the planters of S. Thomé to foreign parts (approximately)	98:448$574	1.200:000$000
Sum total...........		Réis 7:200:000$000

(1) See annexed table.
(2) Remittances by post, and monies brought by the employees themselves on their return home are not included.

The annual current of gold which in a progressive increase flows from the territory of our Islands in the Gulf of Guinea, and converges to the metropolis, being thus distributed, all the classes of the country have their direct or indirect share in it.

The State and municipalities benefit from the high taxes which the Colony contributes to the public revenues.

On the part of the State, according to the Budget of ordinary and extraordinary expenditure for 1909-1910, these revenues are thus distributed:

Salaries of 365 public employees, civil and military, in the Province of S. Thomé and Principe..	229:618$375
Pay of 363 non-commissioned officers and privates, and 23 bandsmen in the Province of S. Thomé and Principe	56:095$840
Return passages of employees..	13:000$000
Expenses of Colonial administration paid in the metropolis....	27:738$600
In the construction of the Trindade railway	286:599$200
Wages to workmen in the Government service, house-rent, stationery, sundries for public works, light-houses, telephones, and other expenses................................	119:752$635
Sum.....................	732:804$650
Assets as per the same Budget.....................	869:956$000
Balance.. Réis	137:151$350

The Government remits to other provinces and especially to Angola this balance and other economies, which doubtless the progressive increase of receipts produces during the year, where they cover part of the deficit of that Province.

The municipal revenues are distributed as follows:

Salaries of municipal and administrative employees	16:447$592
Personnel, plant, and cattle for cleansing, preserving and opening streets.....................................	15:090$000
Rents of schools, law-courts, offices of notaries, police-stations, etc.	4:742$000
Lighting of streets	3:410$000
Reconstructing buildings and repairing bridges, roads, etc.	14:084$288
Water rate, cemeteries and prisons....................	5:722$000
Interest and amortisation of a loan of Réis 34:000$000	4:301$740
Divers other municipal services and charges	15:665$173
Total....................... Réis	79:462$793

The commercial and economical life of labour-furnishing Colonies is kept up by the heavy tax of Reis 500:000$000 which is paid them by the Islands of S. Thomé and Principe for the contracting and repatriation of labourers, together with Reis 276:584$960, the value of the agricultural produce which this Province buys from them.

The national steam navigation for the West Coast of Africa formerly received an annual grant of Reis 200:000$000 from the Government, and the service con-

Native planters and their children. Island of S. Thomé

sisted only of one voyage monthly between Lisbon and Mossamedes, in steamers of less than 1.500 tons and making 7 knots. The navigation for the East Coast which received the annual grant of Reis 372:000$000, also ran once monthly between Lisbon and Mozambique in steamers of 3.000 tons running 12 knots.

At present there are three voyages monthly for the West and one for the East Coast, connecting our two great provinces of the African Continent with one another and the other smaller Colonies and with the metropolis, carried out in magnificent steamers of 2.200 to 3.000 tons, and running 10 knots in the voyage to Tiger Bay, and in steamers of 4.000 to 6.000 tons, running 13 knots in the voyage to Mozambique, every modern improvement being found in those steamers as well as all the comforts found in similar steamers of the most advanced maritime nations. This excellent service is gratuitous for the State.

To complete the longer voyages, there is a coasting service in the Provinces of Cape Verde, Guinea, S. Thomé, Angola, and Mozambique, carried on in steamers of less tonnage connecting the smaller ports of the respective Provinces with the principal ones, there being time-tables fixed for the transhipment of passengers and cargo from the larger to the smaller steamers. This special service is carried out by the same company, that receives an annual State grant of Réis 10:000$000 in the Province of Angola, Réis 36:000$000 in Mozambique, the service being gratuitous in S. Thomé, Cape Verde and Guinea.

The personnel employed on board the steamers and the office employees of the Empreza Nacional average, as per accompanying map, 1.467 individuals, generally heads of families, which at the rate of four for each family represents the important number of 5.868 people, living on the proceeds of work furnished by the Portuguese steam navigation to Africa, a number which may be calculated at more than 6.000 persons, if we take into consideration those employed by the same Company in their sailing service.

All these benefits are obtained for the national community free of charge for the State, seeing that the reductions obtained by the latter in the price of passages for its officials and for Government stores have reached sums exceeding the Réis 46:000$000 of the grants; such benefits, in part, are certainly due to the excellent and rigorous administration of the Empreza Nacional, but it is also no less certain that they are chiefly derived from the tribute which our Colonies pay in passages and freights, among which the Province of S. Thomé and Principe takes the first place.

The stores and provisions which the steamers buy at home also form a valuable asset to national agriculture and commerce.

The wine trade which gives employment to so many people in our country is likewise benefited. The value of the wine, vinegar, and spirits consumed in 1908 reached the amount of Réis 300:733$004 and this sum ought to increase from year to year if the present protection tariff be maintained (1).

----

(1) In 1909, 4.000:000 litres of wine in barrels were shipped to S. Thomé in the Empreza Nacional Steamers and about 300.000 litres, or approximately 10.000 casks, in sailing vessels.

We have no means of calculating the quantity of bottled wines and spirits shipped in 1909, but certainly that quantity was not less than in the preceding year. — (See annexed map.).

Other agricultural products and their derivatives find a sale in S. Thomé and Principe the value of each being as follows: — Cattle for traction, Reis 45:782꠸666; salted and prepared meats, lard, butter, Reis 64:099꠸520; flours, bran, biscuits, Reis 128.396꠸026; cereals including millet, Reis 79:751꠸010; dried and fresh fruits and plants, Reis 4:942꠸933; vegetables, Reis 129:410꠸751; straw, Reis 1:999$066; cheese, Reis 2:840꠸266; potatoes and onions, Reis 24:733꠸865; — and the agriculture and industry of Cape Verde, Angola and Mozambique receive in exchange for cattle, Reis 59:917꠸333; for corn, Reis 14:699꠸466; for dried and salted fish, Reis 188:407꠸073; and other products, Reis 13:561꠸088 (1).

National capitalists find an excellent and safe market for investments, which obtain a higher rate of interest than in the metropolis, important sums being thus employed.

The Réis 450:00꠸000 which S. Thomé and Principe contributed in 1908 for repayment of borrowed capital was distributed in Réis 147:179꠸261 paid to the Ultramarine Bank, and Réis 302:820꠸739 to other Banks, to trade and private persons. This sum ought to be exceeded in the year 1909, and in the future may be much higher to the advantage of borrowers and lenders, if — losing their proverbial timidity — national capitalists would launch out on a larger scale for the encouragement of new enterprises and for increasing the existing ones.

The salaries of the European employees, both public and private, support numerous families. It is no exaggeration to state that, out of the 2000 Europeans resident in S. Thomé and Principe, four-fifths exercise functions ranging from the high positions of governors, magistrates, and managers of plantations to the more humble callings of shop assistants, farm stewards, or foremen of labourers, and that the important sum of Réis 300:000꠸000, to which the annual transference of the salaries of private employees amounts — so far as we could learn, — added to sums unknown to us, and those which public officials transfer, represent in their totality, a respectable amount which we cannot state precisely, but suppose is more than Réis 400:000꠸000, which amount is sent home monthy for rents, payments of school fees, the support and other expenses of the same employees' families.

Supposing that each family consists on the average of four members, we have 6.400 persons living in the metropolis supported by the salaries of the public and private employees working in the Colony. This money reaching the hands of the interested parties in duo-decimal fractions, helps them in their periodical necessities, and their fractional division prevents waste from improvidence or extravagance.

The residue of the salaries generally accompanies the employees on their return from Africa, the larger portion being occasionally spent at home, and part invested in land, houses, or scrip, public wealth as well as taxable matter being thus increased.

---

(1) All these amounts are taken from the imports of the year 1905, which are the last statistics published, (Official Bulletins of S. Thomé, n° 30 of 1908, and appendix of n.° 11, 1909) a third being added which was the total increase in the national imports in 1908 as compared to 1905.

STEAMERS OF THE NATIONAL STEAM NAVIGATION CO. TO PORTUGUESE AFRICA.

S. S. «Cazengo»

One of the steamers used in the transport of labourers from Angola and Cape Verde to S. Thomé and Principe

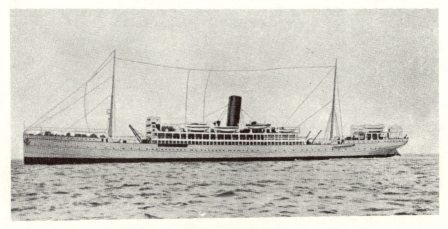

S. S. «Lusitania»

Which transports labourers from Mozambique to S. Thomé

S. S. «Africa»

Which transports labourers from Mozambique to S. Thomé

The dividends paid by the Companies also benefit numerous families. There are 12 limited Companies that carry on agricultural enterprises in the Province all having their head-offices in Lisbon, where they employ the respective staffs.

The total capital of those Companies is Réis 11.751:100$000. Five pay a dividend which amounted last year to the sum of Réis 503:000$000.

We could not obtain the exact number of shareholders of these institutions, as there is a considerable quantity of shares payable to bearer; but, considering the dissemination of public wealth in Portugal, it is easy to deduce that the very large capital of these Companies is distributed amongst a considerable number of families that live partly or exclusively on the revenues.

In the value attributed in the statistics of foreign merchandise imported under the national flag (via Lisbon or Oporto), of Réis	823:971$886
there is a difference for the national navigation of	50:000$000
which is approximately the share which belongs to our flag of the amount of freight received, and which is included in the value of that merchandise.	
This correction being made, the sum paid to foreigners is reduced to Réis	773:971$886

In these numbers we have not taken into account the circumstance which it would be as well to note; that is the goods for re-exportation to S. Thomé and Principe, brought to Lisbon by foreign steamers, and the re-shipment from Lisbon of our cocoa to the ports of consumption, thus increasing the amount of foreign shipping entering the Port of Lisbon, which is very advantageous for our trade and the national economy in general.

Foreign goods imported direct are of the annual value of Réis 327:579$540, but of this amount the Treasury only receives the augmented duties collected in the respective Custom Houses.

Voyages abroad. — The sum of nearly Réis 100:000$000, which is the amount calculated as spent by planters away from Portugal, cannot be considered as useless for the country. Many of these voyages are undertaken from the need of undergoing cures at watering-places, medical treatment, or simple hygienic excursions to mountainous regions, etc., to which Europeans who have resided in S. Thomé or Principe submit themselves for the benefit of their health, and to strengthen their constitutions weakened and impaired by the depressing effects of the African climate.

The health and robustness of those who work and produce are also a national asset, and their preservation deserves some monetary sacrifice.

The salutary influence of our valuable Colony in the economic life of the nation is not limited however to what has been mentioned.

The chief planters of S. Thomé and Principe reside in the metropolis, and here spend their income in maintaining themselves and families, employing the residue, — those who possess it — or the capital obtained on credit, in most varied investments, such as cultivating farms and other agricultural enterprises on a larger scale, in building houses in the capital or in the provinces, in industrial enterprises on their own account, or by joining their capital to the work of others, or even in shares representing capital employed in industries or trades, in Government scrip, etc., etc.

Many people living at present in Portugal are helped by the money which comes from S. Thomé and Principe, and very important is the assistance that money renders to Portuguese industries, commerce, and agriculture, and if it were possible to penetrate the veil enshrouding its action, one would see how widespread and beneficent it is. But the planters and merchants of S. Thomé and Principe do not turn over only the Réis 7.200:000$000 of their annual gross receipts.

As may be clearly deduced from the amount of interest annually paid, they have large recourse to credit.

Supposing that the average interest on those transactions be 7 °/₀, the capital corresponding to the Réis 450:000$000 of interest would be 6.429 contos (round numbers). Having recourse to credit, the planters do not accumulate money in their safes for the mere sickly pleasure of gloating over it in the solitude of their strong-rooms; it is clear therefore that those important sums are all put into circulation, part being intended to increase and add to the value of estates in S. Thomé and Principe which do not yet yield a profit, or only an insufficient one, and part also intended to acquire, exploit, and increase the value of property in the kingdom, as well as other investments, including transactions on the Stock Exchange, thus the increase of business transactions becomes advantageous to all the economy of the country.

We will now conclude this summary individualisation of the various applications to which the money of S. Thomé is put, and appreciate the question under another aspect.

Exchange.

By its natural influence on the exchange market — and the natural influences are always the best in these cases — the cocoa-gold which the Islands of S. Thomé and Principe export, exercises a preponderating and normalizing action on exchange, an important factor in the financial and economical life of the country, and serves as a curb to speculation.

Let us see how this preponderating and normalizing action is exercised.

As we have shown in this study, the average value of cocoa and coffee in each year is Réis 7.200:000$000; but as all the coffee and 218.400 kilos of cocoa do not leave Portugal we will discount their value, which is respectively of 449 and 76 contos, from that sum, (it is well to remark that if this produce did not remain here, we should have to pay in gold for what would be imported in its place) and we have Réis 6.675:000$000 left, which is equivalent to gold, although subject to the fluctuations of the respective exchange.

Let us now examine what are the requirements of that great client that purchases gold, that periodical, certain, and tangible client against whom are directed the greatest efforts of speculators — the State — on what occasion and in what proportion it requires to furnish itself and let us at the same time examine when are the occasions, and in what proportion the gold of S. Thomé and Principe appears in the market to offer its assistance.

General Calheiros Street, during the visit of H. R. H. The Crown Prince Luiz Filippe.

On the right, the office and residence of the National Navigation Co's agent. Island of S. Thomé

Gold bought by the Government, and value in gold of the cocoa of S. Thomé and Principe entered into Lisbon during the economic year of 1908-1909

Gold bought by the Government			Arrivals in Lisbon of cocoa from S. Thomé and Principe	
Dates	£	Values according to the medium prices and ex- changes of the last decade. £	Dates	Number of bags, each 60 kilos
1908			**1908**	
July 11.........	20.000	49.058. 6.8	July 8.........	14.500
» 18.........	20.000	26.535. 9.8	» 12.........	7.843
» 25.........	25.c00	38.309. 9.8	» 25.........	11.323
August 1.........	25.000	37.585. 9.0	August 6.........	11.109
» 8.........	25.000	324.16.0	» 11.........	096
» 14.........	25.000	21.660. 2.0	» 16.........	6.402
October 10.........	25.000	48.073.15.8	» 22.........	14.209
» 17.........	25.000	45.631. 0.0	September 8.........	13.487
» 24.........	25.000	51.399 12.0	» 22.........	15.192
» 31.........	25.000	45.035.11.0	October 8.........	13.311
November 7.........	25.000	51.416.10.4	» 20.........	15.197
» 14.........	25.000	42.961.11.4	November 7.........	12.698
» 21.........	25.000	15.363.14.4	» 10.........	4.541
» 28.........	25.000	60.341.15.0	» 22.........	17.835
December 8.........	25.000	25.490. 0.8	December 7.........	7.534
» 12.........	26.150	47.021.11.4	» 13.........	13.898
1909				
January 16.........	20.000	200.371. 3.0	» 14.........	59.223
» 23.........	20.000	33.515. 6.0	» 19.........	9.906
			1909	
» 30.........	20.000	39.233. 2.8	January 6.........	11.596
February 6.........	20.000	65.864. 0.8	» 13.........	19.414
» 13.........	20.000	63.914.11.0	» 24.........	18.891
» 20.........	25.000	33.011. 3.8	February 7.........	9.757
» 27.........	25.000	96.123.17.8	» 13.........	28.411
March 6.........	25.000	67.061. 1.0	» 20.........	19.821
» 13.........	25.000	32.831.17.4	March 9.........	9.704
» 20.........	25.000	19.217. 6.8	» 13.........	5.680
» 27.........	25.000	36.543. 7.8	» 20.........	10.801
April 3.........	25.000	37.507.12.8	April 10.........	11.086
» 17.........	25.000	20.157.18.0	» 17.........	5.958
» 24.........	25.000	33.775.16.4	» 18.........	9.983
May 1.........	25.000	40.620. 6.0	May 6.........	12.006
» 8.........	25.000	37 595.12.0	» 12.........	11.112
» 15.........	25.000	38.126.15.0	» 20.........	11.269
» 22.........	25.000	51.501. 2.0	June 6.........	15.222
» 29.........	25.000	25.422. 1.4	» 11.........	7.514
June 5.........	25.000	32.151.16.4	» 19.........	9.503
» 22.........	30.000	—		—
	896.150	1.610.574.18.8		476.032

OBSERVATIONS. — According to the system adopted in this work, which is to apply the medium of the last decade to all calculations relative to cocoa, we have taken the same basis for the above table:

Medium price for 15 kilos, in Portuguese money (round numbers)..... 4$540 Réis
Price in sterling for 15 kilos, at the medium exhange of 44ᵈ ¾ for Réis 1$000 (round numbers)... £ 0.16.11

As is shown by this table, the State comes periodically to the market, twice, thrice, or four times monthly, to buy the gold necessary for its foreign payments, and the Province of S. Thomé and Principe comes also periodically to the market, twice, thrice; and four times monthly to offer the gold of its plantations in a much larger quantity than the State requires, and at the moment when its presence is necessary.

After the State requirements have been satisfied, a large sum remains which is offered to the market, together with the gold received from other sources, to assist the requirements of trade. Thus our cocoa performs the double mission of covering an important part of the economic deficit of the metropolis, and preventing speculators from increasing the premium on gold beyond certain limits.

The moderating action in the exchange markets of the gross values of cocoa and coffee from S. Thomé and Principe, and the manner in which these values are distributed in money, demonstrate their beneficent influence on all the branches of national wealth.

There is therefore every foundation for affirming that the Province of S. Thomé and Principe is now an indispensable factor in the economic existence of the nation, and we must preserve and develop it at all costs.

In the actual conditions of the country, with an economic deficit which in our commercial balance shows the sum of Réis 3o.ooo:ooo$ooo with a deficit in the budget of Réis 3.746:ooo$ooo (1) and with a premium of 1 1 °/₀ on gold, we must not lose this great element of equilibrium; we ought even to endeavour to increase it, and find others to balance our economic accounts, without which neither will the premium on gold disappear, nor the State finances be based on solid foundations.

We have valuable Colonies which, if governed and exploited judiciously and economically, can assist the metropolis to overcome the difficulties with which it struggles.

The Province of S. Thomé and Principe stands prominent amongst all, from its special and double condition as a genuine Portuguese and exclusively agricultural Colony, producing articles for export of great commercial value and of easy placement in foreign markets and which are paid in gold, and can be greatly increased as there are many plantations, as yet unproductive or only beginning to produce, and also much land suitable for cultivation, but not yet cleared, where lie new sources of abundant wealth waiting for the hand of man to exploit them.

(1) Average for 5 years.

Native type. Island of Principe

Type of half-caste. Island of Principe

Native type. Island of Principe

The Islands of S. Thomé and Principe must have a surface of 120.000 hectares (1) thus distributed:

Cultivated holdings		62.288
Spaces occupied by buildings, roads, and waterways		6.603
Forest lands { For cultivation	35.000	
{ For building, roads, etc.	5.891	
		40.891
Lands unsuitable for culture (sands, rocks, etc.) (2)		10.218
		120.000

Taking into account the increase of production in the existing plantations, and what can be obtained in lands not yet cultivated, it will be no exaggeration to state that when all are cultivated and in full production, and the methods employed in the plantations, which in many leave much to be desired, are improved by the teachings of science and experience, there will be an increase of 70 % on the actual production, and thus the Réis 7.200:000$000 which we now receive will attain Réis 12.240:000$000.

So important an addition of gold-capital to the national assets would determine a great reduction in the economic deficit of the metropolis, and at the same time influence the rate of exchange by reducing the premium, which fact alone would cause an appreciable improvement in the situation of the Treasury.

Now to reach this desideratum, so that S. Thomé and Principe may attain their limit of production, many years are not required; to obtain that result rapidly it is sufficient to resolve the question of manual labour, so that all hands required may be supplied under such conditions as do not handicap or destroy agriculture, and in circumstances counselled by the liberal and humanitarian sentiment, and the public convenience of the Portuguese nation, but not according to the morbid mentality of exotic philanthropists, or the exclusive interests of egotistical foreigners.

To solve the problem the whole nation must work unitedly, seriously facing the dangers of the situation, energetically and persistently pursue the path already traced, join their efforts in a common action, and not abandon the subject until it is completely resolved.

In addition to what is already accomplished, we think that it would be advisable to avoid present and future difficulties by the following means:

1st — To assure as speedily as possible the emigration of labourers from the Province of Guinea;

2nd — To strengthen the current already started of labourers from Mozambique, by defending it against all the manœuvres and intrigues of those, natives or foreigners, who endeavour to stop it;

---

(1) 1 Hectare = 2·4711 acres.

(2) These figures are not mathematically exact, as no agricultural maps of the Province exist. They are based on information received from planters and calculations on the produce; they cannot be far from the real ones.

We compute lands unsuitable for culture at 20 % of those left for cultivation.

3rd — To initiate, according to the precise terms of the regulation of 17th July 1909, the emigration of the subjected «Sóbados» of the Province of Angola, and to endeavour that in the first contracts the legal terms be anticipated for some of the natives, repatriating them partially and successively beginning at the end of one year, so as to put an end, as quickly as possible to the legend of discredit of the emigration for S. Thomé, which convenience, ignorance, or bad faith has endeavoured, and still endeavours to spread amongst the inhabitants of the subjected regions of that Province;

4th — To maintain the option in force by which labourers on the termination of their contracts can, if they so wish, freely re-engage themselves for a new period, subject to the conditions stipulated in the respective regulations;

5th — To establish coercive measures to make use of those natives of S. Thomé and Principe living in idleness, endeavouring to make them work by kindness and persuasion, before having recourse to violent means;

6th — To concede the option of renouncing his birthplace to any native labourer of the Angola hinterland, brought to the Province before the law of 17th July 1909 was put into force, who having resided for 5 years or more in S. Thomé or Principe wishes to renew his contract, the act of renunciation being effected by a declaration included in the contract indenture and registered in the «Curadoria» (curator's office), he having the right to receive henceforward the amount credited to him in the Labour and Repatriation Fund, in annuities of Réis 10$000;

7th — To regulate and execute the Decree of 21st May 1892, of Ferreira do Amaral, relative to military recruitment and repression of vagrancy, or issue and execute any other measures tending to the same effect, and completing them with the organization of a good rural police-force.

Such are the measures which in our opinion should be adopted with firmness and perseverance to complete the system organized, and take advantage of the efforts expended, until in time, the problem may encounter its natural and definite solution by utilizing the hands existing in the Province and by the settlement there of a population sufficiently numerous for the principal requirements of agriculture.

To work to guarantee the present and secure to the Colony a solid future, free from doubts and embarrassments, is the duty of the Governments, as well as a convenience to the planters and the supreme interest of the nation. The present is guaranteed by facilitating immigration under conditions and charges compatible with the means of the planters, and faithfully carrying out, as has been done to the present, the terms agreed with the labourers; the future is prepared by consolidating a current of temporary emigrants to fill the gaps in the manual labour required by agriculture, and promoting the employment of the natives of the Islands and the forced settlement in the Colony of the labour elements existing there, aborigines of the Angola hinterland, which they may wish to adopt as their native country, and also as the birthplace of their children.

In all times and in all countries, farseeing Governments have endeavoured to constitute in fertile and productive regions centres of permanent settlers, who make the land valuable by their labour, thus securing their well-being and contributing to the prosperity of the nation to which they belong.

Without seeking examples in more remote eras, we will mention those in more recent times which occur to us, namely:

Manager's dwelling, Agua Izé Plantation. Labourers waiting for the payment of their wages. Island of S. Thomé

The fabulous sums spent by Brazil in promoting immigration from the most varied sources, and making every sacrifice to introduce and perpetuate the emigrant in Brazil;

The U. S. America, in the period of their repopulation refusing to celebrate extradition treaties, conceding safe refuge to criminal fugitives from other countries, and compelling naturalization on immigrants after a short residence in the country;

England, exporting to Australia shiploads of women to obtain the settlement of colonists by means of the formation of family ties;

Transvaal, exempting from taxation the labourers of Mozambique who have resided more than one year in that country, paying all expenses to attract them thither, but omitting the obligation of paying their return passage, surrounding the repatriation with difficulties and not even assuring them the certainty of their repatriation at their own expense by reserving a portion of their wages for protecting them against their natural improvidence.

Let us imitate therefore the good example of these countries, masters in the art of modern colonization, by favouring the definite installation in our Colony of the actual labourers of the Angola hinterland; let us endeavour to gain over for work the natives of the Province; let us make a trial of emigration from the subjected regions of the Province of Angola, with the corresponding optional repatriation; let us have recourse in the same conditions to the emigration from Guinea, and let us not neglect that one already started under such good auspices from the Province of Mozambique.

At the same time, let us persevere in the desire of identifying ourselves more and more with the immigrants; let us increase, if it be possible, the advantages which they and their families enjoy, surrounding them with comforts, and creating new attractions so as to turn their stay in the Islands as agreeable as possible, and in order that, in the comparison which they may make between the conditions of life we proportion to them and those offered by their birthplace and any other region to where they may emigrate, it will not be easy to find a combination of advantages equal to those encountered by emigrants in the Province of S. Thomé and Principe.

By proceeding neither hastily nor impatiently, we shall gradually and entirely obtain their full confidence, and when they know and can appreciate us properly, no intrigues or manœuvres will be able to prejudice us in the minds of the natives of any part; we shall then be able to rely on the assistance of the working family of all our Colonies, and the problem, at present difficult, of labour in S. Thomé will be satisfactorily and for ever solved; we shall then completely put a stop to all pretexts for causing us international difficulties raised by interests opposed to ours, and the nation will be able to rely without the least fear, on the powerful assistance rendered by capital drawn from the soil of S. Thomé and Principe.

After having indicated some measures which surely would improve the system now in execution and intended to solve the manual labour problem, we propose to conclude this chapter with a summary demonstration of the economic state of agriculture in the Islands of S. Thomé and Principe.

We will not refer in that demonstration to the special situation of any planter, though some obtain sufficiently remunerative incomes, whilst others close their balance-sheets with a deficit, sometimes considerable, as our aim is to give a general notion without entering into details.

In the charges of agriculture we shall have to include all the taxes and rates paid to the State and municipalities, for as agriculture is the only mainstay of the public and private revenues of the Province, all tributes directly or indirectly, whatever may be their designation, fall on it.

Let us explain therefore the situation:

Taxes for the State, Réis..........................	950:000$000
Ditto for the municipalities	79:462$793
Wages, maintenance, clothing, medical and hospital attendance to 40:000 labourers (not including Angolares) and employees, at the average annual rate per head (including expenses incurred with the children) of Réis 90$000..	3.600:000$000
Contracts and repatriation of labourers	500:000$000
Freights, packages, insurance and other expenses up to delivery in Lisbon or Funchal of 504:350 bags of cocoa and 15:331 bags of coffee (less duties in the S. Thomé Custom House) (1)...........................	812:880$675
Interest on building and other loans, transferences, etc. paid to the Banco Ultramarino........................	147:179$261
Half of all the other interest (it is calculated that the other half is spent in the kingdom in expenses foreign to the S. Thomé plantations)........................	151:410$365
New installations in the plantations and preservation of the existing ones, 5 % of the gross revenue...............	360:000$000
Sundry expenses, 3 % of the gross revenue..............	216:000$000
Réis	6.816:933$094

These charges absorb more than 94·5 % of the gross revenue, which is, as has already been stated, according to the average of the last ten years, of 7:200 contos of réis, having been only of 6:800 contos of réis in the year 1909, owing to the low quotations of our cocoa in that year, and if we consider the works for increasing the cultures executed more or less annually in all the estates still incompletely cultivated, require new capital, we arrive at the conclusion that, in the years in which the price of cocoa does not rise beyond the average adopted for our calculations, sums approximately equal to all the revenues of the plantations of S. Thomé and Principe are swallowed up by the expenses arising from their maintenance or enlargement, and by the taxes paid, for if some of the larger planters have favourable balances in those years, the larger number close their accounts with deficits, which are covered by borrowed capital.

---

(1) The number of bags taken for this calculation is that corresponding to the imports in Lisbon and Funchal from 31st of January to December 31st 1909.

J. A. Wyllie, F. R. G. S.

Lieutenant-Colonel of the Indian Army (on half pay)
Portugal's defender in the English and North American Press, in the S. Thomé
manual labour question

This situation is not only difficult for the smaller number; for the majority of planters, who can only emerge from it with economy and time, when the new plantations arrive at maturity, it is still embarrassing, at least temporarily, and is naturally aggravated in the years of low prices for cocoa, like 1909, for in such a case the revenues, which we calculated according to the average of the last decade, would be considerably reduced, without the corresponding decrease in the charges.

In these circumstances, to increase charges of any kind, in this or in approaching years, would be to condemn the larger number of the planters to certain and inevitable ruin, and to this would have to be added all the losses which the repercussion of that disaster would determine in the entire country, if the State should not decide to compensate the planters with a proportional reduction in the high taxes collected, which would cause another disaster, even if of less importance, as it would reduce the revenues of the improverished public Treasury.

The Province of S. Thomé, the population of which is calculated in round numbers at 68:000, pays a tax per head of réis 13$963, whilst the corresponding rate in other parts of the country is réis 7$350, and in foreign countries, like Spain réis 7$753, France 12$300, England 11$700, Germany 11$340, Italy 6$150, Belgium 6$500, Roumania 6$000, Sweden 5$700, and in Holland 4$700. But as there are 40.000 labourers with 6.987 children who do not pay any tax whatever, and as the greater part of the natives of the Island, Angolares or others, are in the same circumstances, the rates fall only on a very reduced number of individuals, and in this case the tributary burden for each real tax-payer reaches truly unheard of and absurd figures.

Thus our Province of S. Thomé and Principe bears the palm in taxation matters over all the nations of Europe — great and small.

Let the public authorities therefore consider, let the nation consider, and especially let those consider who have interests leagued to the Province of S. Thomé and Principe, the danger of the situation if — acquiescing in the new demands of foreigners — we promote measures to aggravate the charges of agriculture.

All that could be reasonably asked for in the name of liberty and humanity has long been done in S. Thomé. The last governmental measures complete the ultra-protection system of the black race that emigrates to that Province, and we dare affirm that no country, possessing Colonies in Equatorial Africa, has up to to-day done more or better. Let us limit ourselves therefore to executing and causing to be executed our model laws, let us continue to facilitate the entry to our plantations to foreigners desirous of visiting them, and — strong in our conscience and with the testimony of those who wish to give an impartial account of what they observed — let us proceed serenely and tranquilly along the civilizing and humanitarian path which has been and which will continue to be the aim and the motto of our people, sure of having done our duty and certain of obtaining a favourable sentence in the tribunal of History.

And if our defamers continue in their unjust campaign let us reply to them with the Arab proverb. . .

L. Mac Hale

English merchant in Manchester.
Portugal's defender in the English Press, in the S. Thomé
manual labour question

CHAPTER VI.

Conclusion.

The idea of our writing the present work arose, as has already been stated, from the charge with which we were honoured to make an exposition relative to the conditions of production and manual labour, and the manner in which agriculture is exploited at present in the Islands of S. Thomé and Principe.

Various reasons, principally those of a patriotic nature and of general interest in which local and private ones absolutely and perfectly form an integral part, owing to our want of time and professional resources, have led us to dilate more widely, and perhaps without due order, on subjects dispensable to the restricted study of the question, although they are naturally deduced from, and identified with, the same.

Amplifying, with a separate work, the honourable charge entrusted to us, we had in view, whilst we endeavoured to execute it, the defence of the country and the interests specially aimed at, demonstrating with the small resources at our disposal what the Province of S. Thomé and Principe has been and is at present, and the strenuous efforts employed by the Portuguese at different times to clear the forests, civilize the inhabitants and preserve so precious a jewel in the national patrimony.

And really, from what has been stated we think the following conclusions may be drawn:

That shortly after its discovery up to the present date, the efforts and sacrifices of the Portuguese have been constant to colonize and exploit the Islands of S. Thomé and Principe, having placed at the service of its progress, principally (after the second half of the last century), a colonizing capacity composed of unbreakable tenacity, of intelligence, and activity methodically applied and of unsurpassed sentiments of humanity, attested by the complete public tranquillity which has reigned there for very many years, and the enviable prosperity which the Province enjoys;

That these facts give to the Province the right of being considered a model Colony amongst all similar possessions of African regions;

That in all times, some foreigners of different nationalities moved by covetousness or envy, certain English having made themselves prominent within the last few years, have attempted to overthrow our dominion, others to suffocate our activity and the measures employed to introduce progress and civilization in the Province, now endeavouring to snatch it from us by force, now practising crushing hostilities against the boldest and most legitimate enterprises, or promoting campaigns of discredit thoughout the World, from motives of unconfessed egotism, disguised by a philanthropy which is as misplaced as it is absurd;

That the Portuguese colonization, and its administrative and professional methods of agricultural enterprise in the Islands of S. Thomé and Principe notwithstanding the embarrassments of every description and the defamations of various order which envy or interest have brought on them, have served as a school and model to similar Colonies in English and German Africa;

That in no other African Colony of any nation, emigrants, servants, labourers, or employees encounter centres of production and activity which offer a combination of advantages, expressed in the conditions of labour, treatment, dwellings, remuneration, forethought, and assistance, equal to those offered in the plantations of S. Thomé and Principe, together with the sincerely paternal benevolence and toleration which the employers generally show their labourers;

That Portuguese legislation enriched by the last measures decreed by the Government of the metropolis, contains all the requirements for guaranteeing the liberty, rights, privileges, and other means of security relative to recruitments, contracts, transports, treatment, wages, and repatriation of the natives of any origin that may emigrate to S. Thomé and Principe, conceding besides this dispositions for protection, assistance, security, and justice which are not exceeded or equalled in any other African Colony, and the execution of which by the private individuals and authorities is realized to the content of those chiefly interested — masters and labourers;

That the proceeding, both austere and tolerant, of the Portuguese authorities and the strictly just and benevolent attitude of the Estate owners of the Islands give us the right to affirm before the whole World that we are absolutely justified in our expectation to see maintained that meritorious work of the agriculturalists of S. Thomé and Principe, which constitutes the well-being of the working population in the whole Province, and to verify that all the measures will continue to be enforced rigorously which impose duties on that population and assure rights, privileges, protection, and liberty;

That the prosperity of S. Thomé and Principe is a factor of first order, an emporium of work and production which exercises a powerful influence on the financial equilibrium and economy, both public and private, of the nation, and that the latter has the greatest interest in encouraging that prosperity, by not permitting its destruction, its stagnation, or decadence;

Finally, that no Government of this country, in the just defence of the national dignity and interests confided to it, and of which it must be zealous, ought to make new concessions to the unjustified exigencies of morbid philanthropy which attacks and insults us, and that its action should be limited to adopting, when it deems it necessary and convenient, the measures which the liberal character, the traditional honour and interests of the country counsel, without pre-occupying itself with the opinion of egotistical foreigners, who may wish to injure us.

And notwithstanding the excessive length of some considerations expressed in the preceding chapters, may it be still allowed us to make brief reference to some points not yet touched upon, which appear to us worthy of the attention of the Government, the country, and the Island Estate owners, and what it is as well to accentuate, so as to appreciate more fully the financial and agricultural situation of

Private railway in the Santa Margarida Plantation. Island of S. Thomé

the Province, the insufficiency of its rural population and the value which the Colony represents in the common wealth.

As we have already said, of the total surface of the Islands of S. Thomé and Principe — 120:000 hectares (1) — 35:000 hectares of land suitable for culture are not yet cleared, there being approximately 20:000 hectares suitable for the culture of cocoa, 5:000 hectares for coffee, and 10:000 hectares for Peruvian bark, rubber and other produce.

The cultivated surface contains plantations in full maturity, plantations which have not yet attained their maximum producing power, and others which have not yet commenced to produce. We must count therefore, during the first decade, upon an increase of annual production resulting from work already done, which it will be no exaggeration to calculate at 3 $\%$ of the actual annual figures (the increase in cocoa in each of the ten previous years was, on the average, of nearly 12 $\%$ calculated on the harvest of 1900); so that by treating and preserving what is already made we shall have within ten years raised the figures representing the annual production of cocoa to 39.339:300 kilos, and those of coffee to 1.395:121 kilos, or in other words 654 kilos per cultivated hectare of coffee and cocoa. (2)

Of the cocoa produced, a particle of 6 $\%$ corresponds to thefts committed on the plantations by vagrants, or to the work of the small farmers who are nearly all natives (3); the remainder belongs to the important planters.

To look after the existing plantations which occupy 62:288 hectares these planters employ 40:000 contracted labourers and 2:000 Angolares, and to cultivate the remaining zones suitable for culture, the extent of which is over 35:000 hectares, they require proportionately more than 23:600 hands. But as there exist scattered throughout the plantations, and in the sandy zones of the coast, many millions of palm trees producing palm oil and cocoa nut, and also cocoa plantations the majority of which are abandoned owing to the want of hands, it would be as well to consider in computing the number of labourers which the Province still requires, how many would be necessary to exploit that wealth, a great part of which is wasted; and supposing that 2:400 labourers would be sufficient to work that branch of agriculture in the Province, we shall arrive at the conclusion that the Islands of S. Thomé and Principe require to increase their rural labourers by 26:000 to develop the exploitation of native produce, up to the limits of which the extension of the two Islands is susceptible.

The labourers we require can be supplied in part by the native population of S. Thomé, and the remainder by our Provinces of Angola, Mozambique, Guinea, and Cape Verde, by means of temporary contracts, the repatriation to be always paid by the employers when the labourers, on the expiration of their contracts, choose to return home.

---

(1) 1 Hectare = 2·4711 acres.

(2) The computed average production of the two articles together is of 40.734:421 kilos, and the surface is of 62:288 hectares for each article: separately they would be cocoa 690 kilos, and coffee 230 kilos per hectare, the cocoa plantations covering the surface of 56:923 hectares, and those of coffee 5:365.

(3) This calculation is based on the approximate quantity of «paiol» cocoa (in stock) sold first hand in Lisbon in 1908.

In homage to the philanthropy of our English accusers, let it be permitted that the Congolese, Turks, Moors, Persians, Arabs, and Kaffirs continue to exploit the outcasts of the extreme Angola hinterland, until our Government can realize the effectual occupation of those regions. In the meanwhile, let us not contract in Angola, or accept thence, only labourers proceeding from subdued tribes, as is determined by the regulation of July of last year, and according to its articles.

To obtain the number of labourers lacking, to install them and attend to the numerous and costly exigencies of the regulations and charges of exploiting, large capital is required.

It is natural that a part of the wealthier planters of the Islands should contribute to these charges, even though it be but by completing the clearing of their properties; another part will certainly find assistance in private capital, but the remainder who are still many, will require to ask for the intervention of the Government, not for loans or guarantees, but simply that by agreement with the «Banco Ultramarino», an increase of transactions, relating to predial credit, be promoted, and the limit of colonial predial debentures be increased by several thousands of pounds, and by facilitating the investment in new transactions, of the debentures, as they are paid off by the instalments of loans effected.

However, no new enterprises of any importance will be initiated, nor will any fresh capital assist the development of those useful undertakings if, as far as possible, the just remuneration of the capital and labour expended be not assured, and for this it is necessary to diminish the cost of the estates, increasing the facilities of sea and land transports, and stipulating reduced tariffs. Therefore the State can and ought to put into execution, as soon as possible, the following measures; to turn effective daily coasting steam service in S. Thomé, and establish it weekly in the Island of Principe; to organize a network of narrow gauge railways completed by roads, to the interior of S. Thomé, which cannot be served by the maritime route; to levy no more taxes, nor to permit the municipalities to do so.

On the other hand, it is the duty of the planters to promote the bettering of their incomes by improving the methods of culture, and developing the productive power of their properties; to improve the qualities of the fruits, by the care lavished on the trees and soil, and turn their products more valuable, by perfecting the fermenting, drying and selecting processes; and still further promote the lessening of the cost of manual labour, by having recourse to machinery in every case in which mechanical labour can substitute manual labour.

As a complement to the measures which the Government ought to take, and of the means which the estate owners ought to put into practice, to increase revenues and decrease expenses, we have already indicated the organization of a rural police force to guard the plantations and repress vagrancy.

To prevent losses annually suffered by the planters, caused by the theft of ungathered fruits, generally carried out in the confines of the properties, is tantamount to increasing their income. To repress vagrancy in the fields corresponds to employing the numerous hands in the plantations, which are idling in the Province, at the same time putting an end to the demoralizing example given to those who are at work.

The Province of S. Thomé and Principe is actually a pacific region devoted completely to a laborious and tranquil agricultural life, the thefts to which we have

Manager's dwelling, Boa Entrada Plantation. Island of S. Thomé

alluded being excepted, and they arise from the idleness in which a part of the native element and the «Angolares forros» live, the latter being vestiges of a population, whose moral sense became perverted by the example of the criminals who during centuries the metropolis shipped to the Colony, and whose influence is not yet completely eliminated.

Excepting this case of social pathology which cannot be considered as arising from evil instincts, from reaction against tyranny or bad treatment, crime in S. Thomé is insignificant, as may be seen by the following table of the list of prisoners in the gaol during the year 1908, which are the last statistics published.

That list was:

Prisoners in gaol on the 1ˢᵗ January 1908.................... 28
Ditto entering during 1908............................. 89
                                                        ——— 117
Ditto leaving during 1908 81
Ditto remaining in gaol on 31ˢᵗ December 1908 36

Therefore, during the year there were 89 crimes or infringements of the law causing imprisonment, a number which, in a population of 68:000 souls, corresponds to the insignificant proportion of 1·4 per mil; in addition to this, 81 of the prisoners were freed during the same year, from which it may be concluded that the reasons for imprisonment were all infractions of minor importance, this fact evidently demonstrates not only the good traits of the people, but also the excellent social regime in which they live.

In a population composed of 97 % of blacks, 3 % of whites, and with a public force which in S. Thomé never exceeds 250 soldiers, nearly all blacks, it would be impossible to maintain order and secure all the rights of citizens, in the calmness of a peace which has lasted without interruption for more than 50 years, if the black population, which has the enormous advantage of numerical superiority should feel itself constrained, tyrannized, or enslaved as somewhere have stated some badly informed or evil intentioned English. The best reply to so absurd an affirmation lies in the peace which the Colony enjoys, and in the constant progress in which it has advanced for half a century.

These circumstances, therefore, being admitted, nothing else is required to complete the moralization of native customs, except to employ in regenerating and dignified work the scattered remnants of a population, contemporaries or successors of convicts still suffering from the influence of the dissolvent centre in which they lived or have inherited the tradition. It is our conviction that the hope indicated, can be easily realized, once the rural police are organized, and a good law for the repression of vagrancy is put into execution, the chief penalty of which to consist of enforced labour.

Our English detractors would have us send back from S. Thomé to the hinterland of Angola, whether voluntarily or otherwise, the labourers who came thence, together with the families they formed in our Island protected by our liberal laws; they further wish us to increase still more the wages of the labourers, which had already been done in 1903 by the regulation of Teixeira de Sousa, and again in 1909 by that of Terra Vianna, without the interested parties having asked for it (the same labourers earn 3o Réis per diem in Angola, or Réis 9oo monthly, which is about a third of what is paid in S. Thomé, (1) without English philanthropy making any claim in their favour); and they also wish that the working hours which are 9 ½ should be shortened, whilst our rural labourers in the metropolis work 10 hours in the winter, and 12 in the summer.

These three pretensions all tend to the same end, which is to determine the immediate rise in the cost of producing Portuguese cocoa, to such proportions, that we should be placed in a situation of great inferiority, the British West Indies and English Colonies of the Gold Coast, representatives in the market of cocoa similar to ours, thus obtaining at our expense, an exceptionally advantageous position in the countries consuming that produce.

If we could not, and ought not to acquiesce to such exigencies, even if they should proceed from a more impoverished country than our own, much less could we, or ought we to satisfy them at the cost of our poverty and of our smallness, for the benefit of the wealthiest and most powerful nation in the World. The exigency of our crumbs demanded by the British Colossus, would be the height of egotism; the surrender on our part would be the height of incapacity.

But if it is our duty not to commit suicide, so that the English who have cocoa plantations in Trinidad, Accra, and Lagos may live in opulence, we have also no right to help in the game of such interests, against the universal consumers of this now so necessary and popular article of food, nor have we the right to raise difficulties to free competition, by contributing to establish a kind of monopoly in favour of the mentioned English Colonies, to the detriment of North American, German, French, Swiss, Dutch, Italian, Spanish, Belgian, and other manufacturers, who would have to buy the raw material for their industry at a higher price.

We must, therefore, reply to such exigencies with a firm «non possumus», and defend our legitimate interests and the properties which constitute an important part of the national patrimony.

The gross revenue of the landed property of the Islands of S. Thomé and Principe, as has already been stated, shows an annual average of 7:2oo contos of réis during the last ten years; only with the works already carried out on the estates, that revenue, always progressively increasing, should attain within the next decade 9:36o contos of réis; if we rapidly clear the remaining land suitable for culture, it can reach later the sum of 12:24o contos of réis, without taking into account the value of oleaginous produce, the exploitation of which can also constitute important revenues in gold. Calculating the value of property in that Colony, according to the official system adopted in the kingdom, and notwithstanding an important part of the net revenues being employed, as we have stated, to amplify the same properties, we will take off, in the hypothesis of the largest reduction, 6o % of the annual gross revenue, or 4:32o contos of réis, and there will remain a balance of 2:88o contos of réis, which — multiplied by 2o — produces the respectable sum of 57:6oo contos of réis, by which amount the Islands of S. Thomé and Principe ought to be actually represented in the assets of the national public wealth.

---

(1) Art. 23. N.º 2 of the Regulation of 16th July 1902.

Children of labourers at play, Boa Entrada Plantation. Island of S. Thomé

Within a decade, if we limit ourselves to the existing cultivations, the Islands can represent 74:880 contos of réis; and fourteen or fifteen years later, they will represent 97:920 contos of réis if — within the next three or four years — the virgin forests which still cover part of the most prolific soil give place to new plantations.

The nation has there a most valuable patrimony, which, principally due to its great worth, gives rise to' envy and produces rivalry, inspires spite and determines collisions of varied interests which — under the cloak of philanthropy — give vent to their fury with a violence, which would have compelled us to capitulate long since, if Portuguese tenacity had to bend, having on its side, as it has, reason, right, and justice.

The colonists of S. Thomé have given ample proofs of that tenacity, and of that force of resistance in an unequal struggle which has lasted for many years; and our antagonists having always seen that the efforts employed for impeding the progress of our Islands were in vain, now play an audacious game, investing the hostilities with a universal character which, until recently, were restricted to a dispute between English and Portuguese.

To discredit us before the civilized World, presenting us as being employed in, or consenting to, the criminal traffic of slavery, and under this pretext isolate us, as though we were morally infected, thus more easily to annihilate the prosperity of our Colony, is the last phase of the English campaign. They will not however, achieve the result aimed at by their iniquitous act, for neither the civilized World is so badly informed as to help the game of our detractors, nor will the energy of the S. Thomé and Principe planters succumb to the new and audacious assault, nor will the Government of this country consent that foreigners come in their own interests to snatch that important asset from the national patrimony.

In the formidable strife of human ambition, interests, and passions, if often wealth, audacity, and power, by supplanting right, reason, and justice, obtain an unjust victory, on other occasions, and history registers not a few, poverty, weak and unprotected but energetic, firm in its right and in its justice, emerges conqueror from the contest.

We neither provoke nor desire conflicts with anyone. Ours is a peaceable, working and honourable nation, that endeavours to carry out the natural and social duties imposed by humanity, to provide for its support and physical, moral and intellectual progress by its own efforts, respecting the rights and the honour of other nations without causing injury to anyone, and without feeling hatred or envy for those who are wealthier or more powerful.

This mode of proceeding on our part gives us right to reciprocal treatment from those countries with whom our nation holds correct and friendly relations. Therefore we do not beg a favour invoking that right, and we are convinced that with the exception of some maniacs worthy of figuring amongst the patients of the successors of that scientific luminary named Lombroso, our appeal will find a sympathetic echo in all cultured nations, for whom reason is not a negative value, right a vain formula, and justice a myth; and of these the first will be as soon as she is impartially informed, our old ally and ancient and modern friend, sensible and practical England.

Labourers' dwellings and installations for the drying of cocoa on the Porto Real Plantation (West). Island of Principe

The manager's residence on the right

Post-scriptum.

M.r Cadbury's Book.

On concluding this work, we received by post, from M.r William A. Cadbury, his book, *The Labourers of S. Thomé,* Portuguese edition, and an album of photographs taken in Africa.

We thank M.r Cadbury for his present, and as one good turn deserves another, we take advantage of the opportunity, not to make a criticism on the book, because this is not the right place for that criticism, but to say a few words respecting the intervention of the English firms in the system of agrarian labour in that Province.

We will begin, therefore, by declaring frankly and loyally, that we never attributed neither do we attribute, the origin of the English campaigns initiated in recent years against us, to the chocolate firms, nor do we believe, that the repercussion through the World, which their intervention caused, had for its object the advertisement of their industrial products; and having read in the Lisbon Press, signed by a Portuguese personal witness, (1) that the only words favourable to our country, pronounced in the Birmingham Court on the occasion of the *Standard* lawsuit,

---

(1) «The Labourers of S. Thomé». — «Unfortunately for us, this question is and promises to be for a long time without a final solution, to the great discredit of our name and our finances. Is not this due to the want of a complete and impartial study on the part of all those persons direct or indirectly interested in the subject? In Portugal the question is imperfectly known and erroneously stated. The proof of this lies in the manner in which we accompanied that extraordinary lawsuit realised last month in Birmingham and how we commented on the final sentence.

«Called upon to give evidence as a witness of the meeting in which I acted as interpreter, and which took place at Lisbon in 1907, between William A. Cadbury and a Committee delegated by the planters of S. Thomé and Principe, I was present from the beginning to the end of the seven long and most interesting sessions of the High Court of Birmingham. I had occasion there to follow closely all the details of this campaign and to know its chief personalities. They were real revelations to me.

«This lawsuit which in England was quite an event, and which was of such great interest to us, passed almost unnoticed in Portugal. The description and history of this trial has still to be made amongst us. I may perhaps do it some day, but for the present I merely wish to accentuate how contrary to the truth of the facts is the opinion formed here. We were rudely

were spoken by M^r. Cadbury, and we believing such was the case, lament however, that as he, M^r. Cadbury, gave a wide publicity in England to the conclusions of the conference in Lisbon with the delegation of S. Thomé planters, he did not give an equal publicity to the text of the respective minutes for his readers to know, that in a discussion with him and M^r. Burtt, the accusations contained in the report of the latter gentleman were refuted, and the accuser silenced (1).

The campaign started before M^r. Cadbury and his colleagues interfered in the matter, and, as we have already said sufficient in the preceding chapters to state our opinion on its probable causes, we will not repeat it.

We even admire the courage of M^r. Cadbury in coming first to Portugal, and going afterwards to our African Colonies with the intent of harmonizing, in face

---

attacked there. At times I confess, I had to blush on hearing the insults directed to my country. But there was also present one person who defended us to a certain extent, and recognised our difficulties and affirmed that we were not all, as has been insinuated, a nation of slave-dealers.

«I return to Portugal and what do I behold? The eulogium of our greatest enemies and detractors and hatred for those who defended us! Any one reading the references made by the Portuguese Press to the trial *Cadbury* versus *Standard,* could only remain under the impression that the *Standard* was our defender and Cadbury our accuser. Well it was exactly the reverse.

«The *Standard* which in the article originating the lawsuit had been most violent against us, called us in court through its lawyers the most opprobrious epithets, describing the conditions of S. Thomé and Principe as the worst that could be imagined, and hours were spent, demonstrating that the Portuguese were unworthy of credit. For the *Standard,* S. Thomé and Principe were the scene of the most atrocious slavery. Cadbury deserved to be shot and the products of his industry rejected, for having trusted in the promises of reform given by the Portuguese and for having, in the last 7 years, bought 6.000 contos (£ 1.200.000) of Portuguese cocoa for his factory at Bourneville.

«Cadbury on the contrary always referred to the Portuguese in courteous terms. even going to the length of praising them, although convinced that labour in S. Thomé and Principe is not free, owing to the manner in which the recruitment is carried out in Angola and by the want of option in the repatriation; he described the installations in the Islands as models, and did justice to the efforts and honesty of many Portuguese with whom he came in contact. Cadbury was in my opinion, to a certain extent, our defender. Owing to his wish to show benevolence to us he had to suffer during four days, this rude combat of sarcastic and captious questioning. Notwithstanding all this, Cadbury is pointed out as our greatest detractor!

«The final sentence was given against the *Standard.* The court recognizing Cadbury's honesty and sincerity, sentenced the *Standard* to pay damages of one farthing. Here in Portugal, we almost rejoiced at the insignificance of the damages even taking the part of the *Standard* against Cadbury. It appears as if we preferred the condemnation of Cadbury, forgetting that this would entail a greater condemnation for us,

«We also did not perfectly appreciate the importance of the sentence. In addition to its moral significance that farthing involved the payment of costs which amount to £ 10.000, this being at least the sum which the *Standard* has to pay. What shall we gain by twisting the truth of the facts? It appears to me that it is on that account and because we have not studied the question thoroughly that it is still and likely to be unsolved. But it is the fate of this poor Portugal to call white black and black white.

«(Signed) *Alfredo A. da Silva.*»

(From the *Mundo* of 25th January 1910).

(1) See minutes *of the meeting held in Lisbon,* which are published in the appendix of this book.

Type of half-caste. Island of S. Thomé

Type of female half-castes. Island of S. Thomé

Type of half-caste. Island of S. Thomé

of the campaign of his contemporaries, his own and his friends' business interests and those of the promoters of that campaign by means of concessions obtained from the Portuguese Government and the planters of S. Thomé.

The conviction which M^r. Cadbury was under as to the possibility of success, showed that his clear intelligence was, on that point, obscured by the dense veil of illusion concealing from him the situation in England, so that he could not see the impossibility of conciliating, at our exclusive cost, the interests connected with a campaign which certainly many people believed in good faith, but whose promoters and hidden auxiliaries would not be, peradventure, disposed to give way in the face of other concessions except the ruin of S. Thomé and also, perhaps the discredit of the English chocolate firms.

The planters of S. Thomé, whom M^r. Cadbury met in Lisbon, although only morally interested in the subject gave him a reception such as in identical circumstances, we are convinced, no Portuguese would have met with among planters of English Colonies, and was received in like manner at S. Thomé and Principe, when with the same end in view he visited our plantations to observe what took place there with regard to the labourers.

Mr Cadbury did not obtain from the authorities of this country both in the kingdom and in the Colonies, as much as he wished because his pretensions were so exorbitant that no self-respecting official could satisfy them completely, but much greater condescension and facilities than we would have graciously afforded in identical circumstances to any Portuguese subject, and that also any Portuguese would have encountered among English authorities whether metropolitan or colonial.

But Mr Cadbury, notwithstanding those facilities, did not obtain his desideratum; and he did not obtain it because anyone prevented him in Portugal or made themselves inaccessible to him, which would have been fully justified in presence of the violent English attack, and would have caused the failure of his conciliatory projects, but because on the opposite side, that of the English, only conciliation ruinous for S. Thomé was desired, or none at all.

The English accusations can be resumed to two capital points:

1st. Cruelty and violence against liberty, practised by irresponsible men in the recruitments in Angola, and no measures facilitating the repatriation of the natives who may wish it on the expiration of their contracts;

2nd. Detention of labourers in S. Thomé for an unlimited period and against their wish.

On 17th July 1907 the Portuguese Government countersigned a decree in which was stipulated:

Relative to S. Thomé.

«Art. 95.th — When the contract legally expires, the repatriation need not be carried out, if at the labourer's request a new engagement is made.

« § 1.st — The renewal of the contracts to be allowed only after the Curator is convinced that it is by the express wish of the labourer, without outside pressure of any description, the following rules having to be observed:

a) Planters, manufacturers, merchants, officials, or private individuals employing labourers and wishing to renew the contracts to apply for permission to the Governor of the Province of S. Thomé, and to the Governor of the district of Principe;

b) The Governors to consult the Curator-general if the application is made at S. Thomé, or his delegate if it is made at Principe, who will give written information as to whether the petitioner has been found guilty of attacking the freedom of the labourers;

c) The crime referred to above is punishable with six months prevention to contract natives, and if the offence be repeated with one year;

d) When the Governor has granted the petition he will forward it at once to the Curator or his delegate and these magistrates will publish edicts which will be affixed at least a week previously on the door of the office, announcing the date, hour and locality where the contract is to be made, and the name of the person employing the labourers, and inviting the presence at this act of all those interested or desirous of being present;

e) As the renewal of the contracts is public, all those who wish to be present, to be admitted either by the Curator when the contract is made in his office, or by the planter if it be made on his estate, as long as they do not disturb the proceedings in any way;

f) The renewal of labour contracts can only be effected before the Curator-general at S. Thomé or before his delegate at Principe in the presence of an employee of the Curator's office, two witnesses, and a sworn interpreter, the latter never to be chosen from the personnel of the employer, and the labourers.»

After the promulgation of these regulations which guarantee the greatest liberty to the labourers and permit everyone, natives or foreigners, to be present at the renewals of the contracts and verify whether the labourers are forced to remain, or if they do so spontaneously and uncoerced, can anybody without having been present at those acts, and which have thus been carried out for some months truthfully say that the blacks are in S. Thomé against their wish and enslaved?

Relative to Angola.

As has already been stated in this work, Chapter V. of the aforesaid Regulations of 17th July 1909 determines:

That the recruitment of labourers, which till then had been effected in the interior without any supervision whatever, (embracing all the Province, including the savage regions of the extreme hinterland), can only be carried on in determined regions, submitted to the effective authority of Government officials, and that, within those regions it is only permitted in the zones, which the Governor of the Province determines by an edict, and even to the number of individuals fixed yearly by the same authority.

The new law further determines that no one may recruit labourers without having previously obtained from the district Governor permission which can only be conceded to a trustworthy person who proves his Portuguese nationality, knows the native language, possesses the necessary qualifications for the proper fulfil-

Matheus Sampaio Street, during the visit of H. R. H. The Crown Prince, Louis Philip. Island of S. Thomé

ment of the office, and who has deposited a sum of money or given surety for the same.

The recruiter cannot commence his duties until his diploma has been viséd by the local administrative authority, and the latter, after the recruiter has been identified, presents him to the native chief or chiefs of the localities where he has to operate.

The recruitment being concluded, the administrative authority intervenes again to legalize the respective documents and identify the recruited natives, the latter, in charge of the recruiter, journeying to the coast by a route previously determined by an edict of the Governor-general, giving preference, whenever it is possible, to railways. On these routes, and in localities selected by the authorities, there will be comfortable and hygienic installations for the labourers to rest. The recruited labourers may not be compelled to carry loads, but only their food.

On the arrival of the labourers at the coast, the emigration agent is entrusted with their lodging, maintenance and all they may require until they embark, and their names are registered in a large book for identification, which each agency must have; then they appear before the Curator-general, who enquires from them before witnesses, if they wish to be contracted for agricultural work in S. Thomé and Principe, and once they answer affirmatively, the contract is proceeded with, the identifying number of the labourer being inscribed in it, so that later, on the occasion of his repatriation, it may be known from what locality he came, to what tribe he belongs and in which administrative district it is situated.

The birthplace of the labourers, recruited in the conditions referred to, is known, and they can return thither; therefore, the contracts will be effected without difficulty, seeing that by the registered number of identity, particulars are found immediately regarding the place they came from, and the labourers following the same route by which they journeyed to the coast, can return home without inconvenience.

The itinerary is the same, both coming and going, and this makes the route frequented, the constant passing to and fro of travellers and caravans is alone an element of security, and as the established route is always the same, it can be easily patrolled.

Owing to these measures no irresponsible persons can recruit labourers in the hinterland of Angola.

No recruitment can be effected where no Portuguese authorities exist, and in those regions where those authorities do exist, it can only be carried out in the zones determined by law, with the respective restrictions. The caravans of labourers cannot escape the vigilance of the police by choosing devious byways, because they are obliged to follow the route previously marked out for all by the Government.

It is not licit therefore to allege that labourers, thus contracted, cannot return home on the expiration of their contracts, as their birthplaces are unknown, or for want of security on the roads; nor can it be admitted that, despite such rigorous supervision exercised by the authorities, acts contrary to the liberty of the labourers, or cruelties are committed.

The regulations limit to a moderate amount the sum which the employer has to spend on each labourer, including the passage, from the moment he is recruited in the interior of Angola till he lands at S. Thomé; this sum is only half of what it was lately, and a third of what it used to be originally and is only sufficient to cover expenses and reserve a small commission for the agents; it not being possible, in any case, within the authorized sum, to effect any illicit transactions of buying and selling, without immediate discovery and punishment.

And as a further proof of the sincerity with which the Governor and the planters of S. Thomé wish to see the law of 17th July 1909 enforced, not only theoretically but also practically, the suspension of the recruitment in Angola was, by mutual consent, decreed by the Government on the 29th of the same month, and on the 22nd of the following November, that of the contracts, as well as the shipment of labourers for S. Thomé until 31st January last, so that everything should be organized in that Province in the precise terms of the aforesaid law at the moment it began to be enforced.

On the other hand, 18 months have elapsed since the planters initiated the introduction into the Islands of labourers from Mozambique by means of contracts in which more advantageous conditions are stipulated than those imposed by Transvaal. We continue to receive from Cape Verde all the labourers wishing to emigrate thence; we go to Cabinda to seek men for maritime service; we ask the governments to promote emigration from Guinea; we depend on machinery and railways for the economy of hands; all this is done with the deliberate intent of reducing to a minimum the demand for labourers from Angola. By every means agriculture and the public authorities work together in unison, not verbally, but by positive demonstration, to obtain, as far as possible, what the promoters of the English campaign declared to be their desideratum; but did those gentlemen desist, did they declare themselves satisfied in view of our proceeding?

We believe not; at least they have not come forward to declare it. On the contrary, this is the moment in which M[r]. Cadbury, the representative of the English firms before the Portuguese public, chooses to publish in Portugal his book *The Labourers of S. Thomé and Principe,* in which are reproduced accusations from the Burtt report, already refuted (1), and the exigencies of that campaign are maintained, many having been already complied with, and even others, the compliance with which, legally and humanely impossible, would result in the economic ruin of our Island. And the English chocolate firms would not continue to think or to act as if we had done nothing, nor would they maintain the boycottage voted to our cocoa, which causes them much loss, if the campaigners were satisfied.

It appears to us, that we have demonstrated in this book, with documentary evidence, that the English campaign against S. Thomé, having come to light in the beginning of the agricultural regeneration of that Province, has lasted 50 years, and has accompanied all the phases of the progress of our Colony always hindering it when possible. And if it is certain that the English Governments have abstained in recent years from interfering in the dispute, doubtless because they considered the causes unjustifiable, and maintaining officially a correct and friendly attitude with our nation, it is not less certain that some English societies and private individuals continue the interminable campaign of discredit against our Islands, using philanthropic

(1) See minutes of the Lisbon meeting which is published at the end of this book.

The family of the manager, Agua Izé Plantation, visiting the works of constructing a railway on the Plantation, Island of S. Thomé

pretexts, as if those minute atoms lost in the immensity of the Atlantic Ocean, which are called the Islands of S. Thomé and Principe, contained the most unfortunate beings of the Universe.

Peradventure, without going further would not these philanthropists, if philanthropy were really their object, be able to exercise so noble an attribute at home, with more advantage for suffering humanity?

Is there not Ireland? — that beautiful Island, whose population, that in 1841 consisted of 8.175.000 human beings, workers, and worthy of assistance and protection, was reduced by want in 1851 to 6.552.387; in 1861 to 5.798.967; in 1871 to 5.412.378; in 1881 to 5.159.840; in 1891 to 4.706.162; and in 1901 to 4.704.750; whilst, the population of other parts of the United Kingdom, consisting at the beginning of the xix century of 9.000.000 souls, rose in 1851 to 18.000:000; in 1871 to 26.445.922; in 1891 to 33.182.391; in 1901 to 40.905.925; having still further increased from that date to the point of being multiplied five times, in the course of a century, and Ireland reduced in 70 years to little more than half the number of her inhabitants!?

Deducting the half million of souls, which a famine destroyed in 1846 and 1847, what has become of the people of Ireland? They emigrated, never to return to the ungrateful soil of their fatherland; they emigrated to flee from the injustice of man and from the misery of a life, without hope for a better future, these facts having determined the exodus of many unfortunates, who went to seek in alien lands — North America principally — means of livelihood and progress. And why is it that so many emigrants have not returned neither will they return from their voluntary exile?

Is it because they are enslaved there by those who employ them and remunerate their aptitudes and work, or is it because they feel more at home in that hospitable country than in their own, which circumstances obliged them to abandon?

And those noble natures who accuse us of forcibly detaining in S. Thomé the labourers of the Angola hinterland, will they not admit, that these blacks may also prefer the life, ennobled by remunerated work that they enjoy in S. Thomé, to the despotic and degrading savageness, the cruel punishments, and the pitiless mutilations of the barbarous countries where they were born?

But if it is to the Portuguese that English philanthropy wants to apply itself, helping their misfortunes in preference to its own, what a vast field it has in the Portuguese Continent itself for the exercise of its altruism and its philanthropy. Why choose S. Thomé!

Here, at home, we have more than a million of rural labourers of both sexes (in S. Thomé and Principe there are only 40.000, between natives and emigrants from different sources), the men earning as a rule from réis 200 to 240 per day, the women from réis 120 to 140 working 12 hours a day in summer, and 10 hours in winter (in S. Thomé and Principe, they only work 9 1/2 hours all the year round); who earn nothing when they cannot work, or no work is to be obtained, which happens very often; who do not get food, clothing, dwellings, medical and hospital treatment, nor are they housed by the employers when they are old or unfit for work, and have not any of the other advantages enjoyed by the labourers of S. Thomé, such as, gratuitous legal advice, maintenance and clothing for their children, exemption from taxes and military service, etc.

Why is it that our English detractors wishing to exercise their philanthropy in aid of our fellow citizens, do not apply their beneficent action in favour of so many necessitous persons existing in this country, men and women of the white race, which is also their own, and why is it, that they seek in preference, amongst the black race, not the specimens that live under tyrannical conditions in the African Continent, but those who spend a life full of privileges and comforts?

Why wish to compel these people to accept a special happiness, which they do not understand, and which consists in changing the civilized, humanitarian and liberal centre, in which their existence, and that of their families, is peaceably passed, for the savagery of the African wilds?

And if it is the special protection of the natives of Portuguese Africa that the altruism of those sensitive hearts has in view, why do they not join their best efforts to those which their countryman, M^r. G. Henry Somers, is employing in the South African Press, so that a rigorous and impartial enquiry may be ordered regarding labour in the Transvaal mines, and if the accusation be true, an end may be put to the exploration and martyrdom which the blacks from Mozambique, working there, are suffering, as the same M^r. Somers affirms in the article, which we copy from the *Diario Popular* (1).

And if it is not that, if it is the black race in general they have in view, if it

---

(1) *The South African News* of 28th January 1910 publishes the following letter, on which we make no comment. Its tenour is sufficient.

«Sir — In the leading article appearing in your issue of the 13th inst., under the heading «Incredible Scandals», you refer to alleged abuses practised under the famous Mozambique Treaty, hurriedly passed by the Transvaal Government in the interest of the Rand mining houses.

«Anyone acquainted with the methods employed in obtaining native labour in Portuguese East Africa knew that there is no voluntary labour recruited from that source.

«The Witwatersrand Native Labour Association agents are paid by results, the native runners employed by the agents are paid by results, and the petty chiefs or headmen of kraals are paid at so much per native supplied to the agent. The native is not consulted, and does not know what wages he is to receive for his work until he reaches the W. N. L. A. compound on the Rand, where each batch is classified and the Portuguese pass-board of each native is stamped with the amount of wages the officials consider he ought to receive — usually 40^s per month of 30 working days, for natives who have previously worked on the mines; 30^s for strong able-bodied natives who are new to mine work; and 15^s for «piccannins», or young Kafirs.

«The gangs, or batches, are then sent to the different mines where labour is wanted, and then the Government native labour inspector issues to each native a Transvaal pass-board, and informs him of the terms of contract and rate of pay. The native can offer no objection, and is absolutely at the mercy of his employers during his term of contract. Can you wonder that such a system can give rise to grave abuses.

«I do not wish to infer that the Portuguese authorities are cognisant of the methods employed in obtaining native labour in their territories, but the fact remains that the larger the number of natives sent forward each month the greater the revenue according to the agreement under the Mozambique Treaty.

«As regards the treatment of natives on the mines, one often hears, in the semi-darkness of the underground vaults, lighted by dim candlelight only, where the natives work, a pitiful cry of pain and agony, and on inquiry one hears that it is only the cry of a Kulaman (Quilemane native) who is lashed by the «boss boy» for not working properly. The mine managers, in their eagerness to cut down expenses, allow one white overseer to supervise up to 150 natives, distributed over from five to 10 different working places in small gangs, under a native

Habitations for labourers in an agricultural section of the Porto Real Plantation (West). Island of Principe

is the blacks without distinction they prefer in this fever of well doing at the expense of others, why do not such meritorious humanitarians apply to their own Government, so that by their initiative, nations who have neighbouring colonies, may agree and employ in collective or individual action, all their efforts as sovereign powers, to combat slavery and savagery in those central regions of the African Continent which constitute the hinterland of the Portuguese, English and Congolese possessions, and possibly, of some other African power, where the crimes against liberty and the cruelties against blacks, of which Portugal is unjustly accused, are exercised?

It is not in favour of S. Thomé, but rather to the benefit of other countries, that slavery is exercised in Central Africa; this is peremptorily affirmed by an authorized and impartial Englishman — Colonel Wyllie, — in the excerpt from his recent letter to the *Daily Despatch* of Birmingham, which the *Dia* of Lisbon reproduced:

«The slave trade in Central Africa does not exist, as seems to have been assumed throughout all this agitation, in order to furnish labour for the cocoa plantations of the Islands; it exists for the benefit of Turkey via Tripoli, of Morocco, of Persia, of Arabia via the Red Sea Ports, and (according to M.ʳ Burtt himself) of the French Congo following the lamentable lead of her Belgian neighbour. And the brutalities incidental thereto are committed, not by Portuguese at all, but by Africans upon Africans of their own race, regardless of ties of kinship.» (1)

«boss-boy». The «boss-boys», chosen from the ranks of the more intelligent native races, have no sympathy or pity for the poor emaciated newcomers, who for months after arriving from the warm, generous climate of the coasts, suffer from a cough caught in transit to the higher altitude and colder climate of the Rand.

«It very often happens that a native has to put in 40 to 50 working days before his first 30-days' pay ticket is full, which will enable him to draw his first pay, less the price of clothing, etc., supplied and issued to him by the W. N. L. A. officials as soon as he passes the Transvaal frontier. Although the native is under contract for a fixed period at a fixed rate of pay per month of 30 working days, he is put to task work, and is refused his daily pay ticket unless his master is satisfied that he has completed his allotted task. No wonder that the free-born natives of the British Colonies object to mine work on the Rand, and will often suffer great privations, through the failure of their crops during bad seasons, before they decide to seek work on the Rand mines. I must say that, from what I can gather without actual experience, the system at De Beers in Kimberley is most satisfactory, and Colonial natives are eager to seek work where they receive fair wages and humane treatment. The English people, who love to show their sympathy with the oppressed and wronged of foreign countries by refusing the cheering breakfast cup of cocoa because it is alleged that the cocoa plantations in West Africa are worked by slave labour, cannot be aware that the gold and dividends from the gold mines on the Rand are obtained by employment of servile labour, the recruiting of which is legalised and ratified by a treaty signed by the King's representative. If the Union Gonvernment is to start on a clean sheet, the first Parliament should, immediately on assembling, appoint a commission te inquire into the working of the Mozambique Treaty and the treatment of natives on the Rand, and submit a full report to the Imperial Government and a request for the immediate cancellation of the obnoxious agreement.

I am, etc.

«G. Henry Somers».

Gong-Gong, Barkly West, January, 24, 1910.

(1) J. A. Wyllie F. R. G. S. — Lieut-Colonel of the Indian Army (Retired). *O Dia* n.º 2907 of November 17ᵗʰ 1909. (See appendix).

This affirmation of the impartial Colonel Wyllie is not the only news received, as to what takes place in the central regions of the African Continent.

In his notable work on African companies, A. de Preville writes:

«Ces traitants se forment en compagnies commerciales, et leurs comptoirs de vente sont établis dans les principales villes des bords du Nil et de l'Afrique septentrionale. Les plus actifs d'entre eux, dont le nom est pris pour raison sociale, se transportent quelquefois de leur personne sur les lieux d'exploitation; il en vient même de «Tunis» jusque, dans la région des grands lacs, témoin ce négociant tunisien qui portait d'Ou-Nyoro en Ou-Ganda les lettres de Casati prisonnier. (Pag. 3o5.)»

. . . .

«Samory étend actuellement ce genre d'exploitation sur un territoire de «3oo.ooo kilometres carrés; il est, avec son rival Tiéba, le grand pourvoyeur «d'esclaves des marchands de Tombouctou, de l'Adrar, et du Maroc». (Pag. 3 1 2 et 3 1 4).

. . . .

«Puis, la traite des esclaves s'est développée de ce côté d'une façon inouïe, ainsi qu'en temoignent toutes les relations des voyageurs et des missionaires. Non seulement il faut répondre à la demande d'esclaves de l'Arabie, un des grands foyers d'appel de la traite, et de tous les pays d'Orient; mais encore les negociants eux mêmes, vu leur trés petit nombre, sont forcés pour leur propre securité de s'entourer de veritables garnisons, formées d'esclaves armés; la prospérité des affaires d'un négociant s'établit par le nombre de mousquets qu'il peut remettre entre ces mains asservies. De nouveau, des nations entières sont enlevées á leurs anciens travaux, la chasse, la cueillette ou la culture, pour composer des bandes armées; ont peut citer en particulier la population du Manyéma comme ayant presque en entier accepté ce genre de vie. Ce sont les esclaves des marchands, commandés souvent par des métis, qui composent ces troupes de bandits, pillards, incendiaires et dépopulateurs, connues sous le nom de «Rouga-Rouga». Ces serviteurs armés sont matériellement bien traités par leur maitres; ceux-ci les appellent «mes enfants, mes fils», mais ne remplissent point à leur égard la véritable mission de l'autorité paternelle, mission moralisatrice et coërcitive, incompatible avec les services qu'on attend d'eux. Pour les avoir dans la main, il faut les laisser croupir dans la fainéantise et dans tous les vices; il importe de ne pas les élever à la situation de chefs de familles réguliers. On ne les marie point, ils brocantent seulement entre eux et avec leurs patrons les femmes qu'ils ont enlevées. Comme le «farcuk» créé par les marchands du nord, les esclaves et les porteurs des Zanzibaristes sont pour l'Afrique noire, non un moyen de relèvement, mais une cause de désorganisation ajoutée a toutes celles que nous avons constatées jusqu'ici. Autrefois, dans l'Espagne et les Gaules, la levée et passage des soldats mercenaires enrôlés par les chefs Carthaginois ont présenté le même tableau, c'était aussi une conquête commerciale en vue du transit et de l'exploitation.» (pag. 3 1 4 et 3 1 5)

. . . .

«Ce n'est pas à la côte que se rend le convoi d'esclaves; c'est dans le pays ne «Djenndé» ou des Cafres du Sud, dans les contrés où jadis le bon Livingstone rencontra les Makololo. Les institutions régimentaires des Cafres ont fait le vide dans la population de cette partie de l'Afrique; on comble ce vide par l'achat de femmes et d'enfants, échangés contre l'ivoire qui est encore très abondant dans la contrée.

Panoramic View of the Head-quarters of the Boa Entrada Plantation. Island of S. Thomé

Ce nouveau débouché s'est trouvé ouvert «juste à point» pour consoler les Pombeïros de la fermeture des mers à la traite; leur trafic de chair humaine continue d'être aussi actif qu'auparavant.» (pag. 320)

. . . .

«Quant aux colons anglais du Cap, que nous avons aussi rencontrés précédemment, leur attitude vis-à-vis des noirs n'est pas celle de la pure indifférence. La race Anglo-Saxonne n'a jamais fourni des bons patrons de négres, il y a antipathie. Le colon Anglais ou Yankee est exaspéré par le travail «forcément indolent» du noir esclave; ce temps qu'il voit perdre sous ses yeux par des ouvriers qui n'ont aucun intérêt à le bien employer, — ce temps qui est de l'argent, — c'est son bien, c'est sa fortune à lui-même qu'on gaspille en sa présence. Il ne comprend que le travail de l'ouvrier libre, actif et intéressé. Il veut secouer la torpeur du noir, l'acculer au progrès; le noir se révolte, et l'Anglais le fusille.» (pag. 330) (1).

. . . .

Well, is it then the fault of S. Thomé that blacks are enslaved and sold in Central Africa, to populate the harems with concubines and eunuchs, and with slaves the guilded palaces and shady parks which serve as a pastime for the leisure of Moorish, Persian, and Arab magnates, and with females and children the polygamous homes of the Kaffirs? And if some of those unfortunates succeed in escaping from their grim fate and come to S. Thomé, and here get civilized and marry, is English philanthropy to compel them and their kinsmen, to return to that accursed land where they would be pitilessly sold to different masters, and spend the remainder of their lives as slaves, without ever hearing of one another — husbands, wives and children?

Let the honourable M^r. Cadbury meditate on what we have written, let all those in England, who in good faith have joined the campaign against us, who, we well believe, are many, also meditate, and their consciences will tell them, that the attacks against the colonization of S. Thomé cannot be based on simple acts of humanitarianism, in the exercise of which, Portugal has done more for the benefit of the labourers of S. Thomé and Principe, than for her labourers at home, and more and better than any other nation possessing African Colonies.

But the chocolate firms were not successful in harmonising the English campaigns with their business interests, and attribute their failure to the Portuguese Government.

It is not so, and it is M^r. Cadbury himself who shows the truth of our affirmation in the following excerpt of the letter which he wrote to us on 6th July, 1908:

«We have informed you that the English public is thoroughly roused by the present unsatisfactory state of affairs, and may, from one moment to another, refuse to buy cocoa manufactured from the produce gathered in those islands.

«We well know, that such a mode of proceeding would not help to solve the problem promptly, and at the same time, might easily oblige us to cut off all business relations with you; for this reason, we again insist that prompt and energetic measures be taken.»

---

(1) *Les Sociétées Africaines — Leur Origine — Leur Évolution — Leur Avenir* — par A. de Preville.

. . . .

«Another subject, which we should be able to prove to our public, is that you without taking into consideration the cost and inconvenience, repatriated men, women and their families, from the plantations to their homes in the Continent, and that this repatriation will continue regularly in the future.»

That is the question.

We replied, on the 14th July, 1908, to the part of M[r]. Cadbury's letter which we have transcribed, as follows:

«With respect to the repatriation of the Angola labourers, the committee of planters already informed you here, on the occasion of our meeting, held last November, that though obligatory for the planter, it was voluntary for the labourers. Once the latter wish to return home, the former have to send them there, and will not place any difficulties in carrying out this duty; but to send them forcibly, against their will, cannot be reasonably expected, nor do I believe that the Government of this or any other liberal country, would lend itself to practise such an arbitrary act.

«The planters of S. Thomé ardently wish to see the labour question settled in such a manner that, whilst assuring manual labour for the culture of their properties, the campaigns of discredit, which systematically and periodically happen in England, come to an end once and for all, if that be possible, together with that species of tutellage which it is wished to exercise on us, and which only a small and weak nation like ours would tolerate, and they trust that something to that effect. will result from the official enquiry which is being made. That wish and that hope do not arise exclusively from the desire to secure the English market for the consumption of their produce, as they know, that if that market should fail them, others will be opened to them, where the English consumer will have to purchase what he actually buys from us; they are guided by a nobler purpose, that is to assure to their small but honourable Fatherland, the good name which, as a Colonial Nation, it justly possesses in the civilized World, and to remove the last pretexts of plausibility from the English campaigns of discredit in which it is endeavoured to present us as barbarians, we, who without material means of coercion, but principally by kindness to the natives and by their affection, maintain integrally our vast colonial dominion.

«This does not mean to imply that the producers of S. Thomé and Principe would be insensible to the loss of the English market which consumes an important part of their cocoa; but, if they and the rulers of this country are disposed to make sacrifices to facilitate an entente with the English public, they cannot yield absolutely their own judgment and opinion to the judgment and opinion of the English public, as the latter never yielded, nor would yield their way of thinking and appreciating English subjects, to the criterion and appreciation of the Portuguese public.»

. . . .

As is seen, by the excerpta which we have transcribed, the exigencies which the English campaign demanded from the chocolate firms, to satisfy which, the latter, in their turn, endeavoured to obtain from Portugal, because that was perhaps a way of getting out of difficulties at home, were neither more nor less than to compel the return to the Angola hinterland of the greater majority of the working

Dwellings for labourers, on the Boa Entrada Plantation. Island of S. Thomé

population of S. Thomé, leading us to practise a reprehensible action from a humanitarian point of view, and which would lead to our economical ruin; they were, neither more or less, than the abandonment of our valuable plantations by the expulsion of our able assistants which we could not substitute by others, seeing that the substitution of so large a number of Angola labourers would be impossible in face of the English campaign, which styles the respective contracts as slave-trade. And in the period in which the demand was presented, we did not even count on the immigration of natives from Mozambique, only begun later, contrary to all English expectations.

But even if the planters of S. Thomé should find hands in Angola to substitute those they were expelling in homage to English philanthropy, they could not do so without an outlay of some thousands of pounds which would represent at the same time the complete and irremediable ruin of at least 90 % of the estate owners, and the expelled labourers would wander aimlessly about the regions of the Angola coast, distant, therefore, from their native places, or penetrating into the wilds whence they started, would be victims of the savagery which reigns there! (1)

The planters, therefore, could not accede to so unreasonable a demand, nor could our Government countenance it, however much it might injure the entente between the English makers and consumers of chocolate.

And it appears, it was simply due to our inability to yield absolutely to all the demands made by English interests, that the fomenters of the campaign were not reconciled to their fellow countrymen, the cocoa firms, the latter being compelled by the atmosphere the agitators had created, to suspend the purchase of our cocoa. (2)

We sincerely lament the non-success of the efforts of Mr Cadbury and his colleagues, because we are by temperament, convinced partisans of peace and concord, not of the icy peace of Warsaw, but of that which encourages the life and

---

(1) «Mr Burtt, pressed to say if he had heard any labourer manifest the wish to return to his home, and if he thought that, after landing on the mainland, the labourer could reach it with the savings realized by five years work, replied to the first question that he had heard no labourer manifest any such wish, and that, invited by General Faro, manager of the «Agua-Izé» Plantation, to question any of the labourers of that plantation on this subject, he, Burtt, refused to do so; to the second question he replied, that, if any labourer should penetrate inland carrying valuables he would be robbed before reaching his home.»

(Minutes of the Lisbon meeting, page 14.)

(2) Some think, and the last events in England seem to confirm their opinion, that a political campaign is being raised against the great chocolate firms, most influential members of the English Liberal Party, by their Conservative rivals.

When the Conservatives were in power, the Liberals had accused them of permitting yellow slavery in Transvaal. Now it would be the former who, in retaliation, would accuse the Liberal chocolate firms of having knowingly and hypocritically encouraged black slavery in S. Thomé and Angola, by buying Portuguese cocoa with their money. For this end it was necessary to revive the romance of Nevinson, and sacrifice inoffensive Portugal in the interests of the English political parties!

The Conservatives had accused Portugal of slave-dealing to discredit the Liberal chocolate firms, attributing to them complicity with the Portuguese. The chocolate firms would

progress of people in the tranquil repose of home, and in the active exercise of re-productive labour, shielded by law and justice. That is the peace we would wish to see fraternally cultivated in the relations of all nations in general, and more especially between the English and Portuguese peoples.

To obtain this aspiration, the planters of S. Thomé and the Government of this nation have done everything that the national dignity and interests permit.

If the English who attack us are not satisfied, it is not our fault, but of those who, it appears, will only be content when they see the ruin of the agriculture of S. Thomé, and, possibly, also that of the great English cocoa firms.

---

defend themselves by stating that for a long time they had endeavoured to put an end to that slavery. And thus, in the interests of the English political parties, we should be accused by Greeks and Trojans without pity, and with an acrimony, foreign to the temperament of the English people, usually so calm and reflective in their judgments, such is the prerogative which political passions possess to obliterate the moral sense of people, even those better educated to practise justice.

H. H. Prince Alfred of Löewenstein Werthein Freudemberg
Who visited the Islands of S. Thomé and Principe in January 1910

The German Prince Alfred of Loewenstein.

We had this work ready for the Press when we were honoured by the visit of H. H. Prince Alfred of Loewenstein-Wertheim-Freudenberg and his travelling companion, Wilhelm Kemner, director of the cocoa plantations in the colony of the Cameroons.

The illustrious Prince and M^r. Kemner deigned to call on us and thank us for the invitation received from the Company of the Island of Principe, and the Society of Colonial Agriculture, to visit the plantations «Agua-Izé» in S. Thomé, and «Porto Real» in the Island of Principe, properties of the aforesaid companies.

His Highness deigned also to manifest to us his sentiments of warm sympathy for the civilizing work of the S. Thomé and Principe planters, and honoured us with the gratifying mission which we hereby have great pleasure in discharging, namely, to transmit to our colleagues the expression of those sentiments consigned in a letter addressed to us, and published below.

In fulfilling the desire of His Highness, we take the opportunity to express once more our sincere and profound gratitude for the honour of his visit and that of M^r. Kemner to our Colony, and for the noble and impartial words of comfort, encouragement and justice, in which they synthetize their impressions with regard to the Portuguese work in S. Thomé and Principe.

The letter is as follows:

«Lisbonne, le 16 février, 1910.

«Monsieur

«Ayant l'intention de visiter notre colonie allemande de Kameroun sur la côte occidentale de l'Afrique, tout naturellement nous venait l'idée de visiter les belles colonies portugaises qui se trouvaient à proximité de notre route, et qui nous offraient un vif intérêt pour pouvoir apprécier de près la terre natale de nos cultures de cacao de Kameroun. Nous avons donc profité avec grand plaisir de l'aimable invitation que vous, Monsieur, et vos amis ont bien voulu nous adresser.

«Rentrant de notre voyage nous avons a cœur de vous remercier très sincérement de l'excellent accueil, et de la grand hospitalité que nous avons trouvés chez vous.

«Pendant notre séjour aux îles, nous avons eu l'occasion de visiter les plantations Rio d'Ouro, Boa-Entrada, Agua-Izé, Monte-Café, Porto-Real, etc. Nous con-
naissions déjà par reputation l'importance et la fertilité unique de ces deux perles
parmi les colonies portugaises, mais nous confessons que nos prévisions ont été bien
surpassées. Vos plantations peuvent servir de l'exemple pour nous autres cultivateurs.
Nous reconnaissons avec grand plaisir qu'une activité infatigable et une intelligence
visible ont produit des résultats tout à fait suprenants. Il faut relever surtout la manière magistrale comme le planteur portugais a sur instruire le nègre aux travaux
culturels. Les bons résultats de votre système se voient dans la manière comme le
nègre se prête au travail avec aptitude et bonne volonté évident. Partout où nous
etions nous avons observé des conditions, qui sont á désigner comme modéle sous
tous les rapports. Nous apprécions surtout les mésures efficaces que le gouvernement
portugais a appliqué à la question de l'ouvrier nègre.

«Les bonnes impressions que nous gardons de cette visite de St. Thomé et
Principe comptent parmis plus agréables de tout notre voyage.

«En vous exprimant encore une fois nos remerciments les plus chaleureux nous
vous prions de bien vouloir être notre interprête auprés de vos amis et d'aggreer,
cher Monsieur, l'assurance de notre parfaite considération.

(aa) *Alfred Prince de Loewenstein.*
Wilhelm Kemner.

Monsieur Francisco Mantero.
    Lisbonne.

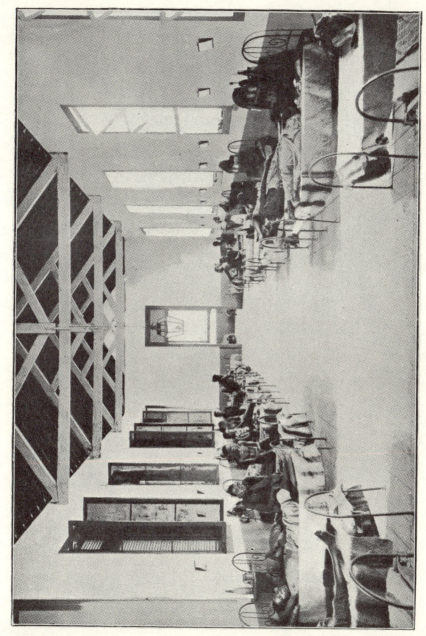

Interior of a ward in the Hospital on the Agua Izé Estate. Island of S. Thomé

Questions and Answers

Relative to

Manual Labour in S. Thomé and Principe.

Small station for the loading of cocoa on the private railway of the «Santa Margarida» Plantation. Island of S. Thomé

Questions and their corresponding Answers.

Centres of production and of agricultural work :
 a) *regions more or less extensive;*
 b) *groups of Colonies;*
 c) *simple individual exploitations more or less isolated.*

The Islands of S. Thomé and Principe constitute, each, a centre of work and production divided into numerous exploitations, some collective constituted into anonymous societies, or simple partnerships between individuals, and others exclusively individual, the conditions of work and production being identical in all.

The Island of S. Thomé is situated 0° 23′ of N lat. and 15° 58′ of E long. and that of Principe 1° 38′ of N lat. and 16° 38′ of E long. of Lisbon, both in the Gulf of Guinea under the Equator (1).

Centres of industrial production economically connected with purely agricultural centres.

In the Colony there are no industrial centres ; in each plantation only oil and palm wine are manufactured in small quantities for household use, and for sale; in some plantations brandy is also manufactured, which is sold for local consumption.

The coffee is all consumed in Portugal, as is likewise nearly all the cocoa and cocoa-nut which supply the Lisbon companies «União Fabril», and «Arrabida», some small quantities being also consumed in the Oporto factories.

The cocoa only supplies national industry with an insignificant quantity (218:400 kilos of the value of Reis 66:002$400 in 1909) of raw

---

(1) Geography of Portugal and Colonies, by J. G. Pery. page 343.

material; it is nearly all exported principally to Germany, via the ports of Hamburg and Bremen; to U. S. America, via New York; to England, via London, Liverpool and Glasgow; and in smaller proportions to Belgium via Antwerp; to Holland, via Amsterdam and Rotterdam; to Italy, via Genoa and Naples; to Denmark, via Copenhagen; to France, via Havre and Bordeaux; to Spain, via Barcelona and Madrid; to Russia via Moscow, Odessa, Riga and S. Petersburg, and to Austria-Hungary via Trieste. From these centres it irradiates to the rest of Europe and North America, after having served the industrial applications of the respective countries.

a) *Industrial centres which employ raw materials furnished by agriculture.*

There are no industrial centres of any kind in the Colony, with the exceptions stated in the answer to the previous question and in Portugal the cocoa industry is very limited.

The consuming centres, national and foreign, are those which are also mentioned in the previous answer.

b) *Industrial centres, more or less independent of the agricultural raw materials, which receive manual labour from the same sources which furnish the agricultural centres.*

Prejudged — vide previous answer.

Information relative to each Island, or to both conjointly, according as to whether circumstances are divergent or identical, in harmony with the following numbers and indications.

I — *Climatic conditions.*

The climate of the Islands of S. Thomé and Principe is unhealthy in the low-lying regions and on the coast, especially in the rainy season — middle of September to the middle of May — with which coincides the increase of solar heat. The most unhealthy months are November and December.

In the interior of both Islands, on the mountain sides, and on the table-lands where the plantations are situated in large numbers, constituting important centres of agricultural produce, and where there are

Head-quarters of the Gue-Gue Plantation. In the background the manager's residence. Island of S. Thomé

great numbers of labourers, the climate is temperate, healthy for Africans and supportable for Europeans, if due care and the prophylatic precautions which science and experience counsel for equatorial countries be taken.

II — *Hydrography*.

S. Thomé.

«The disposition relative to the culminating points is quadrilateral, the vertices of which are the *Peak of S. Thomé,* altitude 2:140 metres, which rises into space, imposing and majestic, covered nearly always by a dense fog, dominating principally the western region of the Island; the *Peak of Cambombey,* nearly 1:350 metres high, dominating the southern regions; the *Formoso* to the east, and the *Calvario* to the north. Corresponding approximately to the centre of this quadrilateral space, is the *Peak of Anna de Chaves,* the spurs of which ramify and join those of the other great eminences.

Indeed, disseminated throughout the Island, there exist numerous other peaks, more or less connected with the principal ones above mentioned and although of smaller elevation they are none the less notable, owing to their manifest preponderance in the formation of the complex and intricate geological and orographical skeleton of the island, determining the great and capricious undulations of its soil, and the formation of its mountain ranges.

«One of these notable for its extension and wealth of cultivation, is that which extends from the *Peak of S. Thomé* in an eastward direction, following approximately the polygonal perimeter which includes in its vast area the «Agua-Izé» plantation. Starting from *Alto Douro* and *Cantagallo* its crest follows the line of *Formoso, Penninha* and *Calvario,* forming up to a certain height the right side of the *Abbade* and the left of *Ió Grande.* Its principal ramifications are the *Morro da Casa* in *Traz-os-Montes,* the notable «cavallete» of *Cruzeiro,* the gigantic Rock of *Mozambóe,* the range of mountains, more or less continuous of *Nova Ceylão, Macambrará, Santa Adelaide, Nova Java, Catumbella, Milagrosa, Valle Paraiso, Santa Clotilde, Montes Herminios* and *Ponta das Palmeiras, Quimpo* and *Santo Antonio,* (Agua-Izé), constituting the left sides of *Rio Abbade,* with important ramifications to the north.

Amongst the mountain ranges which, proceeding directly from the Peak, take a northerly direction, that which separates the rivers *Contador,* and *Pró Vaz* in the regions of *Neves* deserves special mention.

Amongst the numerous undulations and hilly tracts of land, which such an orographic system naturally forms, thousands of water courses exist which, falling first in copious cataracts from the highest points of the vast and steep ridges, percolate afterwards through their sides in deep furrows, between anfractuosities of rugged rocks which occasionally impede their impetuous currents and subdivide them into broad silvery bands, and finally glide, already divided into a thousand calm brooks, between the fields, where they weave the vast network of affluents of the springs of water from which they were originally separated. And it is thus that, meandering through all the Island by hill and dale, they augment the wealth of its most fertile soil, refresh the air with their coolness, maintain the opulence of an incomparable vegetation, and having lavished so many benefits, they, more or less abundantly, more or less impetuously, finally flow into the ocean.

«I referred above to the numerous cataracts which fall from the highest points of this Island. Owing to the vast sheets of water which surge from the mountain springs, it is certainly not difficult to find various cascades, formed by the sudden depressions and uneven ground over-flowed with water. Unfortunately, however, the said waterfalls, notwithstanding their magnificence, are not in conditions suitable for economic and industrial appliances, and although such a disadvantage does not prevent them from being valuable reservoirs of mechanical energy as well as inexhaustible deposits of dynamic force, it is no less certain that the moment has not yet arrived when they can be utilized as such by the initiative of the most daring enterprises.» (1)

Island of Principe.

The orography and hydrography of this Island are identical to those of the Island of S. Thomé; its highest mountains are the *Principe Peak,* the *Preto Peak,* the *Mãe Corne Peak,* the *Barriga Branca Peak,* the *Mesa Peak,* the *Papagaio Peak,* the *Pae Adão Peak* and *Cariote,* whence descend numerous courses of water which, on their way to the sea, divide into a labyrinth of brooks, forming a complex and vast aquatic network, throughout the whole Island, to re-unite near the coast in dozens of streams which flow into the Ocean from all sides.

The orographic ramifications of the Islands, which extend to the sea, determine the formation in different points of the coast, of various creeks more or less sheltered, and some gulfs and bays which offer a sure haven. In S. Thomé the port opened to commerce is that of Anna de

(1) *The Island of S. Thomé and the Agua Izé Plantation,* by the Conde de Sousa e Faro, **pages 20 and 24.**

Types of native women. Island of S. Thomé

Chaves Bay, where is situated the town of S. Thomé, the capital of the Province, but the creek of S. João is the best port of the Island.

In the Island of Principe there are two magnificent ports: that of S. Antonio near the town of the same name, which is the official port, and the Bahia d'Oueste which is the most vast.

III — *The system of construction and hygiene of the dwellings:*

It is subject to rules mentioned in the regulations, preceded by the approval of the plans of construction by the Governor of the Province in council, after consultation with the local Board of Labour and Emigration. (Art. 106 of the General Regulations of 17-7-1909).

The buildings most generally used are: For married couples, groups of houses of only one storey measuring at least 3^m,30 in height (Art. 18 of the provinçial regulations of 29-4-1875), divided into apartments, one for each couple, having at least one door and one window.

These dwellings are constructed of timber, masonry, brick or composite, generally roofed with tiles, and some with corrugated iron, with cement or stone floorings.

Dwellings of two storeys are also used, one or both flats having wooden floors.

For the unmarried labourers the dwellings are in common, but the sexes are completely separated, and consist of great barracks constructed by the same process as that of the houses for the married folk, having in the interior wooden bunks raised from the ground at least 0^m,60 and measuring 2 metres in width, and, at least, 1 metre of space for each person. (Art. 20. of the provincial regulation of 29th April 1875).

The system of huts which Art. 17 of the mentioned regulation of 1875 authorized, is no longer permitted by the authorities to whom the supervision on the matter is entrusted, but the general regulations of 17th July 1909 revive that sanitary measure. The system of huts is, in our opinion, the most hygienic when they are sufficiently large, and even the most picturesque when artistically built. The special nature of these buildings assures a constant ventilation, and the fire, which the black so much likes to have inside his dwelling and which he can make use of constantly in the hut without danger, drives away with its smoke insects, carriers of malaria and other infectious diseases, and attenuates by its heat, the excessive atmospheric humidity which causes rheumatism, bronchitis and fevers brought on by the suppression of perspiration. And further, huts in consequence of their light and economical construction, are advantageous on account of the facility with which the infectious germs can be destroyed, by being periodically burned in groups, and others built on the calcined ground where the former existed.

IV — *Human Races — Number of inhabitants — Density of the native population.*

The most numerous elements of the population comprehending 97 °/₀ of the totality, belong to the black race, the white, bronze and yellow races following in numerical importance according to the order described.

The black population is composed thus:

Natives of the Islands, including Angolares......	19:651
» » » » employed as labourers (1).	4:000
» » » smaller Islands, sons of labourers ..	6:987
» » Cape Verde	1:158
» » the hinterland of Angola	31:878
» » Cabinda (north of the Province of Angola)	544
» » Mozambique and Zambezia	1:923
» » Portuguese Guinea	30
	66:171
Europeans............................	2:000
Natives of Portuguese India and Macau	50
	68:221

The last census taken of the population of the Province refers to the year 1900, there being then 42:130 inhabitants; but, making approximate corrections relative to the nine years elapsed, according to the official and extra-official informations obtained, the actual population may be calculated at 68.221 disseminated over an area of 120:000 hectares the total surface of the two Islands, to which corresponds in density per hectare, 0·551 Africans and 0·017 whites and Asiatics.

V — *Nosology.*

As it was not possible for us to collect official elements to complete the information relative to one year, we give the nosological movement of the military and civil hospital of S. Thomé in the months of September, October and November of 1908, by which an opinion may be formed as to the diseases prevalent in the Province with greater frequency or intensity, and of their results.

---

(1) The official information mentioned 1:724 natives contracted from 1900 up to the present. The 2:216 which we add are those who, owing to the lack of official information, we calculate correspond to the period previous to 1900.

Landing-stage of the Porto Real Plantation (West), West Bay of the Island of Príncipe (in the back-ground Table Peak)

Military and civil hospital of the city of S. Thomé.

Name of the Illness	Patients	Cured	Con-valescent	In the same condition	Deaths
Intermittent ague	63	58	5	–	–
Diarrhæa	23	21	1	–	1
Malarial gastritis	13	12	1	–	–
Ulcers	13	6	7	–	–
Bronchitis	12	12	–	–	–
Pneumonia	11	5	1	–	5
Wounds	11	9	2	–	–
Dysentery	12	9	2	–	1
Syphilis	10	1	7	–	2
Chronic rheumatism	15	4	9	2	–
Malarial anœmia	9	5	3	–	1
Chronic malaria	7	1	5	–	1
Bilious fever (bemoglobinurica)	6	3	–	–	3
Tetanus	6	2	–	–	4
Hydrocelis	6	3	3	–	–
Abscesses	6	5	–	1	–
Ankilostomiase	6	3	2	–	1
Pernicious comatose fever	4	2	–	–	2
Tuberculosis	4	–	2	1	1
Blenorrhagia	4	2	2	–	–
Hepathic abscesses	4	1	1	–	2
Urethritis	4	4	–	–	–
Orchiteis	4	2	2	–	–
Dysidrosis	4	4	–	–	–
Ecsema	3	3	–	–	–
Remittent fevers	3	3	–	–	–
Malarial fevers	3	2	–	1	–
Adénitis	3	2	1	–	–
Chronic bronchitis	3	–	3	–	–
Chronic cystitis	3	–	3	–	–
Influenza	2	2	–	–	–
Pott's disease	2	–	1	1	–
Paresis	2	–	2	–	–
Feigned sickness	2	1	–	1	–
Enteric colic	2	2	–	–	–
Puerperal fever	2	–	–	–	2
Senile cachexy	2	–	–	–	2
Contusions	2	1	1	–	–
Sleeping sickness	2	–	1	–	1
Encephalitis	1	1	–	–	–
Enlargment of the eye	1	1	–	–	–
Chronic endocarditis	1	1	–	–	–
Cardiac embolia	1	–	–	–	1
Valvular affection	1	–	–	–	1
Corysa	1	–	1	–	–
Bright's disease	1	–	–	–	1
Burns	1	–	1	–	–
Hypnosis	1	–	1	–	–
Epulidis	1	1	–	–	–
Malarial cachexy	1	–	–	–	1
Chicken-pox	1	1	–	–	–
Mastoid	1	–	–	1	–
Scalp lipoma	1	–	–	–	1
Chlorosis	1	–	1	–	–
Pericarditis	1	–	–	–	1
Stomatitis	1	1	–	–	–
Hernia	1	1	–	–	–
Boils	1	–	–	–	1
Ulcer in spine	1	1	–	–	–
Dropsy	1	1	–	–	–
Fractures	1	1	–	–	–
Brain sarcoma	1	–	–	1	–
Progressive locomotor ataxy	1	–	–	–	1
Palsy	1	–	–	–	1
Amaurosis	1	–	1	–	–
Jaundice	1	–	–	–	1
Renal insufficiency	1	–	1	–	–
Gangrene	1	–	–	–	1
Zona	1	1	–	–	–
Psoriasis	1	1	–	–	–
Elephantiasis	1	–	1	–	–
	325	202	74	9	40

Geophagia furnishes a large contingent for the nosologic statistics of the rural population, but it is not known in the hospital of the city, where as a rule, no labourers enter.

Native women from the Angola hinterland employed in the Boa Entrada Plantation, with their children

VI — *Means of communication in the Colony and with the exterior.*

Communications in the Colony are carried on by land or by sea.

For maritime communications there is a permanent weekly coasting service round the Island of S. Thomé effected by a steamer of the «Empreza Nacional», and there are also numerous sailing and rowing craft, and some steam tugs; in the Island of Principe there are some sailing and rowing boats.

The communications on land in both the Islands are by means of narrow paths between the different points of the interior and the respective ports of embarkation, in Decauville trucks or in carts, the former being of steam or animal traction, the latter drawn by mules or oxen.

The communications with the exterior are effected by means of a service of the excellent steamers of the «Empreza Nacional de Navegação» three times monthly, which connects the Portuguese Colonies of Africa with each other and all of them with the Port of Lisbon, and by monthly services of the German and English steamers of the Woerman and Elder Dempster Lines.

VII — *Total surface in actual exploitation.*

62:288 hectares.

VIII — *Probability of the increase of the surface in actual exploitation.*

There is an increase every year which is capable of attaining approximately 97:288 hectares, the maximum surface of the soil in the Province suitable for cultivation.

IX — *Principal products—Surface occupied by each.*

Cocoa — Occupies a surface of 56:923 hectares.
Coffee —   »   »   »   » 5:365   »   (1)

(1) The area occupied by the coffee plantations is calculated by attributing actually to each planted hectare, an average annual production of 200 kilos (which in time may be increased to 260) and this average applied to the production of the year 1908 which was 1.073:170 kilos. The space occupied by the coffee plants being thus determined, the remaining planted surface where there exist other small cultures only occupying relatively insignificant spaces, is supposed to be occupied by the cocoa plantations.

X — *Quantity of each product per hectare.*

> Cocoa — 531 kilos per hectare. (1)
> Coffee — 200   »   »   »   (1)

The quantity attributed to each hectare is the average actual production of the cultivated surfaces; but considering that many plantations do not yet produce, or only produce part of what they are capable of doing, and calculating an annual increase of 3 % during ten years, it can be supposed, when all the plantations actually existent are in full maturity that the average quantity of each product, per hectare, will be of 690 kilos of cocoa and 260 kilos of coffee.

XI — *Nature of the work for each kind of production.*

Work common to cocoa and coffee; — clearance of the forests, cleaning the soil, digging holes, setting the plants, pruning and cleaning the trees, harvest, removal of fruit to the open spaces, drying, selection, packing and transport to the port of embarkation.
Special work for cocoa: — breaking the shells and fermentation.
Special work for coffee: — peeling, polishing and separating.

XII — *Quantities exported of each product.*

The exports of 1909, according to official statistics (2) were the following:

Methylated spirits.....................	20 litres
Brandy..............................	73 »
Palm Oil	602 »
Cocoa...............................	31.602:519 kilos

---

(1) The calculation is made by dividing the year 1909 (page 81) by the number of hectares supposed to be planted with each kind, and which are: cocoa 56:923 and coffee 5365.

(2) These statistics are based on the exports of S. Thomé and Principe from 1st January to 31st December and those of page 81 on the imports into Lisbon and Funchal also from 1st January to 31st December; each part therefore refers to exports effected in different periods, from which results the difference noted in the quantities, and also because the Custom House statistics are calculated according to the verified weight, and that of page 81 is based on the average of 60 kilos per bag of cocoa, and 70 kilos per bag of coffee.

Hospital on the Gue-Gue Estate, Island of S. Thomé

Cocoa shells......................	7:738 kilos
Coffee............................	1.315:050 »
Wax..............................	46 »
Cocoanuts........................	73:008 nuts
Cocoa............................	672:060 kilos
Hides............................	12:167 »
Confectionery....................	383 »
Manioc flour.....................	163 »
Kola.............................	1:148 »
Coco pulp........................	8:909 »
Coco-nut ditto...................	13:275 »
Peruvian bark....................	74:054 »
Soap.............................	900 »

XIII — *Number of labourers for each product.*

Cocoa.......................	38:383
Coffee......................	3:617 (1)
	42:000

XIV — *Total number of labourers employed.*

42:000 (including 2:000 Angolares, whose work is intermittent).

XV — *Number of labourers per hectare in each kind of production.*

One labourer per each cultivated surface of 1,483 hectares, coffee or cocoa.

XVI — *Quality and price of food.*

Rice, kilo 72 réis; beans, kilo 65 réis; dried fish, kilo 80 réis; dried beef, kilo 227 réis; bacon, kilo 260 réis; olive oil, litre 332 réis; fresh meat, kilo 600 réis; palm oil, litre 160 réis; Indian corn, kilo 46 réis; wine, litre 140 réis; palm wine, litre 30 réis; Indian corn «fuba», kilo 90 réis; cod-fish, kilo 285 réis. (2)

---

(1) This calculation is based on the average of one labourer for 1,483 cultivated hectares, those planted with cocoa being calculated at 56:923 and those planted with coffee at 5:365.

(2) Prices regulating merchandise delivered in the Agua-Izé plantation in S. Thomé.

XVII — *Quantity of food consumed by each labourer.*

In one day :
2 decilitres of coffee, 3oo grammes of rice, 25o grammes of fish, 2oo grammes of Indian cornflour, 1 decilitre of oil; or 2 decilitres of coffee, 3oo grammes of beans, 25o grammes of fish, 75 grammes of bacon, 2oo grammes of Indian cornflour, 1 decilitre of oil; or
2 decilitres of coffee, 3oo grammes of rice, 15o grammes of meat or cod-fish, 25o grammes of fish, 1 decilitre of oil, 2oo grammes of flour (1).

XVIII — *Wages or system of remuneration of work according to the class of production, nature of the work, race, sex and age of the labourers.*

The system of remuneration, being uniform for all the labourers, is identical for the different kinds of production; it consists of wages paid in cash every month, food, clothing, medical attendance and hospital, all this for the labourers and for their families, the children always receiving food and medical attendance, whether they work or not. The only exceptions to this rule are the Angolares blacks, who clear the land and fell the forest trees by job work.

No stated time is imposed to execute any determined task. The labourer does as much as he can in the working hours and receives the whole of his wages, as well as everything included in his contract whatever be the amount of work produced. To those who distinguish themselves by producing more than others, extra rewards are given, and inexperienced labourers are allowed time to learn their work without loss of their wages.

According to the regulations of the 17th July 1909, no contracts can be made in which the wages in cash are less than 2$500 reis for the men and 1$800 reis for the women, but there are labourers of all races earning more than this minimum. Those of Mozambique, for example, earn the minimum of 3$500 reis for the men and 2$000 reis for the women, and there are labourers of Cape Verde and Angola earning wages of 3$000, 4$000, 5$000 reis and upwards.

(1) These are the quantities according to the regulations, but as a rule up to 5oo grammes are given instead of 3oo of rice and beans, and the labourers are allowed to eat as much as they like of all the fruits cultivated in the plantations, which are many, and rations of red or palm wine, tobacco, etc., etc., are given as rewards.

Transport of cocoa from the plantations to the port of embarkation. — Porto-Real Plantation (West). Island of Principe

XIX — *Dwellings and family life of the native labourers in the centres of production.*

Vide reply to question number III regarding dwellings.

Each married couple of labourers live together with their children, polygamy being abandoned; as a rule they live happily, each one looking after the *ménage,* when work is over. Both single and married labourers pay their tribute to friendship, each having his friends with whom he cultivates familiar relations. Amongst their friends they give special preference to their fellow passengers from Angola to S. Thomé, whom they denominate their *navios* and who are considered members of the family.

XX — *Native labourers working near their centres of habitation.*

All work near their dwellings: in the small properties because the distances are always short; in the large because the agricultural zones are divided into different *dependencias,* each with its own installations and personel, divided in such a way that the labourers may be as near as possible to the plantations where they work.

XXI — *Labourers who have to go some distance from their centres of habitation to their work.*

Prejudged.

XXII — *Number of native centres of habitation.*

If we consider the dwellings of the labourers as native centres of habitation, and bear in mind that the large estates have numerous places of residence, whilst the smaller, which are many, have only one or two, we can, by establishing an average of three for each of the cultivated properties, estimate the centres referred to at 55o.

But if we wish to extend the information to all the natives, whether they be of the Province or not, who do not work or only do so irregularly or intermittently, it is not possible to fix a number of centres, because those natives are scattered over the surface of the Province in small groups or in isolated families.

There are no villages of native labourers.

XXIII — *Physical conditions of the country.*

S. Thomé.

The Island of S. Thomé, in its general outline presents an oblong form, irregular on all parts of the coast where there exist various gulfs and bays, due to the undulated ground. The soil is mountainous all over the Island, there being some ranges of considerable altitude.

The highest peak is that of S. Thomé, which attains a height of more than 2:140 metres, in the centre of the Island, north-south direction; there existing also other notable peaks to the north and south, as well as to the east and west of the first named. These peaks form a chain from N. E. to S. W. which with its spurs causes the undulated surface of the Island, and is 52 kilometres long by 34 broad (1).

Principe.

The Island of Principe is an aggregate of rough mountains of greater height in the south than in the north, disposed in ranges which run in different directions, occupying a surface of little more than 15 kilometres in length by 10 in its greatest width.

The peak of Principe is the highest of its mountains, though much lower than that of S. Thomé. The coast is similarly cut up in various points by bays, gulfs, and creeks. (1)

The centres of habitation of the native labourers are the plantations or farms where they work, situated in the valleys of the low-lying zone and on the mountain sides, or on the table-lands on the banks of the rivers which separate them, and which are formed by the waters which descend from their steep sides.

XXIV — *Character of the race, capacity for work.*

The race of the hinterland of Angola, which predominates numerically is docile and easily adapts itself to agricultural work; the races of Cape Verde and Mozambique possess a prouder temperament, but are

(1) Geography of Portugal and the Colonies by G. Pery, page 343, and *The Island of S. Thomé,* by the Conde de Sousa e Faro, page 17.

One of the pavillions of the Hospital, Agua Izé Plantation. Island of S. Thomé

not disorderly ; that of Guinea is of a warlike origin but as there is only a very limited number in the Province it has no occasion to manifest practically its rebellious instincts, which however are being modified by intercourse with the other races. The Cabindo is very quarrelsome but absolutely harmless. All are more or less subject to indolence—the innate evil of the South African races.

XXV — *Density of the population.*

o,568 inhabitants per hectare.

XXVI — *Means of communication with other countries.*

Vide answer to question n.º VI.

Political conditions.

XXVII — *National and independent sovereignties.*

Only the sovereignty of Portugal exists.

XXVIII — *Government of chiefs more or less independent.*

Prejudged.

XXIX — *Effective occupation by civilized nations.*

Portugal effectually occupies all the Province.

XXX — Protectorates.

There are none.

XXXI — *System of government. Power of kings or chiefs of tribes.*

Prejudged.

XXXII — *Relations between the native peoples themselves.*

Good.

XXXIII — *Character and frequency of wars between the native peoples.*

There have not been any intestine fights for more than half a century.

XXXIV — *Treatment of war prisioners.*

Prejudged.

XXXV — *Crimes. — Penalties.*

With the exception of small thefts, and slight infringements of regulations, crime is very limited. The prison movement in 1908 is reported in the following table:

Prisoners existing on the 1ˢᵗ of January 1908 28
» entered during the year 1908 89
117
» left during the year 1908 81
» remaining on 31ˢᵗ December 1908 36

which, in a population of 68:221 souls corresponds to 1·31 per mil, it being noted that all the crimes were of little importance as may be concluded from the short detention of the prisoners in gaol.

Penalties applicable to natives, whether labourers or not, are the same as are generally applied in Portugal — temporary imprisonment or transportation for great crimes, simple imprisonment for those of smaller magnitude, and forced labour in Government works or money fines for simple infringements. Corporal punishments and life sentences are abolished.

Wilhelm Kemner

Manager of the cocoa plantations in the german Colony of the Cameroons, who visited the plantations
of S. Thomé and Principe in January 1910

Social status.

XXXVI — *Constitution of family.*

The savage form is the one adopted in the majority of cases, but polygamy amongst the labourers is excluded. Family organization according to Christian principles is being introduced, even if slowly, into the native habits.

XXXVII — *Existence of free labourers.*

All individuals working in S. Thomé and Principe are free.

XXXVIII — *Existence of slaves and servants.*

There are none.

XXXIX — *Organization of property.*

As in the metropolis, property in the two Islands is individual or collective, exploited directly by the owners or by tenants, and transmissible in the terms of Portuguese civil law. The Islands are divided into properties of different extensions, the large estates predominating. They are nearly all free and allodial.

Industrial status.

XL — *Game.*

There is very little, and, in general, it is not taken advantage of.

XLI — *Cattle.*

There being no pasture because the fields are preferred for the rich cultivations, cattle-breeding is very limited and consists almost exclusively of donkeys and goats. There is not much more «*creoulo*» cattle, that necessary for consumption and traction is imported from Angola, Cape Verde and Portugal.

XLII — *Agriculture.*

Agriculture is in a flourishing condition and supplies all local necessities; the chief agricultural product is cocoa, but coffee, sugar-cane, Peruvian bark, the oil palm, coco trees, rubber, cinnamon, vanilla, etc. are also cultivated.

The soil also produces Indian corn, beans, vegetables, manioc, yams, bananas, arrowroot and various fruit, but these products are generally cultivated by the farmers only in small quantities for their own use.

XLIII — *Extractive industries of an agricultural or forestal nature.*

There are none.

XLIV — *Other industries.*

There are none.

XLV — *Revenue, repartition, remuneration of labour.*

Prejudged, as no industries exist.

XLVI — *Commerce.*

It is limited to supplying public employees and the part of the native population who do not export or import directly from the metropolis. Local trade, thus restricted, has little importance and no margin for increasing.

Customs.

XLVII — *Habit, taste for or repugnance to work.*

As has been already stated the races introduced into the Islands are indolent by nature, but as a rule they struggle against their innate torpidness, and work.

Of the native race, the educated class either occupy themselves in agriculture or are engaged in business or burocracy, or are employed in different trades; the remainder do little or nothing, all suffer from the same repugnance to work, the former struggling against it, and the latter allowing themselves to be overcome by it.

XLVIII — *Sobriety or alcoholic intemperance.*

The tendency is for alcoholic intemperance, but in the plantations sobriety is enforced by the planters, and generally observed; this enforcement and the prohibition of polygamy constitute two great services which our agriculturalists render to the conservation and selection of the race.

XLIX — *Distances from the centres of native habitation to the centres of production*

The centres of habitation are all situated near the centres of production.

L — *Nature of the country to be crossed.*

There are no crossings to be made.

LI — *Means of transport in the Province.*

By land, Decauville lines, steam and animal traction, and carts drawn by mules and oxen; by water, sailing-boats, launches and steam tugs.

LII — *Nature of contracts of the agricultural labourers, made in the centres of production and labour.*

The contracts are an undertaking on the part of the labourers to render agricultural services for a stated time; and on the part of the employer to remunerate those services with money, food, clothing, medical attendance, dwellings, and return passage from S. Thomé and Principe.

LIII — *Nature of contracts made in the centres of habitation more or less distant from the centres of labour.*

Identical to the preceding answer.

LIV — *System of transport of labourers contracted outside the Province.*

All the labourers are conveyed in the steamers of the *Empreza Nacional de Navegação para a Africa,* both on their voyage to the Islands, and on their return to the home ports.

LV — *Formalities and mutual public guarantees of the contracts. — Legislation and regulations.*

The contracts effected outside the Province of S. Thomé and Principe are made between the labourers, assisted by the Curator-general or his delegate, the natural guardians of the labourers, and the masters represented by the emigration agents, in the presence of witnesses and with the help of an interpreter.

The renewal of contracts in the Province are public acts, effected always in the presence of the Curator-general or his delegate, and also in the presence of an interpreter and witnesses. Both are written and registered in the respective *curadorias* (Curator's office).

The guarantees of the contracting parties consist of the respective laws and regulations, which are:

Law of April 29th, 1875; general labour regulations of November 20th, 1878, of January 29th, 1903, of April 23rd, 1908, of December 31st, of the same year and of July 17th, 1909, and provincial regulations of August 28th, 1876 and August 17th of 1880.

City of Santo Antonio. Island of Principe. View taken from the sea
(Copy of an old-print)

LVI — *If the agricultural labourers return to their native countries.*

Some return, others remain.
(Vide answer to question N.º LX).

LVII — *If so, under what conditions, by what means and with what results is the return effected.*

The return passage to the home port is paid by the employer. The labourers are conveyed in the steamers of the *Empreza Nacional de Navegação,* accompanied by a Government commissary, the bearer of the savings accumulated during the contracts which the former receive on their arrival at the port of destination.

The results are beneficial for all those interested and for the two Provinces. For the Province of S. Thomé and for the agriculturists by the service rendered by the labourers; for their native places by the money which the contracted labourers send to their families, and that which the repatriated spend in local trade; for the labourers by the series of advantages which result from their contracts.

Shortly after their return home, many re-contract themselves to serve in S. Thomé, some in the same plantations where they had served, others under new masters. In the second contract many are accompanied by their wives.

LVIII — *If the repatriated labourers return home with savings.*

According to the terms of the regulations, the labourer receives only half of his wages from which any sums he may have received when contracted as well as the monthly allowance paid to his family are deducted; the other half is deposited by his employer in the Labour and Repatriation Fund, whence it is drawn at the time of the labourer's repatriation, and paid to him when he lands at his home port. A Government commissary sails in each vessel carrying repatriated labourers, and is the bearer of the savings of the latter, and entrusted with their payment which is made in the presence of the agent who contracted the emigrants and of witnesses.

LIX — *If the knowledge of the conditions in which the labourers return home, incites their fellow country men to imitate them, also freely contracting themselves.*

This has been the case in Cape Verde, Mozambique and in Cabinda; and it is hoped that the same will occur in Guinea, when the emigration from that Province is initiated on a large scale, as well as in the south of Angola, when according to the terms of the actual regulation the current of emigration from certain and subjugated regions to which repatriation is possible is established.

LX — *If the labourers conveyed prefer to renew their contracts and even settle in the centres of production to returning home.*

Those who proceed from the savage regions of the hinterland of Angola prefer to remain, and renew their contracts.

The majority of those from other parts return to their homes, and come back shortly afterwards to S. Thomé, many of them accompanied by members of their family.

LXI — *If so, why and in what conditions do they renew their contracts.*

They renew them because finding them favourable and being satisfied with the manner in which the previous contracts were carried out, they encounter advantages in their renewal as they are made in the same conditions as the last ones, or with increased wages; as a rule, the increase of wage always accompanies the renewal of the contract, and the regulamentary law determines that all the wages less than the minimum fixed in the last regulation be made equal, those of former contracts being raised on the occasion of their renewal, and, this measure being concluded, the law also determines that no contract whatever can be renewed without an increase in the wages of 10 °/₀ at least.

LXII — *Institutions in the centres of production and of work for education, instruction, insurance against sickness, accidents and death, and for medical attendance to the labourers.*

In all the centres of labour of any importance the labourers are taught the trades of carpenters, masons, blacksmiths, farm servants, carmen, cooks, gardeners, sawyers, etc.

Labourers from Quelimane (Moçambique) employed in the Boa Entrada Plantation. Island of S. Thomé

There is no insurance against sickness, but by the regulations the proprietors are compelled to provide medical and hospital attendance for the sick during all the time of their contracts, infirmaries, nurses, and pharmacies being established for this purpose in all the plantations, under the direction of a doctor who lives in the respective zone.

There is no insurance in case of death, but according to tradition always observed, the planter takes charge of and maintains the family of the labourers who die, the same practice being observed with those whom old age or any accident makes unfit for work, as well as their families.

LXIII — *Institutions of investment and credit, destined to encourage savings amongst the labourers and make them profitable — Legislation and regulations.*

There is established in S. Thomé a Fund of Labour and Repatriation (Art. 97., general reg. of 17-7-909), where half the wages of the labourers are deposited. This Fund is under the management of the Local Board of Work and Emigration, and the money is deposited in the Agency of the «Banco Nacional Ultramarino» (Art. 91. 2.), the Government being authorized to negociate with the same Bank the remuneration of those funds or to employ them, subject to the vote of the Central Committee of Emigration in first class scrip, uninfluenced by the fluctuations of the Stock Exchange (Art. 14. § 2.). This rule was decreed on July 17th 1909, and commenced to be enforced in November of the same year, but the Government has not yet negociated the form of remunerating the capital in deposit.

LXIV — *If in tropical or sub-tropical countries the work formerly carried out almost exclusively by black African labourers, is actually executed by labourers of pure white races (such as Portuguese, Italians, and Anglo-Saxons).*

Manual labour out of doors is all done by Africans in S. Thomé and Principe. In that climate the European cannot resist the fatigues of manual labour out of doors owing to the excessive heat, and can only be employed as a workman under shelter, or as a foreman of the labourers.

LXV — *If in the countries where agricultural work was formerly executed by labourers of imported races, their descendants tend to disappear or if on the contrary they are increasing.*

S. Thomé and Principe being desert Islands when they were discovered, all the inhabitants are descendants of colonists or imported labourers, freemen, freedmen or slaves. These inhabitants are of the black race, pure or half-caste. The pure race increases, although slowly; the half-castes, having periods of decadence and stagnation, do not increase.

LXVI — *If however they continue to occupy themselves with the same work which they or their ancestors executed formerly as slaves, or if on the contrary the interest derived from that work, freely continued, is insufficient to arouse and maintain the activity of the labourers descendants of former slaves.*

The natives descending from the two last generations of imported agricultural labourers, having received a more modern education, employ themselves in work and continue to occupy themselves, freely contracted, in the same work as their fathers, but the remainder who descend from former slaves or freedmen or even from free men, as a rule do not follow the example of their ancestors. With the exceptions mentioned above and in the reply to question XLVII, the native population does not lend itself to permanent agricultural labour. On the other hand the abundance with which the exuberant nature of the country supplies them with the necessary elements essential for living, and the high temperature of the climate which dispenses with shelter, are such that the indolent natives have no necessity to work for clothing or food; besides this, a false pride hinders them from taking part in paid labour in the fields, because they consider that occupation excessively humble for persons of their *social category,* however, there are already some examples of the natives of the Islands engaging themselves in paid labour, but as yet they form an exception.

LXVII — *If in those same countries the pure descendants of the slaves are being substituted in the execution of agricultural labour by half-castes adapted to local conditions.*

They are not substituted by half-castes because the latter suffer from the same false ideas of the pure race relative to salaried agricultural labour, and because their number is insignificant. The half-caste race does not increase in these Islands, notwithstanding the intercourse of more than four centuries between the black and the white race.

Labourers' compound in the head quarters of the Cantagallo district, Agua Izé Plantation, Island of S. Thomé

Sentence passed on the 9th of November 1877

BY

The Vice-Admiralty Court of Freetown

IN

The Colony of Sierra Leone

Absolving the Portuguese brigue "Ovarense" from the accusation
of slave-dealing

Cocoa Plantation in the Porto Real Estate. Island of Principe

In the Vice Admiralty Court, Sierra Leone, West Coast of Africa.

THE PORTUGUESE BRIG OVARENSE

Manoel dos Santos Casaca, Junior, Master.

———

Judgment.

On the 11th of December, 1876, a Monition was issued in this case returnable on the 18th.

On the 18th, while the Queen's Advocate was moving for the forfeiture and condemnation of the vessel and slaves on board, no appearance having been entered or claim filed, Mr. Bicaise, the Acting Portuguese Consul of this port, applied for time to appear and put in a claim, as the owners, the charterer, and the Master of the brig had not been able to secure the services of counsel, Mr. Montagu, one of the three practitioners then in the Colony not being able at the time to undertake the case, the other two practitioners, the Queen's Advocate and Mr. Lewis being engaged on behalf of the seizor; the Court accordingly granted until the 21st.

On the 21st Mr. Montagu appeared and applied for a week to put in a claim, which was granted, and on the 28th the time was extended to the 3rd of January on account of the number of papers required to be translated.

On the 3rd of January, the claim and affidavits in support thereof having been filed late on the 2nd, the Court was adjourned to the 6th to enable the seizor's Proctor to peruse these affidavits and to determine whether his client would abandon the seizure or allow the case to be determined upon the affidavits filed on behalf of the seizor and of the claimants, and on any further affidavits the seizor might wish to file in reply, or proceed by libel and plea.

On the 6th, the seizor being absent from the colony at the last sitting of the Court and being still absent, the 12th of January was assigned for bringing in the libel.

On the 12th the libel was accordingly brought in, and a day was assigned for bringing in the plea, which was accordingly filed on the 24th on behalf of the Master of the brig, Manoel Dos Santos Casaca, junior, the owners Manoel Rodrigues Formigal and Fernando Oliveira Bello, Merchants at Lisbon, and the charterer Francisco Ferreira de Moraes, of the Island of St. Thomas.

The seizor by his libel asserts that the *Ovarense,* then in the harbour of Freetown, was engaged in the slave-trade, having on board three slaves, and that she was also fitted out and equipped for the slave-trade, having on board a larger quantity of water than was necessary for the use of the crew of 14 persons, and an extraordinary number of empty casks for holding water, for which no certificate was produced that security had been given that these casks were for lawful traffic, and also 73 bags of rice and 32 mats, and that these mats were more than necessary for the use of the crew; and the seizor therefore prayed for the forfeiture of the brig, her tackle and apparel, and of the goods, wares and merchandize on board, and of the 3 alleged slaves, and that the Master be condemned in costs.

The claimants by their plea contend that the *Ovarense* was not engaged in or fitted out for the slave-trade, that she was at the time of seizure an immigrant vessel duly licensed as such, and that the 3 persons on board were not slaves but free immigrants destined for the Portuguese Island of St. Thomas, where slavery did not exist, slavery having been abolished in 1875.

That the rice was in the brig's manifest.

That the 32 mats were not used or intended to be used by the crew, but had been used on previous voyages in lining the vessel to protect coffee, sugar, and salt, and had been left in the brig.

That of the water, 2 tanks and 9 puncheons were in the manifest, the remainder having been taken on board in the harbour of Freetown for the use of the intended immigrants.

That of the empty casks, some had contained stores on board, and the remainder had been taken on board while the vessel was in the harbour here, and were intended for water for the immigrants.

And that in respect to certain shackles alleged in the libel to have been brought from St. Thomas and got rid of in the harbour of Freetown, it was entirely untrue, as there never were any shackles on board.

And they pray that the seizor's suit be dismissed, the brig, her tackle, and the goods and merchandize, and the 3 men called slaves be restored, and that the seizor be condemned in all costs, losses, damages, demurrage and expenses.

The following facts appear in evidence: —

The Portuguese Government by a law passed on the 29th of April, 1875, but to come into operation one year after publication, had abolished slavery in the Island of St. Thomas, on the West Coast of Africa, under which law, however, the freed slaves were to remain in a state of apprenticeship for two years, becoming absolutely free at the expiration of the two years.

A system of immigration of free labourers into St. Thomas from the West Coast of Africa thereupon commenced, in which the steam ships of the British and African Steam Navigation Company, trading and carrying the mails along the coast, were employed by Francisco Ferreira de Moraes, who had contracted with many of the Proprietors of Plantations in the island to procure labourers for them.

On the 23rd of September, 1876, certain regulations were passed by the Portuguese Government for the introduction by Portuguese vessels of free labourers and immigrants into St. Thomas.

Labourers' children in the Boa Entrada Plantation, engaged in sports. Island of S. Thomé

The Portuguese brig *Ovarense,* of the burthen of 309 tons, left Lisbon on the 24th of June, 1876, and arrived at the Island of St. Thomas, the captain says, about 5 or 6 p.m. on the 5th August following, the log book not showing the time of the day, with a cargo of stores for the Government for the erection of a new Government House; and in September 1876 she was chartered by de Moraes for the purpose of procuring and taking to St. Thomas immigrants under the forementioned regulations, and under his contracts with the planters; and for this purpose he received from the Governor of the island a license for himself, and one for the Master of the brig.

The *Ovarense* was then on the 26th of September 1876 cleared out from St. Thomas for the ports of Liberia and Sierra Leone, and her manifest showed as having then on board, shipped at St. Thomas

> 587 Boxes of Gin
> 402 Demijohns of Rum
>   6 Packages of Cotton
> 75 Bags of Rice
> 150 Tons of sand ballast and
>   9 Casks and 2 tanks containing
> 2700 gallons of water, for a voyage of *four months,* as stated in the manifest,

and the Governor of St. Thomas delivered to the Captain a letter addressed to the Portuguese Consul here, informing him that the *Ovarense* was «licensed to carry work people, provided they were free men, to St. Thomas, and to take in water at Sierra Leone for 368 men, or 400, if the Captain adds a small half deck which he proposed to do at Sierra Leone», and the Governor informs the Consul that «the introduction of free men is an urgent necessity, and that the vessel is in order», and he closes his letter by requesting the Consul «to afford her his official protection»; and he also, at the end of the licenses given by him to Moraes and the Captain, requests the authorities at the several ports «to put no impediment in their way, but rather to afford them assistance».

Before the *Ovarense* sailed from St. Thomas, a list of the passengers was signed by the proper Portuguese Authority there according to Portuguese regulations, and this list formed one of the brig's authorized papers to be produced at the next port, and delivered with the other papers to the Portuguese Consul at the port.

On Saturday the 2nd December, 1876, the *Ovarense* having left St. Thomas on the 27th of September with Moraes and some 20 passengers, arrived in the harbour of Freetown between 3 and 4 o'clock p.m., after a voyage of 66 days, having touched at Cape Coast, landing passengers there, and at Cape Palmas, where she also landed passengers, and then left on the morning of the 18th of November, taking 15 days from Cape Palmas to the Port of Freetown.

On her arrival here, she had on board, in addition to the Captain and her crew of 13 white men, including the doctor, engaged by Moraes to attend the immigrants in accordance with his charter party, William Grant, (an African of 14 years of age) who was the steward's boy on board, and 6 Kroomen, vizt. Jim Boy, who had been, and then was, in the service of the charterer, Moraes, as a head

Krooman for looking after the Kroo-boy immigrants, Black Will, Tom Dollar, and 3 others, alleged by the seizor to be 3 slaves, or kidnapped on board at Cape Palmas to be dealt with as slaves, vizt. Grando, Pannick and Yoruba.

On the brig's arrival here on the 2nd of December, the charterer Moraes, who had taken passage in her from St. Thomas, but had landed at Cape Coast with other passengers, and had come on here in one of the Mail steamers, went on board with Mr. Julius John Smith, and they both returned to the shore the same evening, the Captain accompanying them; but before leaving the *Ovarense,* Moraes gave Jim Boy a sovereign, with permission, at Jim Boy's request, to spend 3 days on shore. Jim Boy, however, swears that his request was refused, but that he went on shore that same Saturday evening with Black Will; and Tom Dollar supports him as to the refusal.

The Captain returned to the ship at about 7 o'clock p.m. that same evening, and observing two small trunks broken, containing, or which had contained, goods of Moraes the charterer, he again went on shore and informed Moraes.

The following morning, Sunday the 3rd of December, Moraes went on board the *Ovarense,* and the Captain showed him the broken packages. Moraes then sent for Jim Boy, who was on shore, and on Jim Boy coming on board he was arrested, under an order previously obtained by Mr. Julius John Smith, on behalf of Moraes, from James Craig Loggie, Inspector General of Police and a Justice of the Peace, but was subsequently discharged by the Police Magistrate on the 7th of December.

William Grant, the steward's boy, says that he went on shore on Sunday the 3rd of December, but returned the same day at 7 p.m.; that he saw Jim Boy in the Police station while locked up, but that he «did not talk long with him».

On Monday the 4th of December, the Captain entered his vessel at the Customs, leaving the ship's manifest there, and asking and receiving from the Collector verbal permission to commence taking in water, Mr. Julius John Smith interpreting for him, who, however, has not been examined as to this permission.

The Captain also on that same day left with the Acting Portuguese Consul the ship's papers, amongst which, however, the authórized passengers' list from St. Thomas was wanting, the Captain swearing that Mr. Moraes, the charterer, had the list, Mr. Moraes swearing he thought he had it amongst his papers, but not finding it he must have left it at St. Thomas, the seizor's Counsel complaining of the non-production of this list which would have shown whetther Black Will, an important witness, was on board of the *Ovarense* or not on her passage from St. Thomas to Cape Palmas, as contended by the seizor and his witnesses, but denied by the claimants and their witnesses.

Mr. Bicaise, the Acting Portuguese Consul swears that «before the arrival in this port of the *Ovarense* he knew what her purpose was in coming here, and that he had seen the Governor *officially* on the 30th of November, and again on the 3rd of December 1876, respecting the *Ovarense.* It does not, however, transpire on the evidence, what passed between the Governor and the Portuguese Consul in respect to the *Ovarense.*

Mr. Loggie swears that «about noon on Sunday the 3rd of December, he received information that the *Ovarense* had been shipping too great a quantity of water».

Loggie, however, took no active steps then or on Monday the 4th; nor did he

Labourers' dwellings in one of the agricultural sections, Agua Izé Plantation. Island of S. Thomé

see the Collector of Customs, or the Acting Portuguese Consul, or call on the Governor from whom he received his warrant or authority to visit, seize, and detain
vessels suspected of being equipped for, or engaged in, the slave trade within
British jurisdiction.

The Captain of the *Ovarense* in the meantime, on the said Monday the 4ᵗʰ,
commenced to take in water without a Customs permit in writing for the purpose,
which the seizor contends was absolutely necessary, as sworn to by Hanson, the
Surveyor of Customs, for the shipment of *empty water casks,* but on the verbal
permission which the Captain swears he had received from the Collector of Customs.

It does not seen to me, however, to be necessary under the Customs Ordinan-
ces, or the Order in Council of the 13ᵗʰ of February 1849, that a Customs permit
should be obtained for taking in water on board, or even for taking on board
empty casks for the reception of water for the use of the crew and passengers, a
Customs permit being only necessary for goods, wares, and merchandize.

Early on the Tuesday morning the 5ᵗʰ, at between 5 and 6 o'clock, Mr. Loggie
boarded the *Ovarense* with Mr. Augustus Beale Hanson, the Surveyor of Customs
and Acting Harbour Master, and with about 5 policemen. He says he told the
Captain he «came to look», and that the Captain made no objection; and Hanson
swears that they «went into the hold and they rummaged the vessel». And Loggie
deposes that they found 70 bags of rice, and 32 mats, which he swears «were
underneath some of the packages of rum and gin»; in his affidavit of seizure, he
says «*wholly covered* with demijohns of rum». The mate, however, swears they
were not concealed, though some of them may have been hidden by demijohns of
rum; but neither Hanson nor the policeman, who both assisted in the search, are
questioned as to these mats in support of Loggie's testimony.

Loggie swears he also found below in the after part of the brig

2 tanks, containing about 2.000 gallons of water; and these tanks are sworn
to have been built in the brig.

3 puncheons containing each 100 gallons of water, equal to 300 gallons of
water. And on deck

1 butt containing 200 gallons of water.

6 puncheons, each containing 100 gallons of water, equal to 600 gallons of
water, making a total of about 3.100 gallons of water. Also in the hold, empty

3 puncheons capable of holding 300 gallons of water, and

15 casks of from 30 to 50 gallons each; Hanson says 20 to 30 gallons, the
libel averring them as capable of holding 400 gallons of water; making 18 casks
capable of holding 700 gallons of water.

On his first visit, therefore, the seizor Loggie found on board vessels holding
water equal to

	3.100 gallons	
and vessels for holding about	700	»
equal to...............	3.800	»

Loggie swears he applied to the Captain for the ship's papers, who referred
him to the Portuguese Consul; but the Captain swears Loggie, *on board,* did not

ask him for the ship's papers, nor he refer him to the Consul, and he adds that Loggie did not show him any authority for searching; indeed, Loggie does not say he produced any.

There may be an apparent, but there is no actual contradiction in this evidence, for Loggie does not swear·where it was, or when specially, he asked for the papers, nor does the Captain say Loggie did not *at any time* ask him, but that he did not ask him *on board,* the presumption being that he did ask him elsewhere, and that the Captain then referred him to the Portuguese Consul. This may have been on the 5ᵗʰ, but certainly must have been on or before the 7ᵗʰ, on which day there is no doubt from the evidence that Loggie called on the Consul.

Loggie swears that he saw 3 Kroo boys on board, (proved afterwards to be Grando, Panick, and Yoruba, the 3 alleged slaves) but that he did not speak to them nor they to him. The Captain, however, swears that Loggie did speak to them on this his first visit at 6 o'clock, a.m. It is quite possible that Hanson, who, as Acting Harbour Master, may have seen these boys on his first visit on board when the *Ovarense* entered the port, was the person who spoke to the boys, and whom the Captain mistook for Loggie; or the Captain, having a full recollection of having seen these boys spoken to, was under the impression when he gave his evidence that it was the seizor Loggie who spoke to these 3 Kroo boys. Unfortunately this contradiction was not cleared up or fully maintained by a more close or searching examination, or by questioning Hanson or the policemen who accompanied Loggie or any of the crew on board.

Loggie quitted the *Ovarense* with Hanson at 8 a.m. on that 5ᵗʰ of December, the policemen being left on board with instructions from Loggie, as sworn to by one of them, not to interfere with the work of the ship.

Loggie says that Hanson and himself were alongside the *Cæsar* at about 9 a.m. on the same 5ᵗʰ of December, after leaving the *Ovarense,* when William Grant (the steward's boy of the *Ovarense)* came off to them in a boat with a policeman.

Loggie and Hanson returned to the *Ovarense* on the same 5ᵗʰ of December, at 10 a.m. accompanied by Jim Boy (who had been accused by Moraes and the Captain, and locked up under a warrant from Loggie on Sunday the 3ʳᵈ for theft), by William Grant the steward's boy of the *Ovarense,* and by Black Will, who swears that he came in the *Ovarense* from St. Thomas, other Witnesses of the seizor swearing to the same effect, while the witnesses for the claimants swear that Black Will never came in the *Ovarense* from St. Thomas, but from Cape Palmas only, the Captain having granted him a free passage at the request of Jim Boy.

Loggie on this 2ⁿᵈ visit saw alongside the *Ovarense* and being then taken on board

2 butts containing	400	gallons of water
4 puncheons containing	400	»
equal to...........	800	»
Which, with the previous	3,100	»
made a total of	3,900	»
And empty casks capable of holding...	700	»
in all.............	4,600	»

Forest in the Agua Izé Estate. Private railway for use of the Plantation. Island of S. Thomé

Hanson says he saw 5 large butts on deck, each capable of holding 200 gallons, and 6 alongside in a boat; his statement making the quantity larger.

Loggie swears that he did not receive any information from William Grant, Jim Boy, or Black Will, till after his first visit to the *Ovarense* at 6 a.m., on Tuesday the 5th of December; that it was before his 2nd visit at 10 a.m. on that day, that William Grant told him that the 3 Kroo boys on board were slaves; that Jim Boy and Black Will also told him so; and that Jim Boy further informed him that shackles and irons with padlocks were on board; whereupon he removed Jim Boy from the lock-up, or cell for accused prisoners, and took him on board with him on this 2nd occasion to show where the shackles were hidden; and while on board he sent for a number of labourers; that search was made, and the sand ballast removed and examined, but that no shackles, irons or padlocks were found.

Loggie says he made a 3rd visit to the *Ovarense* at noon on the 5th, and then seized her and brought the 3 Kroo boys on shore, the policemen remaining on board, and that he seized the *Ovarense* on the following grounds: —

1.st For having on board a large quantity of water and an extraordinary number of vessels for holding water, more than necessary for the use of the crew, 14 men all told; no certificate having been produced to him showing that security had been given that the empty casks were for lawful trade.

2.nd For having on board 3 Kroo boys said to be slaves.

3.rd Also more mats than were necessary for the use of the crew.

4.th A large quantity of rice, 70 bags.

The Portuguese Consul swears that, on hearing of the seizure of the *Ovarense* on the 5th of December, he went to the Collector of Customs, and then to the Governor, officially, as Consul; that he did not then know who seized the vessel, but the Governor told him it was Mr. Loggie. That on the 6th he wrote a letter to the Governor and received an answer, that he wrote again on the same day, but received no answer. These letters have not been put in evidence. The Counsel for the claimants says that acting as their Proctor he tendered in evidence the correspondence between the Governor and Consul, particularly as the Governor from whom the authority to seize issued, was absent from the colony, and he had not the opportunity of examining him, but that the Registrar refused to admit the letters, on what ground does not appear, for I see no note made of these letters having been tendered and rejected.

Mr. Loggie says he went to the Portuguese Consul for the papers of the *Ovarense,* who referred him to the Governor saying all the papers were with the Governor. He says he went to the Consul he thinks on the 5th on the 7th and on a subsequent day; but the Consul swears that he did not see Mr. Loggie, nor had he any conversation with him before the 7th.

Mr. Loggie swears that he did not go to the Governor *before* he seized the *Ovarense,* the presumption from this being that he had seen the Governor after he had made the seizure, and this probably would be after the Consul had told him on the 5th according to Loggie, but on the 7th according to the Consul, that the Brig's papers were with the Governor.

These papers were produced in evidence and are:

1. A Royal passport dated Lisbon the 9th of June 1870, with 22 *visés* thereon, showing a trading of the *Ovarense* between the ports of Lisbon and Rio

de Janeiro, Pernambuco, Bahia and the Portuguese Island of St. Thomé, the last *visé* being St. Thomé the 25th of September 1876 for a voyage to the ports of Liberia and Sierra Leone.

2. The Brig's Articles.

3. The «Charter Party» between the Owners and Moraes to take labourers to St. Thomas from the ports of Liberia and Sierra Leone, Moraes the Charterer binding himself to furnish water casks and water, to make a half deck for an additional number of labourers to make up 400, the *Ovarense* being computed to carry, without such additional half deck, 368 persons; also to furnish a person to take charge of these free labourers, and a Doctor and medicine; and to pay monthly to the Owners, as freight, one Conto of réis, equal to £ 222. 4. 6, 20 réis making an English penny.

4. & 5. The licenses to Moraes and the Captain to import free labourers into St. Thomas, already referred to.

6. The letter from the Governor of St. Thomas to the Portuguese Consul here, also already referred to.

It is contended on the part of the Seizor's Counsel that the 3 Kroo-boys found on board, Grando, Panick and Yoruba were received on board as slaves, and were intended to be dealt with as slaves by being taken to the Portuguese Island of St. Thomas and there treated as slaves. He also contends that the *Ovarense* was fitted out and equipped for the slave-trade at the time of seizure.

In support of this he says that it has been proved by the 3 Kroo-boys themselves, Grando, Panick and Yoruba, and by Tor Nah, the Krooman who took them on board at Cape Palmas; that they had expressed to Tor Nah their wish and intention of going to Lagos, one of them, Grando, having been there twice before; that Tor Nah induced them to go on board the *Ovarense;* that while on board they were told to go into the hold to get out cases of gin, and that while there the hatches were closed over them, and that when the hatches were removed and they came out of the hold the *Ovarense* was already under way; that the evidence of these men is supported by Jim Boy, Tom Dollar, Black Will, and William Grant, the steward's boy, one of them swearing that George Cole (to whom Tor Nah had transferred these 3 boys, and who received them for Moraes, and as his agent) said to the Captain «let us fool them into the hold»; while Tor Nah swears that he and his brother George Cole had agreed together to deceive these Kroo-boys and to sell them to the Captain for Moraes and had accordingly sold them, the Captain giving Cole a paper for the money — (paper marked C.)

He further contends that these 3 Kroo-boys were certainly intended to be dealt with as slaves, because not only on account of the way in which they were kidnapped on board, no contracts moreover having been made with them, but also because the persons whom Moraes swears in his affidavit of claim were taken by him to the Portuguese Island of St. Thomas professedly as free immigrants from the various ports, towns and villages along the Liberian Coast were not, at any rate, all of them, free immigrants, that many were slaves and natives of Africa intended to be dealt with as slaves, and that this is proved by the money dealings which passed between Moraes, or his Agents, and the Kroomen, called headmen, who received moneys for these boys, professedly as advances for the boys on their wages, but in reality head money, in other words purchase money, at so-much per

Government House. Island of S. Thomé

head; — by the manner in which they were treated on board, being put into the ship's hold, in one case, the *Formosa,* under open gratings, to prevent them from escaping from the restraint they were under, and from ultimate slavery; — by some being engaged for other ports along the Coast than St. Thomas and then put under restraint in the manner stated and taken to St. Thomas instead; — and by their transfer in the case of the British Steam ship *Formosa* from that ship in the open sea into the *Ovarense* which left the harbour of St. Thomas to meet the *Formosa* outside and away from the harbour, and while in the *Ovarense;* by their being put into the hold, the elder ones being coupled together in chains and landed, so shackled at night under cover of darkness; and lastly, from the fact these immigrants so taken to St. Thomas were there dealt with as slaves.

The seizor's counsel also contends that it has been proved that shackles were on board which were got rid of in the harbour of Freetown, and that these together with the 32 mats found on board, which were only part of 500 proved to have been on board the *Ovarense* when she left Lisbon are strong evidence in themselves, with the water and the number of empty casks found on board, that the *Ovarense* was engaged in the slave-trade, it having been proved that, at any rate, 15 of these empty casks capable of holding 400 gallons of water were on board from St. Thomas to Freetown, and were not in the ship's manifest.

The seizor's counsel also contends that should the judge come to a conclusion on the evidence that it has not been proved that these 3 Kroo-boys were slaves, or that the *Ovarense* was engaged in or fitted out for the slave-trade, and that the vessel must therefore be restored, yet no costs or damages can be given against the seizor,

1st. Because of the 32 mats being more than sufficient for the use of the crew, 14 all told.

2nd. Because of the quantity of water found on board on Loggie's first visit, 3,100 gallons; and of empty vessels 3 puncheons and 15 casks capable of holding, of water 700 gallons, equal to 3,800 gallons. And on his second visit a further quantity of water 800 gallons, making of water and of casks for holding water at least 4,600 gallons, Mr. Hanson making the quantity on the second visit considerably more; no certificate existing of security having been given that the empty casks were for lawful traffic.

3rd. Because there was probable cause of seizure and reasonable grounds for suspicion that the vessel was engaged in the slave-trade. And he cited the case of *The Woodbridge* — Munnings, 1 Haggard's Adm. Reports, p. 63, and *The Winwick* 2 Moore-s P. C. C. p. 19., and

4th. The seizor's proctor contends that no damages can under any circumstances be given against the seizor by reason of the 32 mats and the extra quantity of water, and the extraordinary number of empty water casks found on board at the time of seizure without the necessary certificate, these articles being in the 1st schedule of the Act 36 and 37 Vic. ch. 88, the 4th Section of that Act debarring the claimants from any damages even though the vessel be restored, if any of the particulars mentioned in the schedule be found on board.

The claimants claim the restoration of the vessel with damages and costs on the ground,

1st. That she is an immigrant ship licensed by the proper authorities for that purpose, and is not a merchant vessel, the schedule to the Act applying to merchant vessels only in respect to the articles therein stated.

2nd. That the quantity of water beyond the 2 tanks and 9 casks and the empty casks were all, except those which had contained stores, taken on board in this harbour for the use of immigrants, and that the proper documents for the same would have been obtained at the time of clearing the vessel outwards, the only time it was necessary by law to obtain them.

3rd. That the 32 mats were old mats which had remained in the vessel out of a large number in use in lining the ship's side for protection to coffee, salt, and sugar carried in bags, and were not used or intended to be used by the crew.

4th. That the 3 men on board were not slaves or intended to be dealt with as such, but free immigrants.

5th. That there was no reasonable ground for suspicion, nor any probable cause for seizure, inasmuch as it was in the power of the seizor to to have obtained all the necessary information to satisfy a reasonable mind that the vessel was an immigrant ship, and lawfully so engaged and in no way fitted out for, or engaged in, the slave-trade, nor could be so suspected, and that to a reasonable mind the story given to the seizor about these 3 Kroo-boys being slaves could only have been viewed as a got-up story on vindictive grounds against the master and charterer of the vessel, every other circumstance tending to throw a very strong suspicion against the truth of the story — and he cited the case of *The Richardo Schmidt,* 4 Moore's P. C. C. p. 121. *The Laura,* 3 Moore's P. C. C. p. 181. *The Newport,* 11 Moore's P. C. C. p. 155. *The Barbarossa,* 1 Haggard's Adm. Reports p. 75 (note).

It will be necessary for me in the first place, to state what is my view of the law.

Before the passing of the Act 36 and 37 Vic. ch. 88, the statute 5 Geo. iv. ch. 113 was the law by which we were to be guided in cases of slave-dealing within British waters and jurisdiction, and under that law, and in accordance with decisions pronounced in cases coming under it, the captors were bound to prove, in order to condemn the vessel, not only that she was actually engaged in the slave-trade, or fitted out for the purposes of the slave-trade, but that the owners of the ship were cognizant of the fact or had a guilty knowledge thereof, and that the owners of the cargo on board had also a guilty knowledge of the fact to justify a forfeiture of their goods, but that if there was probable cause for the seizure, that is, if from all the surrounding circumstances there was to a reasonable mind a fair and reasonable suspicion that the vessel was engaged in, or fitted out for, the purposes of the slave-trade, then, although the vessel were restored, no damages could be awarded against the seizor.

In addition to the statute 5 Geo. iv. ch. 113, Acts of Parliament were passed to carry out the various treaties entered into between Great Britain and other Powers for the suppression of the slave-trade, and amongst these, one with the kingdom of Portugal.

In these treaties certain articles are described, which if found on board of, or in the equipment of any vessel visited in pursuance of the treaty, are declared to be *prima facie* evidence that the vessel was actually engaged in the slave-trade, or was fitted out for the purposes of the slave-trade; and by one of the stipulations

Landing of H. R. H. The Crown Prince Luiz Filippe. Island of S. Thomé

of the treaties, such as Article X of the treaty with Portugal, it is declared in the following words: —

«If any of the things specified in the preceding Article shall be found in any vessel which is detained under the stipulations of this treaty, or shall be proved to be on board the vessel during the voyage on which the vessel was proceeding when captured, no compensation for losses, damages, or expenses consequent upon the detention of such vessel shall in any case be granted, either to her master, or to her owner, or to any other person interested in her equipment or lading, even though the Mixed Commission should not pronounce any sentence of condemnation in consequence of her detention.»

Then came the Act, 36 and 37 Vic. ch. 88, the title of which is «for consolidating with amendments the Acts for carrying into effect treaties for the more effectual suppression of the slave-trade» and for other purposes connected with the slave-trade.

To this Act is attached a schedule of Articles described as equipments which are *prima facie* evidence of a vessel being engaged in the slave-trade. The articles in the schedule are the articles which in the treaties so made are described as *prima facie* evidence of a vessel being engaged in the slave-trade with, in some cases, perhaps, slight variations.

Under section 24 of this Act of 1873 the unrepealed portions of the statute 5 Geo. iv. ch. 113, are incorporated with the Act, namely from sections 2 to 11 inclusive, part of section 12, and section 39, 40, and 47.

Section 17 of the Act of 1873 gives to seizors the like benefit of protection as is afforded to seizors under any Act relating to Her Majesty's Customs in the United kingdom.

Section 3 gives to certain persons therein mentioned power to visit, seize, and detain vessels which «on reasonable grounds are suspected of being engaged, or fitted out for the slave-trade».

The Proctor of the seizor contended, and in his reply particularly, that section 4 of the Act of 1873 is a consolidation of articles 9 and 10 set out in the treaty with Portugal, and in other treaties, and that it is intended to carry out the 10th article of the treaty in the very terms of that article, and that if any one of the particulars mentioned in the schedule be found on board, or in the equipment of the vessel, at the time of seizure, no damages can be awarded to the claimants against the seizor, in any case, or under any circumstances, and he urged that this is the view taken by judges in cases coming under the treaties and the Acts by which they were enforced, and he referred to the opinion of Lord Westbury on this point in his judgment in the case of the *Richardo Schmidt* cited by the claimant's counsel and reported in 4 Moore's P.C.C. p. 121 ; and he contended that the 32 mats found on board, and the quantity of water, more than sufficient for the use of the crew, and the empty water casks not in the manifest, and for which no certificate was produced that security had been given that they were for lawful traffic, effectually debarred the claimants from damages if the vessel were restored.

On the argument I expressed my opinion that the decision did not go that length; that though some of such articles should be found on board or in the equipment, yet the surrounding circumstances and every other matter connected with the vessel might remove, rather than excite suspicion, and satisfy any reasonable mind that the vessel was engaged in lawful traffic, and not in the slave-trade, or fitted out or equipped for that trade; and that if in such case the person visiting should detain the vessel for the purpose of condemnation or adjudication simply on the ground that such article or articles were found on board, or in the equipment of the vessel, the vessel would nevertheless be restored with damages against the seizor; and on carefully reading, after the close of the argument in this case, the judgment of Lord Westbury in the case referred to in 4 Moor's P.C.C. I find I am right in the view I took; for at page 137 His Lordship says «there may be great necessity for laying down clear and definite rules as they are laid down in the Statute 5 and 6 Wm. iv. ch. 60, for the purpose of guiding captors at sea; for there the transaction is of necessity a hurried one, admitting of no very minute examination; and the Legislature therefore defines certain things in that Statute which if they «*are not plainly accounted for*» (those words are very explicit) «shall constitute an amount of probabilis causa» (words showing also that probable cause must be shown) "sufficient to exempt the captor from consequences even if the vessel be not condemned." His Lordship is there speaking in reference to a statute for enforcing a slave-trade Treaty; and I take it that what His Lordship says further in the same paragraph would have reference not only to a vessel visited in the harbour, under the Statute 5 Geo. iv. ch. 113, but also to a vessel visited at sea under a slave-trade treaty, making it obligatory on the person visiting not to detain or further detain, but to release the vessel, and not proceed to adjudication, if he is satisfied that the articles are «plainly accounted for» or that the vessel, is (again using His Lordship's expression) «actually and plainly engaged in *bona fide* trade.» And the language of His Lordship in this latter portion of the paragraph, when in speaking of a vessel seized in the harbour under 5 Geo. iv. ch. 113, he says, «the obligation on a seizor to justify what he has done is a very strict obligation, and one that cannot be discharged by reference to circumstances which *per se* have not an overpowering weight on the mind when the seizure was made,» applies equally and as forcibly to a vessel seized in a British harbour under the Statue 36 and 37 Vic. ch. 88. If my construction of that statute is correct, it was passed, as the title shows, to consolidate *with amendments* the slave-trade Treaty Acts, and they are, in my view, amended in this respect that the obligation on a seizor to justify what he does, and to exempt him from the consequences of his act is now made more strict, even under the slave-trade treaties, and that the prohibited articles will not *per se,* and on slight suspicion only, be sufficient to justify his forcing on to adjudication a vessel he may have visited or detained; but that he must look into all the circumstances and satisfy himself, as a reasonable being would, whether the grounds of his suspicion have become strengthened, or verified, and that the circumstances confirm him in the belief that the vessel is engaged in or fitted out for the slave-trade, and not for lawful traffic.

I take it that the Act of 1873 must be construed not only with the unrepealed portions of the statute 5 Geo. iv. ch. 113, but with its various sections taken together; and sections 3, 4, 5, and 17, are those which are specially to guide me in coming to a right conclusion.

In the first place, under section 3 there must be reasonable grounds of suspicion to render it lawful for any person duly authorized by the Statute «to visit and seize and detain».

Children of labourers at play, Boa Entrada Plantation. Island of S. Thomé

Under the 4[th]Section, if the vessel detained in pursuance of the Act be proved to be «fitted out for the purposes of, or engaged in the slave-trade, she would under Section 5 be condemned and the goods on board also; but, according to the decisions pronounced in slave-trade cases, only if the owners of the vessel and of the goods are respectively proved to have had a guilty knowledge that the vessel was so fitted out or engaged, this Act and the Statute 5 Geo. iv. ch. 113, being read and construed together; but if there was «probable cause» for the seizure the seizor would have the benefit of Section 17 of the Act, and no damages would be awarded against him under Section 5.

If, however, there were no reasonable grounds of suspicion or probable cause for seizure, or the seizure was made by a person not duly authorized, the restoration would be with damages, *notwithstanding that one or more of the particulars or equipments mentioned in the Schedule were on board at the time of seizure.*

If, however, under Section 4, any of the particulars mentioned in the Schedule are found in the equipment or on board of a vessel visited, seized and detained in pursuance of the Act, it would then be necessary on behalf of the claimants *to prove* that the vessel was *not equipped for, or engaged in,* the slave-trade to entitle them on restoration of the vessel to damages, even though the seizor should not attempt or proceed to show «probable cause».

It may, however, be fairly contended that from the words «in pursuance of this Act» contained in the 4th Section, it must be *first shown* on the part of the seizor that he was *duly authorized* by the Act to visit, seize, and detain, and also that there were *reasonable grounds of suspicion.*

I apprehend that, if he was not a person *duly authorized* by the Acts under letter A or B in the 3rd Section, the seizure would be wholly illegal, and the vessel would thereupon be restored with damages and costs against him.

It might also be contended that it would *not* be «lawful» under Section 3 (letter A) «to visit, seize, or detain» a vessel in *British jurisdiction* which is *not a British vessel* «on reasonable grounds of suspicion» only, but that she must actually be *engaged in the slave-trade,* otherwise the words (under letter A) «engaged in the slave-trade» would be redundant and useless; that these words, being there, must have been introduced for some purpose; for if not, and if «reasonable grounds of suspicion» alone would be sufficent to render it «lawful», the wording would have been equally efficient without the words «engaged in the slave-trade; and that accordingly if a *foreign vessel* within British jurisdiction (as in this case of the *Ovarense*) is visited, seized, and detained on «reasonable grounds of suspicion», but it is not shown to be «engaged in the slave-trade», or is proved to be «not engaged in the slave-trade», she must necessarily be restored under Section 5, and restored with costs and damages, even if, under Section 4, any of the particulars mentioned in the 1st Schedule be found on board; unless, indeed, under Section 17, the seizor, if he proves probable or justifiable cause, is necessarily freed from costs and damages notwithstanding the *unlawfulness* of the seizure, arising from the vessel not having been proved to be *engaged in the slave-trade*. In the *proviso* in Section 5, the same words are used «and which has not been *engaged* within British jurisdiction *in the slave-trade*».

Under Section 3 it would also seem that the detention of a person on board of any suspected vessel must be for the *purpose of the slave-trade.*

A question might therefore arise whether canoes, coming from any of the neighbouring places or traversing British waters with canoe-men and attendants who are simply *domesticated slaves* can be *lawfully* seized and brought to adjudication unless there are reasonable grounds for believing that they are «slaves *for the purpose of the slave-trade*;» and that if this purpose be not proved, a canoe so seized would be restored with damages against the seizor, unless he could show justifiable or probable grounds of seizure.

It this were not so the trade with the natives adjoining the British Settlements might possibly be greatly impeded, and this provision and expression «for the purpose of the slave-trade» may have been advisedly introduced by the Legislature. Of course any of these domesticated slaves could on entering British territory readily claim their freedom, and they could not in such case be restored to their owners.

I now have to consider and determine

1st. Was Mr. Loggie duly authorized to visit, seize and detain?

2nd. Had he reasonable grounds for suspicion?

3rd. Were any of the particulars mentioned in the Schedule found on board or in the equipment?

4th. Was the vessel fitted out for or engaged in the slave-trade?

5th. If not so fitted out for, or engaged in the slave-trade, was there probable cause for seizure and for proceeding to adjudication?

6th. If so engaged or fitted out, had the owners a guilty knowledge thereof to justify condemnation of the vessel and of the goods; and had the charterer a guilty knowledge also to deprive him of the goods belonging to him?

That Mr. Loggie was duly authorized no question has been raised.

Assuming that the *Ovarense* was engaged in or fitted out for the slave-trade, there is no evidence adduced to show a guilty knowledge on the part of the owners, and therefore the vessel on that ground would necessarily be restored.

Having disposed of the 1st and 6th questions, the 2nd, 3rd, 4th and 5th, rest upon the evidence adduced on both sides, and upon all the circumstances bearing on the case.

On a careful perusal and close examination of the evidence I find inconsistences and contradictions in the evidence of the witnesses on each side, some reconcilable, others difficult to reconcile, upon matters material as well as immaterial; that not only do the witnesses on one side contradict the witnesses on the other on matters material as well as immaterial, but also where there could not be a possibility of doubt or question as to the actual fact, satisfying me therefore that gross perjury exists on one side or the other; I allude more particularly to the evidence given as to the meeting at sea beyond, or outside the harbour of St. Thomas, of the two vessels the *Ovarense* and the British steam ship *Formosa,* and the transfer of the Kroomen some 215 from the *Formosa* to the *Ovarense* and to the evidence given whether the Krooman Black Will was, or was not, on board of the *Formosa,* and afterwards on board of the *Ovarense* on her passage from St. Thomas to Freetown harbour.

I am therefore constrained to look at the probabilities and improbabilities and to ask myself:

1st. If the *charterer* of the *Ovarense* and his *agents* and *servants* on board of the two vessels, the *Formosa* and the *Ovarense,* and the captain and crew of the

Manager's house. Porto Real Plantation (East). Island of Principe

On the left, dwellings for labourers

Ovarense have a motive and an interest in denying the meeting of the two vessels, and the transfer of the Kroomen from the one to the other, and that Black Will was on board the *Formosa,* what motive or interest can the men of the *Formosa,* who gave evidence, the mate Baker the quarter-master Reid, and the steward Lardner an African, have? They derived no benefit from the transactions of Moraes, at any rate no attempt has been made to show this; they belonged to the *Formosa,* and were in the service of the Glasgow Steam Ship Company ; could that company have been engaged with Moraes, or have knowingly been assisting him in the nefarious traffic of kidnapping Kroomen along the coast, and dealing with them as slaves? Is it likely, and could it have been possible that for the ordinary passage money of these Kroomen as deck passengers, some £ 2 10 s. each, the owners would risk the loss of their vessel worth thousands of pounds? and would their servants on board perjure themselves for their employers, and without any benefit or profit to themselves, and no attempt has been made to show any compensating advantage to the owners of the *Formosa* or their servants; and moreover, would these persons also run the risk of the heavy penalities and punishments which would follow detection? then

2nd. What could have been the motive or the interest of the witnesses of the seizor, and what could have influenced them to swear as they have sworn in respect to the *Formosa* and the *Ovarense,* and that Black Will was on board, if he was not, namely, the witnesses Jim Boy, William Grant, and Black Will himself. Jim Boy, we find, was accused by the captain and charged and locked up by Moraes for theft, and William Grant swears he was the servant of Moraes the charterer for a considerable time, and had to quit his service because he did not pay him his wages; and Black Will swears he was employed by Moraes with Jim Boy, that Moraes promised to give him, an agreement, that he never gave it to him, that he never gave him a penny except 10^s of the sovereign he gave to Jim Boy between them, and that Moraes now owes him £ 9; is this Black Will's motive then? (Moraes denies having employed Black Will or of even knowing him).

And 3rd. If these 3 men were not actuated by any motive or by any vindictive feeling, as the claimants' counsel contends they were, why did they during the 3 days they were in the port of Freetown delay communicating to M^r. Loggie or to the authorities in Freetown that the 3 Kroo-boys on board, Grando, Panick, and Yoruba, were slaves? Why have delayed till after they saw Loggie go on board and make a search on the morning of the fourth day of their arrival and leave policemen on board? Jim Boy knew they were slaves if Grando speaks the truth, for he says Jim Boy told him they would be taken to S^t. Thomas and there made slaves of; and if Grando speaks the truth, and did not wish to go to S^t. Thomas, and was kidnapped to be dealt with as a slave, why did he not on the arrival in this port of the *Ovarense* communicate the fact to the pilot, or to M^r. Hanson, the Harbour Master? to the two white gentlemen who came on board on Saturday evening the 2nd, Julius John Smith and Moraes; for he swears he did not know who Moraes was, why not to M^r. Edwin who went on board on Monday and measured the *Ovarense!* and why not to M^r. Loggie himself when he went on board with Hanson on Tuesday the 5th, searched the vessel and left policemen in charge? and why not after Hanson and Loggie left, why not to the policemen on board, under whose protection and safe-keeping they must have known they would be, for one of them, Grando, had twice before gone to Lagos in the English steamers and knew the protection he would receive from the British authorities in any British settlement? Jim Boy, too, is a Krooman long resident in Sierra Leone, why did he not communicate to the policemen at the Police station either on the Sunday the 3rd, when locked up, or on the Monday, that these 3 Kroo-boys on board, were slaves and that there were shackles en board, and give the account he afterwards gave to Loggie about the meeting of the *Formosa* and the *Ovarense,* the transfer of the Kroo-boys from the *Formosa* to the *Ovarense* and the chaining of the elder ones in couples, and their being landed at night under cover of darkness, shackled?

These are all matters of grave import when considering the question of reasonable grounds of suspicion and probable cause for seizure, and for proceeding to adjudication, coupling them too with the fact that the papers in the hands of the Consul, and afterwards of the Governor, showed that the *Ovarense* was licensed by the Portuguese Authorities as an immigrant vessel to convey free labourers from the ports and places along the coast of Liberia, where slavery does not exist, to the island of St. Thomas, where slavery had been abolished in 1875, and that she had cleared out from St. Thomas expressly for the Port of Freetown to have a half deck built, and to take in water for the immigrants, and which she was actually doing the day previous to and at the time of seizure.

And I ask myself the further question, Is it reasonable to suppose and is it probable that the captain of a vessel bound to Sierra Leone would kidnap 3 Kroo-boys on board at Cape Palmas for the purpose of being taken to St. Thomas against their will, and there dealt with as slaves, would then bring them on to Sierra Leone to take them back to Cape Palmas and then on to St. Thomas? And while in Sierra Leone would he, and the charterer Moraes, charge with theft and lock up one of their countrymen, Jim Boy, cognizant of the fact of these 3 Kroo-boys being slaves, as he swears, and telling one of them that they would be taken to St. Thomas and there dealt with as slaves, and cognizant of the fact also that his employer who had so incarcerated him had, as he further swore, been kidnapping other Kroomen and dealing with them as slaves? Would such a proceeding be the act of slave-dealers whose actions would be governed by prudence and caution to prevent disclosure of their dealings, or would they quietly bear the loss of the stolen goods which moreover appear not even to have been carried off in the alleged attempt to steal them?

And I would again ask myself the question, If the immigrants taken to St. Thomas are there treated and dealt with as slaves, and if the immigration is a system of slave-dealing, why then transfer these Kroo-boy slaves from one vessel to another outside of St. Thomas? Why land them in the dark, and land them shackled? When once there they cannot escape.

Then again I would ask, If slavery exists at St. Thomas, if the immigrants taken there from April 1875 to the time of the departure of the *Ovarense* from St. Thomas in September 1876 are treated and dealt with as slaves, how is it that the fact has not become known before? What has the British Consul in that quarter been doing? And the other British Authorities, and the captains of cruisers in that locality, have they been idle? And these very Kroomen who have been relating to us these slavery proceedings at St. Thomas, how is it that *they* have been allowed to quit the island? If slavery was carried on there, as they swear, would

Shed and trays for drying cocoa, Porto Real Plantation (East). Island of Principe

On the right, dwellings for labourers

they have been permitted to leave at the risk of their disclosing these slavery doings?

Taking, therefore, all these matters into consideration and weighing all these questions, to what conclusion would a reasonable mind arrive? Would he think the story a probable one which is related by these Kroomen, and by the boy William Grant, and the Kroomen Tor Nah, who swears he holds the charterer Moraes responsible for the killing of his wife at St. Thomas? Would he believe in the truth of it?

Then as to the water, the empty water casks, and the 32 mats, would he come to the conclusion that they were on board for the purpose of the slave-trade, or for the use of immigrants which the vessel was licensed by the Portuguese Governor to carry? Would he, as a reasonable being, say or consider that the Portuguese Government, in treaty with Great Britain for the suppression of the slave-trade, was, or that its Governor at St. Thomas was, conniving at and encouraging that trade, and granting licenses professedly for the immigration of free labourers, but, as the seizor contends, only as a blind for slave-dealing?

Weighing all these matters and answering all these questions, I can, as a judge, come to no other conclusion — the witnesses on the one side positively contradicting the witnesses on the other, and the ship's papers in the hands of the Portuguese Consul, and then of the Governor showing that the *Ovarense* was an immigrant vessel — than that the story of the Kroomen witnesses of the seizor is a made up story, is an unreasonable and improbable one, and has no foundation in truth; and that there were no reasonable grounds for suspecting that the *Ovarense* was either engaged in, or fitted out, or equipped for the purposes of the slave-trade, either at the time of her seizure in the harbour of Freetown, or since her departure from St. Thomas for this port, and no probable cause for seizing her, or for bringing her to adjudication, and that no reasonable mind could think otherwise.

What course then, it may be asked, should Mr. Loggie, or any other reasonable being, when informed that the vessel was taking in too much water, have adopted in order to satisfy himself that there were reasonable grounds of suspicion against the *Ovarense?*

It must be borne in mind that Mr. Loggie is Inspector General of Police, and has been so for a number of years, that he is a Justice of the Peace, and has on several occasions acted as Police Magistrate.

There being a Slave-Trade Treaty between Great Britain and Portugal, and a Consul of that State in Freetown, it appears to me that, before acting on the suspicion that was aroused by the information given on Sunday the 3rd of December in respect to water being taken on board in too great a quantity, the seizor Loggie should, on Monday the 4th, when he did nothing, have gone to Governor Kortright, from whom he received his authority to search and seize, and should have made known to him the information he had received in reference to the water. The Governor who had twice on previous days, the 30th November and the 3rd December, officially been seen by the Portuguese Consul in reference to the *Ovarense,* might probably have been enabled then to have informed Mr. Loggie that the *Ovarense* by her papers was an immigrant vessel, that she was licensed as such, that her papers were stated by the Governor of St. Thomas to be in order, and that she had come to Sierra Leone to take in water, and to have a small deck built for an additional number of immigrants to make up 400; at any rate this information could have readily been obtained before seizure by the help of the Governor if Loggie did not wish to arouse suspicion of his intentions by himself applying to the Portuguese Consul.

Mr. Loggie could also have ascertained from the Collector of Customs, on Monday the 4th, what the manifest of the *Ovarense* contained, and might also have asked him if he had given the captain a permit to take in water, and in what quantity, and for what purpose; and had he gone prudently to work in procuring proper and reliable information, vigilantly watching the actions of the master and the crew while seeking for every procurable information, he probably never would have had the information given to him about the shackles on board, and the 3 slaves, which it would have been madness in the captain to bring here, if slaves, or kidnapped on board at Cape Palmas to be made slaves of, enabling them in such case to make known their condition, they having countrymen innumerable in this city.

But his going on board and searching the brig at 7 a. m., on Tuesday the 5th, set Jim Boy, the Krooman charged with theft on Sunday the 3rd by Moraes and locked up, and his countryman Black Will, and William Grant the steward's boy (with a grudge against his former master, Moraes) to make up and enhance the story about natives of Africa being engaged by Moraes for various places along the coast, taken on board English mail steamers, kept in the hold of these vessels and conveyed direct to St. Thomas and there treated as slaves; and about the 3 Kroo-boys being entrapped on board the *Ovarense* at Cape Palmas, sold to the captain and cajoled into the vessel's hold, and there kept until the brig had left Cape Palmas; and also of natives of Africa taken on board the British steam-ship *Formosa*, kept in the hold with gratings over the hatches, taken to St. Thomas, and at sea transferred from the *Formosa* to the *Ovarense*, and when on board the *Ovarense*, chained in couples and carried on to St. Thomas and landed there at night under cover of darkness, shackled; all which has been contradicted by a number of witnesses, some of more credit from having no interest or motive, and in my view of the evidence — all the circumstances in the case taken into consideration — disproved and wholly untrue.

But Loggie the seizor having gone on board with Hanson the Harbour Master on Tuesday the 5th at 6 a. m. on suspicion from information about the water that the vessel was engaged in the slave-trade, and seeing, as he swears, 3 Kroo-boys, he could have ascertained from his companion Hanson if the captain had brought and reported any passengers; and he then could have ascertained from these 3 Kroo-boys, each apart, how he came on board, where he was going to, and for what purpose; and he might then have ascertained the truth as to these 3 Kroo-boys; but having omitted making this proper and judicious inquiry, he might yet, when he received information from William Grant just before his second visit to the *Ovarense* at 10 a. m. on the same 5th of December that the 3 Kroo-boys *were slaves,* immediately with Hanson have taken each of these Kroo-boys apart and carefully examined them to ascertain if they were slaves, or were being treated as such, as I have stated should *at the first* have been inquired into; but this was not done till afterwards when all these men had had the opportunity of meeting and making up together their story.

Having come to the conclusion that there was no reasonable grounds of sus-

A cocoa plant with fruit, in the Gue-Gue Plantation. Island of S. Thomé

picion, or probable cause for seizure or for proceeding to adjudication of the vessel, it is hardly necessary that I should express any opinion whether the quantity of water and the number of empty casks found on board, and the 32 mats all mentioned in the Schedule of the Act of 1873 as *prima facie* evidence of a vessel being engaged in the slave-trade, would apply to a vessel not strictly at the time a merchant vessel, but duly licensed as an immigrant or passenger ship; nor is it necessary for me to determine whether, as such immigrant vessel carrying a license as such, it is necessary that security should be given that the empty casks are for lawful trade, and that a certificate should be produced that such security has been given; I hardly think, however, that it would be deemed necessary that the captain of even a merchant vessel seen to be taking in water and casks on board in the harbour would be required to produce such certificate before he had completed taking in his necessary supply, nor until he was about passing his entry outwards after lading his vessel; nor do I think under the circumstances would the taking of the water and casks on board be a ground of suspicion against the vessel, or being found on board would *per se* render her liable to be visited or detained.

With regard to the 32 mats found on board and admitted to have been the remainder of 500 on board on a former voyage to Lisbon, and that they were not used by the crew or intended for the use of the crew, would it be necessary to enter them in the manifest of an immigrant or passenger ship conveying immigrants on the coast of Africa, such description of bedding being regularly used by African labourers, and not being entered on the manifest, would such mats be deemed *per se* a good ground of suspicion against the vessel, rendering her liable to seizure, mats being one of the particulars mentioned in the Schedule of the slave-trade Act of 1873? According to the view which I have taken of that Act and of the decisions pronounced even in reference to the Statutes enforcing the Treaties for the suppression of the slave-trade, I do not for the reasons I have already expressed on that point think they would; but even if they did, I think that the seizor swearing that 32 mats were more than sufficient for the use of a crew of 12 sailors, such a sworn statement would not be deemed sufficient evidence or proof that they were actually more than sufficient, no evidence having been given of their size, or as to whether one, two, or more would be required by each sailor; nor any evidence having been given by any other or competent witnesses, such as captains of vessels, that they were more than sufficient.

I may, perhaps, properly here observe that the evidence being taken by the Registrar, and not by, or before the judge, the judge in drawing his conclusions as to the truthfulness of the respective witnesses has laboured under very great disadvantages; he has not had the opportunity of searching into the countenance of each witness while under examination, or of observing his deportment, and noting down the manner in which he has answered questions, and how far he has shown a leaning towards either of the parties.

The Judges of Appeal, should the case go before them, will labour under the same disadvantage and difficulty, and therefore I think it unnecessary to contrast the evidence of the numerous witnesses in the case, or to comment on their various statements. In doing so I might prevent a more careful and searching examination of that evidence by the Judges of Appeal, who might be weighed by my comments, conceiving that they were made with a better knowledge of local circumstances and of the character of the witnesses, particularly of those of this colony and of the Kroo country. I consider that it will conduce more to the ends of justice that I should avoid a contrast of, and comment upon, the evidence.

I may, perhaps, with reason remark that had the practice in the Vice Admiralty Court been similar to the practice in other Courts of Law in this and other colonies, which requires that the judge should in trying every case have the evidence taken before him, I might at an early stage of the evidence, and indeed would — had occasion arisen for so doing — have expressed my view of the law as I take it to be under the existing slave-trade Acts, particularly as I believe that this is the first case adjudicated under the Act of 1873. That view would then have been well considered by counsel on both sides, and perhaps argued before the judge at a very early stage of the examination. I might also have asked, or thrown out for the consideration of the seizor's proctor, if he was prepared with evidence of guilty knowledge of the slave-dealing on the part of the owners, for otherwise the vessel would necessarily be restored; and with the expression of that opinion the vessel might very early have been restored, and the seizor relieved of the heavy damages he has incurred if my judgment be affirmed. The evidence might also have been considerably shortened if taken before the judge. Before the Registrar it is extended to very close upon 5 months, and the judge did not receive it from him till six weeks after.

It is not likely, however, that a judge who is paid by fees only will be induced to relieve the Registrar as examining officer, and to sit for days together, and in some cases, perhaps weeks, (this before the Registrar has lasted nearly five months) examining witnesses without remuneration, the Registrar receiving the fees allowed for such examination; as it is the Court was held for hearing argument in this case 17 days, the judge being unpaid for those days, but receiving £2 for his interlocutory decree.

There is no doubt, as the counsel on both sides have urged, that the practice of taking the examination of witnesses before the Registrar is not conducive to the ends of justice. I speak more particularly in reference to the colonies where the Masters of the Supreme Court who become therefore the Registrars in the Vice Admiralty Court are usually not legal men. In this case the Registrar is an English attorney, but that does not render him fully qualified for the task; there is so little business and practice in the Vice Admiralty Courts in the colonies to keep alive his legal attainments, for he does not, indeed he is not allowed to, practise in the other Courts in the colony.

With these observations I close this case by expressing my opinion that the seizor has failed to support his libel, and that the claimants have established their plea, and that my decree must be according to the prayer in the plea, restoration of the brig *Ovarense,* her tackle and apparel, and the goods and effects on board, and of the 2 surviving Kroo-boys alleged to be slaves, with damages and expenses against the seizor, to be paid by him to the owners, and also to the charterer of the vessel, and with full costs of suit, and I decree accordingly.

9th November, 1877. (Signed) *Horatio James Huggins*
Judge

I certify that the foregoing is a correct copy of my Judgment in the case of the Portuguese brig *Ovarense,* seized on suspicion of being engaged in the slave-trade.

(Signed) *Horatio James Huggins*

Chief Justice and Judge of the Vice-Admiralty Court.

Conference held in Lisbon on the 28th of November 1907

BETWEEN

Wiliam A. Cadbury, accompanied by Joseph Burtt

ON THE ONE SIDE

and the delegates of the planters of S. Thomé and Principe

ON THE OTHER SIDE

The meeting with William A. Cadbury,
who was accompanied by Joseph Burtt, took place
on the 28ᵗʰ of november 1907 in one of the rooms
of the Colonial Centre, and commenced by the
reading of the two letters written by Cadbury, of
the same date and which are as follows:

Lisbon, 28ᵗʰ November 1907.

To the Proprietors of the Cocoa Plantations of S. Thomé and Principe.

Gentlemen

I thank you for having met here to-day, and for giving me this opportunity to express the opinion of my own firm, and of other firms, makers of cocoa, mentioned in my letter of the 12.ᵗʰ inst.

On the occasion of my first visit to Lisbon in 1903, some of the chief planters of S. Thomé, whom I had the honour of meeting, questioned me as to the truth of certain reports, which I had heard, and repeated in their presence, as to the conditions of native labour, in the cocoa plantations in the Islands of S. Thomé and Principe and as to the processes employed in recruiting this labour in the African Continent. I had then to admit that I had but scant trustworthy proofs of the veracity of such reports, and therefore promptly accepted your proposal to send one of our representatives to make a full investigation. As I could not personally spare the necessary time to learn the Portuguese language, and carry on the investigation myself, I asked M.ʳ Joseph Burtt a personal friend of mine of 20 years standing, but completely unacquainted with the cocoa industry, to undertake this work for me.

His investigations lasted nearly two years. Dr. W. Claude Horton, of Brighton, was the companion of our representative during all his travels through Angola.

In my letter I had already taken the opportunity of thanking you and your agents for all the kindness shown to M.ʳ Burtt. I do so once again and feel most grateful for this magnanimous hospitality, which in England we have accustomed ourselves to connect always with the name of Portugal.

The report of Messrs. Burtt. and Horton has already been handed over to you and therefore it is useless for me to go through it again.

This report, however, establishes the following facts for us:

The great majority of the natives of Angola who are taken to S. Thomé, are brought to the coast and shipped to the Islands against their wish, and therefore when they are induced to engage themselves on the coast, it is owing to force of circumstances, and not by an act of their own free will.

The good laws which establish their being sent back to their homes, are still a dead letter, and therefore the labourers are still deprived of the benefits of these laws, because Cabinda excepted, the natives have never been sent back from S. Thomé to Angola.

In addition to the evidence and essential statistics which we now possess there are, and there will always be until you introduce free labour, innumerable «offenses against the natives» which it is impossible to discover but which is the inevitable result of the actual system.

I desire now to refer to that part of M.ʳ Burtt's report respecting the Islands. It was a great pleasure to us to be able to state that the treatment of the labourers in the Islands is excellent in many plantations. We are greatly interested in the reading of the English publication entitled «The Plantation of Boa Entrada», and we had some copies distributed amongst our friends. We rejoice greatly that at the present moment the English public has the opportunity of studying this good work on the excellent treatment of the labourer on a S. Thomé plantation. But the death rate, even on this model plantation, seeing we are considering an adult population, is terrible, notwithstanding that the good and generous owner is doing his very utmost we believe, to lessen the mortality.

Even admitting that all the other plantations have also a model management it is a fact that the system you employ in the Islands, produces a very high death rate, and the birth rate is so low that every year it is necessary to import thousands of labourers to substitute those who die.

The doctor of one of the best managed plantations affirms that the principal diseases which cause the death of the labourers are anæmia and dysentery, diseases which are peculiar to people who are suffering from mental depression. It is also a fact that the mortality is greater amongst the newly imported natives, and this is exactly what could be expected, seeing that they are taken forcibly from their homes to go and work far away, across the Ocean, without any hope of returning again.

It is not necessary to repeat the fact that, excepting the natives of Cabinda, no others return to Angola.

The steamers which go full of natives to S. Thomé do not bring them back again to their homes. As long as this state of affairs exists, there is no argument which will convince the World that this is free labour.

Much will have to be altered before things become absolutely perfect, and reforms cannot be effected all at once, but two essential guarantees of liberty should be conceded immediately. These two guarantees are: — Free contracts, and repatriation equally free.

That this is not impossible, is proved by the fact that the law determines this, and that the Portuguese province of Mozambique carries it out, to its honour be it said. Although the work in the mines is harder than in the cocoa plantations, there is always an abundance of natives ready to be engaged in Mozambique to go and work for a limited term and at a reasonable wage in the Transvaal mines. The English Colonies of West Indies, make a contract with the Indian Government for the supply of labour, and thousands of coolies, men and women, are taken across two oceans, but after serving five years they return with their families to their homes, bringing with them a fair amount of savings.

Once the system of repatriation is established, the natives that return home, men, women and children will inspire their friends with confidence to go and work in the plantations. The Islands will no longer be regarded as graves, from whence nobody returns. The good food, easy work, and the care taken of them in the plantation of Boa Entrada and others, will serve as subjects for conversation in the villages of the interior.

The labourer on his return will be the best agent in favour of emigration, and there will be no lack of natives offering themselves to go cheerfully and freely, because they know they can return to their friends with some money in their pockets. Arriving without coercion at the plantations, the cases of anæmia and dysentery will diminish, and labourers will enjoy better health and spirits in the hope of return. In many plantations where the treatment is not yet perfect, a better management will have to be established, because the owner will know that the labourers will publish everywhere, whether they have been well or badly treated.

What we ask you is not any new principle of liberty, unknown to the Portuguese. Many years ago, Portugal honourably signed together with England and the chief powers, the Act of Brussels, moved by the firm wish of protecting efficaciously the native population of Africa and to put an end once for all to slavery in her dominions.

We are sure that the abuses which are still practised in the province of Angola, by no means indicate that the Portuguese nation has abandoned this high standard of liberty, they are rather the last vestiges of a bad system, which you all deplore, and which we beleive you will cast out with a strong hand, so that the word slavery can never more be associated with the glorious name of Portugal.

We were always buyers of the S. Thomé cocoa and in the hope of continuing our commercial friendship, we again advise you to carry out the requisite reforms which necessarily must establish the principles of free labour and free repatriation in all the Province of Angola and in the Islands. Unfounded assertions as to our object have been published in the Portuguese newspapers, due no doubt to the lack of information on our part. The idea of commercial rivalry is as absurd and as far from the truth as the idea that the English cocoa manufacturers wish to buy the plantations of S. Thomé. Our capital is necessary to us for our business. There are many other assertions falsifying our ends, all, once more we repeat, owing to mere ignorance of the whole subject, and as they appear to us to be so out of place, we trust you will pardon our putting them on one side.

An abundant production of good cocoa is a boon to manufacturers, and for this reason we can only rejoice at the continuation of the progress of the plantations of S. Thomé.

However much it may cost us to leave off buying your excellent cocoa, and although we know it will cause a loss, that is speaking in the name of our own firm, we must say that our consciences will not permit us to continue buying the raw material for our industry, if we have not the certainty of its being produced for the future by a system of free labour.

We conclude by asking you to take immediate action, and we confidently expect it from the planters who having by their intelligence and energy raised S. Thomé in a generation to a first class colony, will know how to complete their work, collaborating with their Government to eradicate from their plantations these remains of a bad system and establish in the Province of Angola an era of true liberty, worthy of the country which first landed on the African shores, and which to-day is still one of the principal colonial powers of the World.

In the name of the English cocoa manufacturers,

I remain, Gentlemen,
Yours truly,

William A. Cadbury.

Lisbon, November 28ᵗʰ 1907.

To the Proprietors of the Cocoa Plantations of S. Thomé and Principe.

Gentlement.

Although I have not had time to consult my friends in England since I received your reply, some days ago, to our report on the work of the labourers in S. Thomé, I have carefully read and studied it.

The reply treats at some length respecting the rights of a nation on the natives of its colonies.

It appears to me that what you state, suggests the idea that any nation has the right of removing the natives of any of its colonies to others of its dominions, and to keep them there always.

It is my duty to express my strong disapproval of such a principle and I believe, even, the planters of S. Thomé have not the intention of asking their Government to put such a theory in practice in their colonies.

With reference to the visit of M.ʳ Burtt to the Islands, I beg leave to remind you that the object of his visit was clearly explained to the planters resident in Lisbon, and these same had the goodness to give thirteen letters of introduction for the definite purpose of facilitating his investigations in Africa. The following is a specimen of the others:

«Ex.ᵐᵒ Sr. Paulo de Mello Magalhães — S. Thomé — I take the liberty of introducing to you M.ʳ Joseph Burtt, who is going to S. Thomé on a mission to study the manner in which the labourer is treated in that province.

I remain
Yours truly

Conde de Valle Flór.

It is with pleasure that I take note of your assertion that the introduction of measures by your Government to effect a satisfactory system of reforms will be agreeable to you and beneficial to your interests.

I wish to conclude stating once more my belief that the interests of the cocoa manufacturers are identical with those of the planters, and my only wish is that you will assist your Government to establish a system of work on a just and lasting basis, which will help to benefit and insure your financial interests, the welfare of the natives and the honour of Portugal.

I remain, Gentlemen
Yours truly

William A. Cadbury.

Lisbon, December 4th 1907.

To William A. Cadbury Esquire

In the name of your honoured firm, and in that of your colleagues Fry and C.º and Rowntree and C.º, you requested a meeting with us in the presence of M.ʳ Joseph Burtt, for a discussion on matters which interested the firms referred to and the planters of S. Thomé and Principe, and together with your letter you forwarded to us a «Report on the condition of the black labourers employed on the cocoa plantations of S. Thomé and Principe, and the means employed in recruiting them at Angola», written by M.ʳ Joseph Burtt.

You having fixed upon the 28th of November for the meeting, we assembled on that date at middy in one of the rooms of the Centro Colonial of this city, and you having made the excuses of your colleagues for their absence, especially M.ʳ Fry, who would have had much pleasure in being present at the meeting, but was prevented owing to the necessity of a voyage to Australia.

The meeting commenced, by the interpreter M.ʳ Silva reading two letters written in Portuguese, the first being an exposition on the subject mentioned in your letter, and the other a reply to the memoir which was made out in the name of the planters of S. Thomé and Principe as a reply to M.ʳ Burtt's report.

All these documents have now been published.

The three documents presented by you were widely discussed, and all items requiring explanation and replies were explained by you and M.ʳ Burtt, and replied to by us.

We will therefore make a slight resumé of what took place at that meeting, as it is materially impossible for us to translate it at full length, and this will be the best way of replying in writing to your letters and to M.ʳ Burtt's report.

EXTRACTS OF THE MEETING.

Previous Questions.

FIRST.

M.ʳ Cadbury requested this meeting on his own account, and on that of his colleagues Fry & C.º and Rowntree & C.º with the sole intent of cooperating in a friendly manner with the planters of S. Thomé and Principe in the solving of the agricultural problem of that colony, which is of great interest to his industry and general business, and this has been his attitude ever since he occupied himself with the subject, and he has never taken upon himself to provoke the planters, cause them any losses, or interfere in any way in the private concerns of the Portuguese nation.

SECOND.

M.ʳ Cadbury having presented Burtt's report to the English Government and requested its intervention before making it known to the planters who gave him facilities for his enquiries, and the planters having for this reason published their memoir before this meeting, M.ʳ Cadbury explained the powerful motives which caused him to act thus, and between the two parties satisfactory explanations were exchanged on the subject.

Appreciation of the documents presented.

FIRST — S. Thomé and Principe.

The Committee affirmed that the Burtt report, with regard to S. Thomé and Principe, contained omissions and errors of facts and judgment, which are reproduced in resumé by M.ʳ Cadbury in his letter. The Committee after discussing them thoroughly, noted:

a) That in the mention of the month allowed to the female labourers after their confinement, it is necessary to state that they do not lose their salaries;

b) That for the appreciation of the mortality in S. Thomé and Principe, it is necessary to bear in mind their geographical situation under the Equator, and comparisons should not be drawn with Great Britain, but with similarly situated countries, and in our special case with the native country of the labourer, which is unquestionably much more unhealthy, and to prove this, it is only necessary to mention the sleeping sickness which has caused so many victims there; moreover the Transvaal Statistics, which M.ʳ Cadbury presented, prove that the percentage of mortality in that country is approximately the same as that of S. Thomé.

c) That the heavy work of the «derrubada» when carried out by the natives of Angola is given to the strongest labourers, but that generally speaking, in this work only natives of the Island, known as *Angolares* who come of a very strong race, are employed, and execute their task by piece-work and therefore work only when, and how they like;

d) That in the chapter *Salaries,* M.ʳ Burt only speaks about the amount each labourer receives monthly, which is 2/5 of his salary, omitting to mention the remaining 3/5, which are deposited, and which constitute his savings when the contract finishes, and which he will receive later according to law;

e) That corporal punishment is not inflicted as is stated in the report, and M.ʳ Burtt being urged several times to say whether he had seen it inflicted, or anybody provided with the instruments to carry out those punishments, and on what estate he saw the former or the latter, replied that he had not seen anything of the sort in any of the plantations where he had been, but he was convinced that such acts took place owing to information which numerous people had given him, and being urged to name his informers, replied that he did not wish to mention names but that the information had been obtained in S. Thomé or Angola;

f) That the respect the labourers have for the managers of the plantations, does not arise from the fear that the almost unlimited power of the latter produces, as M.ʳ Burtt affirms, but comes from the moral authority which with their good treatment the managers obtain over the people they direct, seeing they have no other means, nor do they require any, to make themselves respected;

g) That flights of labourers which sometimes occur, nearly always among the newly arrived ones, are generally due to quarrels between the men themselves or to superstitious causes;

h) That the natives of Angola who work in the Islands enjoy the privileges which the law allows them, namely wages paid monthly, food three times a day, two sets of clothing each half year, a healthy habitation, free medical attendance, medicine and dietary, passage paid to the Islands and back to their homes if they wish to return when their engagements terminate. They are not subject to military service, do not pay taxes, have the right of leaving the plantations without permission, to complain to the authorities against infringements of their contracts or bad treatment, in the actions which these complaints give rise to, and which are summarily and rapidly disposed of, do not pay costs, have free legal advice given them by the curator general (on whom the law imposes this duty) even in criminal cases in which they may be implicated.

That in addition to this, they enjoy hospitality from the planters in their old age and when physically incapacitated to work, their keep, clothing, habitation, and medical attendance for their children, rewards for good conduct, instruction in agriculture and other trades and callings, they are encouraged to give up idolatry, prepared for their baptism and that of their families, the planters acting as sponsors in these solemn acts of Catholic Christianity, and encouraging them in the suppression of polygamy and to form family ties. They are encouraged to form habits of temperance, until they completely give up the vice of drunkeness.

The laws and regulations in force do not allow, even to the authorities, corporal punishments, or the suppression of food. With all these advantages and privileges and with the fatherly interest and assistance which is given them in their daily lives, these labourers when they finish their contracts, having enjoyed comforts they were far from having in their native lands, prefer to make their homes in the Islands rather than return to Angola, this, and no other, is the reason which causes their non repatriation.

They remain therefore in the Islands by their own voluntary act. The agriculturists have never hindered the repatriation, nor would the authorities allow such a thing, and the former would rather some should return to their homes to encourage, with the news of the good treatment received, the emigration of their countrymen, but it would be illegal and inhuman to oblige them to go away against their own wish, and the planters would not have the power for so much nor ought they to exercise it. Liberty and humanity would go into mourning if such a thing took place.

Mr Cadbury having been asked, if a labourer in receipt of these benefits, and his contract being at an end, wishes to remain in S. Thomé should be forced to return to Angola, replied that to wish such a thing under such circumstances, would be absurd.

i) That Mr Burtt, urged to state if he had heard any labourer express a wish to return to his home, and if he thought that by landing on the mainland the labourer could reach his home with his savings of five years work, answered, to the first question, that he had never heard that wish expressed, and that invited by General Faro, manager of the Agua-Izé estate, to question some labourers of that estate on this subject, he, Mr Burtt refused to do so; to the second question he replied, if any labourer ventured to go into the interior carrying any valuables, he would be robbed before he reached his home.

j) That by what is stated in paragraphs «h» and «i», and by all that has been said on this subject and by the strict exactitude with which the Colonial Authorities carry out the labour laws, it is proved that the natives of Angola who renew their contracts in S. Thomé do not remain there against their wish, and much less are they slaves.

k) That the abatements which the law orders to be taken off the wages of the labourer have been carried out, and the money deposited in the safes of the respective employers, guaranteed by the same privileges and special securities, in benefit of the labourers, that serve as a guarantee to the State in the collection of taxes and other national outstandings, but the employers solicited from the Government, the transference of these amounts to the State coffers, the Minister of the Colonies having given the necessary instructions for these transferences, they ought to be concluded on the 31st of December this year. It is estimated that the sum of the deposits will approach £ 100:000.

l) That during next year, the first contracts with the labourers from Angola, carried out according to the terms of the law of 31st January 1903 will finish, and that loyally and openly, as always has been done, the planters will allow them to choose freely between returning to their homes or making new contracts in the Islands. In the first case they will receive the amount of the accumulated abatements, which will average about Réis 90$000 per man. In the second case, they will continue to earn the former wages with an increase of 10 % and in addition to this, their first deposit will be returned to them in quarterly instalments, the savings being made up afresh and increased with the abatements of the second contract, which will be larger than the first ones, because they will be taken off earnings increased by 10 %.

SECOND — Angola.

The Committee not possessing local knowledge nor special competence to appreciate in detail that part of M^r. Burtt's report which refers to the province of Angola, abstained from discussing it, but nevertheless they wish to call attention to a capital point connected with it.

The report as to the ill treatment of the natives and attacks against their liberty which M^r. Burtt relates to us, take place, according to his description, in regions where no permanent government or police authority exists.

Without entering into the merits of these assertions, the Committee think it would not be strange if among a savage population left to its own instincts certain abuses and crimes against liberty should be committed; in any case the remedy would be, the effective occupation of these territories and police permanently established there. This is what our Government commenced to do, some months ago, and will shortly conclude. Four military expeditions have operated and are still operating in that province to effect its occupation — one in the South, and the other in the west — which have just successfully terminated their campaign, the former occupying the region of the Cuamatas, and the latter, that of the Dembos. The third and fourth columns were at that moment proceeding in like manner in the northern regions, situated between the districts of Loanda and Ambriz, and in the territories of Lunda bordering on the Free Congo State. With these Government proceedings the patrolling of the vast regions of the Angola hinterland will be assured. The committee are informed that the Minister of the Colonies has instructed the chief official of his department to sail by the steamer leaving here on the 7th January prox. for that colony, to regulate the best method of recruiting labourers in that province, and an official fiscalisation in the interior.

THIRD — Mozambique.

With regard to the emigration for Mozambique to the Transvaal, M^r. Burtt's remarks are ultra-optimistic. The labourers offer their services enthusiastically, he says, and return to their homes.

The committee was pleased to learn that things were on such a satisfactory footing there, but it is their duty to add, that they are informed that not all the blacks who went from Mozambique to Transvaal returned to their homes, and if some went back with money, others came empty-handed, and not a few returned crippled by accidents in the mines, or owing to excess of work.

The planters of S. Thomé and Principe are also considering the advisibility of resorting to the same methods of engaging labourers under the same conditions as they are hired for the Transvaal, so as to complete the requisite amount they need, and which Angola cannot supply them with. After selecting and re-capitulating as far as we can recollect, the chief points discussed at our meeting, and noting the justice with which the Burtt report speaks as to the good treatment, moderate work, good food, the excellent medical and hospital attendance, and comfort of the dwellings, and passing over all the other subjects of minor importance satisfactorily explained, so as not to make this letter excessively long, we will still refer to two items, one which was discussed, and to which owing to its importance we wish to answer here specially, and another which was not discussed owing to forgetfulness, and as we also consider it very important, we should like it to remain definitely settled.

You stated that you feared the gravest consequences if the principle were put into practice, that a nation can remove workmen from one of its own territories where they are not required, to another where their presence is necessary, mentioned in the memoir of the planters, which you consider to mean perpetual banishment, and fear that it is intended to be applied to the natives of Angola and Mozambique. To this we will reply, that the doctrinal exposition of that principle derived from national sovereignity which remark was made from the beginning, with the restriction *within the rule of legally established labour,* and this in the terms of our agrarian legislation signifies the obligation of repatriation and can either be applied to the economic necessities of a country, or to the security of its institutions, or to the exigencies of its defences, but does not imply however in any way, the idea of demanding its execution in the present emergency, and much less does it force labourers of determined localities to be perpetually banished from their native country.

Capital and corporal punishments, and penal servitude for life, have long been wiped out from Portuguese legislation; in Portugal and her colonies only temporary penalties exist. It would not therefore be the citizens of a country, which even to the greatest criminals reserves the right and holds out the hope of return to their native land, who would take upon themselves to put into force against innocent men penalties which are not even applicable to ordinary criminals.

Your fears therefore are unfounded, and the planters of S. Thomé and Principe in affirming the sovereign right of their country to make laws for its subjects, solving as it thinks best the labour problems of its workmen, did not then, or later, have any intention of asking their Government to enforce that sovereign right.

The other question we desire to settle, is the one which under the heading *«Clandestine Traffic»* appears in M^r. Burtt's report.

We are firmly convinced that the information given to M^r. Burtt is completely erroneous, and that these facts are not exact. We should be greatly obliged, if M^r. Burtt would give us the particulars of the information he obtained, so that on this basis, this Committee may solicit from their Government a rigorous enquiry, and the requisite steps be taken to abolish these abuses, if, contrary to what we believe, the facts alleged should have any foundation.

Mutually congratulating Mr Cadbury and ourselves on the result of our meeting held on November 28th last, and at which wrong and misleading impressions were cleared up, we bring forward the conclusions arrived at:

Conclusions.

I

That the planters are sincerely possessed of the same humane and liberal sentiments as Mr Cadbury, and it is entirely contrary to their intention to place any difficulties in the way of the repatriation of their Angola labourers, who may wish to return to their homes, and they would be glad if some would wish to return and take back to their country a good account of the treatment they received in the Islands.

II

That Mr Cadbury frankly acknowledges the ample proofs of good treatment on the plantations, and admits that on these conditions the labourers be there now of their own free will, and that a large number of them prefer to remain in S. Thomé and enjoy the advantages of regular work and pay, to returning to a precarious existence in Angola.

III

The repatriation fund amounting now to about £ 100,000 will at the request of the planters be transferred to the Ultramarino Bank in S. Thomé, as agents of the State, up to December 31st of the current year, to be administered by the local emigration committee under the surveillance of the Government.

Each repatriated labourer will receive about £ 20 on landing in Angola, those who wish to renew their engagement will receive 10 per cent increase in their wages, and their capital above referred to will be returned to them in quarterly instalments of 6 per cent. A new repatriation fund will then be started for each labourer. The first contract made according to the law of January 1903, will expire during the first half year of 1908.

IV

The planters of S. Thomé and Principe have no intention of asking the Government in future emigrations of labourers from other Portuguese colonies, that the right of repatriation under any circumstances be excluded, a right which is already granted by the existing laws.

V

It is stated that the Colonial Minister intends sending to the Colonies on the 7th of January, the chief official of his department, to remedy any irregularities which may be found to exist in the present system of recruiting.

VI

That the Portuguese Government has taken action and is still proceeding in an energetic and efficacious manner to implant respect for the law, in those regions of the Province of Angola which formerly were not under its control.

VII

That the information obtained by Mr Burtt, regarding S. Thomé and Principe, and which this gentleman believed in all good faith, was not always the exact impression of the truth.

Concluding our exposition, we greet in the person of Mr Cadbury the glorious English nation our old friend and ally.

The Committee appointed by the planters of S. Thomé, assembled together on November 14th 1907.

Alfredo Mendes da Silva.
Henrique José Monteiro de Mendonça.
Joaquim de Ornellas e Mattos.
José Paulo Cancella.
Nicolau Mac. Nicoll.
Francisco Mantero.

January 21st 1908.

Gentlemen

I am in receipt of your favour dated January 14th 1908.

Allow me in the first place to express my regret that you have not received the reply to your original note of November 28th. This was posted from my firm (on whose behalf I have acted in every case) on December 10th, and I now enclose copy. May I add my personal appreciation and acknowledgment of your favour.

On behalf of my firm and their friends, I now acknowledge with satisfaction the evidence of continued interest in the question of repatriation of the S. Thomé labourer, as shown by your kind letter of January 14th, and the copy of the memorandum addressed by you to his Excellency the Minister for Marine and Colonies.

I am, Gentlemen,

Yours faithfully,

(signed) *William A. Cadbury.*

Francisco Mantero, Esq.
Joaquim de Ornellas e Mattos, Esq.
Henrique José Monteiro de Mendonça, Esq.
N. Mc. Nicoll, Esq.
José Paulo Cancella, Esq.
Alfredo Mendes da Silva, Esq.
        Lisbon.

COPY

December 10th 1907.

Messrs The Proprietors of Cocoa Estates of S. Thomé and Principe, per Francisco
   Mantero, Esq. Lisbon.

   Gentlemen

   We thank you for the report of your meeting held on December 4th, and
have read your statement with much interest. We have also received copies of the
Lisbon papers of December 5th giving an account of this meeting, for which also
accept our thanks.
   We thank you for your very kind reception of Mr Willianm A. Cadbury and
Mr Joseph Burtt, who have arrived in England and given us personal account of
their interview.
   We are very thankful to see that substantial measures of reform are now in
hand that we hope will remove the serious difficulties of the past, and assure you
of our best thanks for your share in this action.
   We shall within the next week make a public statement to the Press in England, we hope will do credit to the action that the Colonial Minister and you, as
estate proprietors, have recently taken.

We are, yours faithfully,

(signed) *Cadbury Bros Limited.*

Some of the articles

Published by Lieut-Colonel Wyllie in the English Press

Alleged Slavery in St. Thomé.

---

1 — Hope Terrace,

Edinburgh, September 5th, 1909.

To the Editor of *The Times*.

Sir, — I have only now, on return from St. Thomé and Principe, had access to the file of *The Times* containing the full text of Mr H. W. Nevinson's letter to you of June 4, an inaccurate version of which, telegraphed to the Lisbon Press, has caused some annoyance there as well as at St. Thomé. But inaccuracy is not, I see, confined to the Lisbon Press. Has the case for the St. Thomé planters ever been fairly stated to the British public? When asking this question I do not forget the summary in Mr W. A. Cadbury's Press-note of December 16, 1907. The seven paragraphs into which he condenses the St. Thomé reply to Mr Burtt's indictment of July 4 are a model of what such a summary should be. But a *précis* requires interpretation to be appreciated in all its bearings. Had this been given at the time, many wild assertions since made could never have obtained credence.

Taking Mr Nevinson's letter of June 4, 1909, if the report he refers to means his work entitled «A Modern Slavery», the task of placing his facts, fictions, and conclusions in their true light would require, not a single letter to the Press, but a volume equal to the original. For the present, however, permit me to examine three of his statements to you, viz.: — .

1) That the labour system in Angola and St. Thomé is an atrocious system of slavery, hardly concealed under legal forms.

2) That the *serviçaes* are bought and sold, the planters giving recognized prices for them.

3) That the Portuguese defence (namely, the reluctance of labourers married and with families comfortably settled in St. Thomé to return to barbarism in Angola) is part of the stock-in-trade of all slave-holding communities.

Point (1). Angola *and* St. Thomé? In his zeal for the cause of the black man, I fear Mr Nevinson too often fails to do justice to the white. A reader unfamiliar with the West African coast does not always realize that these two Portuguese colonies, lumped together for the purposes of this accusation, stand widely apart, nine or ten degrees of latitude and from five to ten of longitude intervening, not to mention an absence of land communication, making the distance practically enormous.

They are not even under the same administration. So that it is as reasonable to hold the planters of St. Thomé, as kindly and intelligent a body of men as can well be found, responsible for atrocities committed by savages, black, brown, or white, in the *Hinterland* of Angola or on the boarderland of the Congo Free State as it would be to hold an Oxford-street tradesman answerable, in virtue of business transactions conducted by correspondence, for the personal misdeeds of some customer of anarchist leanings, say, in Barcelona or Madrid.

I am in no way concerned to defend *serviçal* recruitment in Angola, though as to legal forms it is but fair to note that the question is not one of flaws in an admittedly well-drafted piece of Portuguese legislation, so much as of abuses as severely punishable by Portuguese law as by the law of any other civilized nation; abuses, moreover, of an order only too familiar wherever settled Government has not yet established itself. But when I read of steps taken for an extension of the cacau boycott on this pretext to the United States, whither the St. Thomé produce is supposed to have betaken itself now that the British markets are closed to it, I would ask, Are the good people, thus committed to a policy of persecution, aware that Portugal has for some time closed Angola to recruitment? If they are not, I am in a position to assure them that this is so, for I have it direct from the lips of the Portuguese Colonial Minister himself, who assuredly did not communicate it to me as a State secret. M.ʳ Nevinson is surprised and indignant that the planters should regard the boycott as inspired more by a commercial than a humanitarian spirit. But is this so very unnatural, however erroneous it may be, on the part of a body of foreigners unacquainted with the workings of the British temperament, men who have hitherto regarded boycott as a peculiarly un-English weapon — the stock-in-trade of the Calcutta seditionist rather than of the British humanitarian?

Again, has the public mind ever grasped the essential fact that Angola only furnishes a portion of the labour required for the islands; or that the older *roças* now fully planted, have for years been independent of all imported labour, their *moleques* or negros born and bred on the estates providing all the hands they want? M.ʳ Nevinson has visited the islands himself; and even in his time a considerable proportion of the estate labour must have been other than Angolan — Cabo-Verdean, Cabinda, and Moçambique. These classes are being increasingly introduced; and in their case there can be no question that enlistment is voluntary and repatriation regular. I have made a special point of ascertaining this by personal inquiry among the men themselves, not only in the islands, but on board the boats of the Empreza Nacional de Navegação carrying them. Yet the boycott sweeps all into the same net; all *serviçaes* are slaves; all planters are slave-drivers to be exterminated by all possible means. M.ʳ Nevinson himself, whose antipathy to the Portuguese leaps to the eyes from every page of his book, is compelled by the evidence of his senses to admit that the treatment of the blacks on the islands is good; I consider he should have gone a step further and placed the saddle on the right horse once for all. Angola is not St. Thomé, all S. Thomé's labour force is not Angolan.

Gross cruelty has been practised in the African interior. To this fact we have the testimony of the *Voz de Angola,* a courageous and convincing little paper published at Loanda, the substance of whose charges have, I understand, been officially confirmed and the necessary action taken. But not one of St. Thomé's critics, as far as I can discover, has recorded or even recognized the obvious fact that every mutilation, every death on the way down to the coast, be it through violence or neglect, is, putting it on the lowest ground, a fraud on the St. Thomé planter's pocket. It represents so much money uselessly thrown away in travelling expenses, not to speak of the injury to the national good name. The humanitarians who clamour for the ruin of the planter forget that he is as keen as they are (more so, indeed, being a business man injuriously affected) upon the repression of these evils; and that if he has failed it is through no fault of his, the interests of Angola as a colony being not merely distinct from those of St. Thomé, but largely antagonistic to them. His constant complaint is that his own Government will do nothing for him; he has, while conducting his own onerous business, to fight single-handed against fraud in one quarter, misrepresentation in another, and boycott in a third.

Point (2). *Serviçaes* bought and sold. — Just as fair as to say that the Indian coolies for Ceylon or Burma are bought and sold. On the same showing, the humanitarians might equally boycott the Rangoon rice trade; for what is done in that town differs in no essential detail from the St. Thomé system. The practice there is to give a *maistry* (recruiting agent and overseer in one) a cash advance reckoned at from 15 to 20 rupees per head imported, and to send him across to India to collect men. How he gets them is his affair. They come over in their thousands, mostly creatures of the lowest type, and are put through the form of signing-on, the *maistry* himself signing-on at the same time under an act of the Indian Legislature which possesses few of the safeguards of the Portuguese decree. *Maistry* and men are alike kept under *advances* to prevent their absconding, and are sent to work in the rice-fields during the reaping season, returning to the riverside mills during the milling season, their personal liberty being neither, more nor less than that of most factory hands. Of their housing in Rangoon outside the mills, of the malaria of many parts of the paddy-land where they have to work, and of the epidemics (plague and cholera) which scourge them from time to time, the less said the better. Should they abscond, as at times they do, the law provides for their arrest and commitment to gaol till they see the advisability of completing their term of contract work. In Ceylon these provisions extend even to the case of domestic servants; but in pratice they are rarely resorted to except by bad masters. To argue that such a law is unnecessary or wrong in principle, in the case of the coolie at least, is to ignore the vital distinction between East and West, white and black; but my point at present is that we Britons are not in a position to fling stones at the Portuguese in this fashion.

Point (3). Against repatriation. — A very short visit to the islands will convince any impartial inquirer of the *bona fides* of this defence. It is not the planter's fault that the present *serviçal* of the islands cannot possibly be repatriated for want of a record of his original habitat. The Angolan in the native state is an absolute animal — he has neither home nor family — please grasp this fact firmly, for it is essential to the question. His case is that of a monkey taken to a Zoo, with this important difference, that the Zoo may be (generally is) in the most unsuitable of climates for monkey life, whereas the Angolan's new abode is the very reverse. The islands, deadly as they may be for Europeans, are a veritable paradise for the blacks, or would be so could the Angolan but realize his ideal — absolute idleness, plenty of rum, and no care for the morrow. He is malaria-proof, and if it be objected that negro mortality is still high, the answer is a two-fold one; first, that comparison of West African vital statistics with those of any, English city population is manifestly misleading; second, that the truth has not been told as to the causes of this high mortality. Dr. Salgado Motta, a Lisbon physician, personally known I understand to Mr. Nevinson, and who resided in St. Thomé from 1903 to 1906 has placed on record the results of a careful study of the subject — namely, that the mortality on the *roças* among blacks is due to two causes almost exclusively, alcoholism and geophagy. He adds that, were it possible to do away with these two vices on the part of the negro, his mortality would be reduced by 90 per cent.

These things being so, what does the Angolan gain by being sent back to his pristine savagery, assuming it possible to obtain the present address of the tribe to which he once belonged? The first-fruits of an established repatriation will be in all probability the shipment off to the mainland of all sickly Angolans to save the cost of nursing them back into health in the hospitals of the estates.

Have the humanitarians taken all these points into account? If not will they do so now? It is not too late.

I am, Sir, your obedient servant

J. A. Wyllie, F. R. G. S.
Lt.-Col. I. A. (Retd.)

Article published 1ˢᵗ November 1909.

(Re-translated into English by the writer himself)

To the Editor *Birmingham Daily Despatch* — Birmingham.

1, Hope Terrace, Edinburgh, 3o October, 1909.

Slavery on cocoa plantations.

A letter containing statements deserving of attention has appeared under the above heading in your issue of the 23ʳᵈ inst. Let me assure your readers and your correspondent that the latter has been totally misled as to the conditions of labour in the cacao islands (S. Thomé & Principe); a circumstance he himself will doubtless regret, the more so that the cause he has at heart, and which has my entire sympathy, is quite sound enough to dispense with the support of perversions of fact.

To begin with, the alleged Note of the British Government to Portugal is mythical. This cannot be otherwise, bearing in mind the answer given by Sir Edward Grey in Parliament 13ᵗʰ July last. But for that error your correspondent is not responsible. Nor I trust, for the distortions of truth he has accepted and repeats as gospel, namely :

I — That the negro labourers (why employ the question-begging term «slaves»?) are flogged mercilessly by the planters;

II — That those labourers are confined in great compounds, where they are constantly watched by huge and savage dogs;

III — That the planters have become millionaires by battening on the misery of the negro.

I — *The Corporal Punishment Story* is a terrible lie, dating from the publication of a series of fantastic tales by an American Review, re-issued later on in book form under the title «A Modern Slavery». In the islands, where the English language is but little known, the existence of these publications passed unnoticed until Mʳ. Joseph Burtt returned to the charge at the Conference which took place at Lisbon on the 28ᵗʰ November 1907. He was promptly challenged to furnish his proofs of this malpractice or to withdraw the calumny — a very grave one, for as a matter of fact no European nation has succeded in establishing better relations with the negro or with any other coloured race than the Portuguese. According to the minutes of the Conference, which are before me as I write, M^r. Burtt refused either to cite his witnesses or to retract his accusations, though compelled to admit that he had no personal knowledge of a single instance of such punishment having been inflicted on the islands, his information being mere hearsay. Is this altogether just?

II — *The Big Dog Myth* can be traced to the same source. I have myself visited at least a dozen roças (plantations) on the islands, not to mention the numerous *dependencias* of these, and am in a position to defy anyone to produce from any part of the island a dozen dogs larger than a fox-terrier. As to the closing of the compounds at nightfall, that is but the extension to S. Thomé of the mediaeval custom still in force in Lisbon itself, where (as everyone who has lived in a flat in that city knows) the policeman on duty locks up the common door of the stair of every house at a certain hour and keeps the key with him on his beat till the morning. If this is coercion, it is equally so for the European and the native; but it is really a traditional formality rather than anything else.

III — That the law prescribes or permits a man-hunt by the planter for the capture of fugitive labourers is a fable which a reference to the Portuguese Code will at once dispel (vide Regulamento geral da Emigração, art. 113). I have before me not only the Portuguese but also the British Colonial legislation on this point, and can assure your readers that the measures prescribed are to all intents and purposes identical. To those who know the black labourer and his ways, the need for rules is self-evident; to those who do not, I can but suggest a little personal contact with the negro before proceeding to apply theories of liberty which may, or may not fit the case. The whole of this vexed question is in reality due to the confusion of two sets of entirely distinct facts: — the Slave Trade in Central Africa (hinterland of Angola), and the Labour Condition of S. Thomé and Principe. The first of these is a gigantic international abuse, in the suppression of which Portugal is as ready to co-operate as is any other nation, but upon which the most energetic action of the most energetic nation has up to now had not the least effect. The second is not an abuse at all, but on the contrary a beneficent and well-digested enterprise for compensating the imported labourer for whatever sufferings he may have undergone through the existence of the first.

IV — The planters, be they millionaires or not (the community does not possess more than two or three such, and includes many harmless negroes and mulattoes cultivating their own little patches of cacao who will be the first to suffer under this ill-advised crusade), far from battening on the misery of their black neighbours, have done all in their power to secure the comfort and happiness of the latter. Of this I can speak positively from personal study of the conditions of labour on the islands themselves, and should anyone be disposed to doubt my disinterestedness or the accuracy of my observations, I can but ask him to go to the island and see for himself.

One word in conclusion. The slave trade in Central Africa does not exist, as seems to have been assumed throughout all this agitation in order to furnish labour for the cacao plantations of the islands; it exists for the benefit of Turkey via Tripoli, of Morroco, of Persia, of Arabia via the Red Sea Ports, and (according to

Mʳ. Burtt himself) of the French Congo, following the lamentable lead of her Belgian neighbour. And the brutalities incidental thereto are committed, not by Portuguese at all but by Africans upon Africans of their own race, regardless of ties of kinship. To hold the planters on islands thousands of miles away responsible for the misdeeds of those savages (many being cannibals) is as logical as to hold the colonists of Newfoundland who employ Irish labour reponsible for agrarian crime in Tipperary. Be just to the planters; they are doing their best to obtain a labour supply free from all tinge of compulsion, and they have to a very large extent succeeded already. But so long as the atrocities of the Belgian Congo are tolerated, the Slave Trade in Central Africa will continue to flourish. There is where the headquarters of the enemy is to be found, so far as any European Power can be held responsible for an abuse so inveterate.

I am, etc.

J. A. Wyllie, F. R. G. S.

Lieut-Colonel Indian Army (Retired).

EXCERPTA

FROM

Two letters from the emigration agent in Quilemane

ADDRESSED TO

The Company of the Island of Principe and to the Colonial Agricultural Society.

Excerpt from the letter dated February 7th 1910 from the emigration agent in Quilimane addressed to the Board of Directors of the Colonial Agricultural Society.

Twenty-two (22) labourers are sailing by the steamer *Africa* contracted for the estates of the Society which you direct, situated in S. Thomé, 11 labourers being contracted for two years, and the remaining 11 for three years.

Included in that number are a woman and one repatriated labourer, the latter proceeding from the *Santa Margarida* plantation, who arrived here in December last and desired to return thither. When the repatriated arrived in December, your representative in S. Thomé wrote to me with instructions to re-engage those labourers if they should wish to return.

This is the first one to sail and it is natural that the remainder will shortly imitate his example due to the favourable impressions which they brought of their stay in *Santa Margarida*. I hope, therefore, that as soon as they have spent the savings brought with them, they will come to seek new contracts.

As regards the woman, she has her husband there, and he sollicited through the medium of the manager of the *Santa Margarida* plantation that his wife might go there also, to which she agreed to at once gladly. She, therefore, goes to join her husband.

The acting emigration agent

(s.) *Celestino Fernandes Monteiro.*

Excerpt from the letter dated February 7th 1910 from the emigration agent in Quilimane addressed to the Board of Directors of the Company of the Island of Principe.

I confirm my telegram of January 11th ulto, as follows:

«Repatriated with families desire return Agua Izé. May I contract?»

In fact, some days previously, a party of individuals who had returned from Agua Izé called on me requesting to return to S. Thomé to the same plantation where they had already been employed, some of them stating that they wished to be accompanied by their families. I felt I ought not to refuse, as my refusal might force these individuals to seek their livelihood elsewhere, which would be of bad augury for the consolidation of the current of emigration so auspiciously started to our colony, and which deserves all my attention, therefore I sent you the aforesaid telegram, and it was with great pleasure that I received your reply authorizing me to contract them. I sent for the interested parties at once, to give them the good news which was gladly received, nor could it be otherwise, seeing that they had the greatest wish to return to the same house whence they had come, which evidently proves that they are happier there than here. They are in the majority accompanied by relatives, and some of them take their wives. (1) They are all contracted for three years.

The acting emigration agent

(s.) *Celestino Fernandes Monteiro.*

---

(1) The group contracted was composed of 65 labourers of both sexes, some married couples being accompanied by their little children.

INDEX

———

NOTE

One conto of réis is egual to £ 222.4.4 at the rate of Réis 4:500 per £, calculated at par exchange viz: 53 $^1/_3$ d. per 1:000 réis.

Labourers from Mozambique landed at S. Thomé, from the commencement of the emigration July 1908 to 30th January 1910

Dates	Steamers	Proceeding from	Number of labourers	Name of planter
1908				
July 30	Lusitania	Quelimane	83	Companhia Ilha do Principe.
»	»	»	21	Henrique J. M. Mendonça.
August 29	Africa	Mozambique	174	João Baptista de Macedo, Limitada.
September 29	Portugal	»	123	Jeronymo José da Costa.
October 28	Lusitania	Quelimane	54	José Ferreira do Amaral.
»	»	»	16	Companhia Ilha do Principe.
»	»	»	4	Agencia da Empreza Nacional.
»	»	»	2	Henrique José M. de Mendonça.
November 30	Africa	»	20	Sociedade d'Agricultura Colonial.
»	»	Mozambique	20	Lima & Gama.
»	»	»	21	Salvador Levy & C.ª
December 30	Portugal	»	25	Marquis de Valle Flor.
1909				
January 29	Lusitania	Quelimane	157	Ditto.
»	»	»	64	Salvador Levy & C.ª
»	»	»	30	D. Claudina Chamiço.
»	»	»	59	Companhia Ilha do Principe.
March 1	Africa	»	58	Marquis de Valle Flor.
»	»	»	14	Companhia Ilha do Principe.
»	»	»	32	Salvador Levy & C.ª
March 29	Portugal	»	8	D. Claudina Chamiço.
»	»	»	3	Salvador Levy & C.ª
»	»	»	42	Companhia Ilha do Principe.
»	»	»	53	Marquis de Valle Flor.
»	»	Mozambique	109	Ditto.
April 28	Lusitania	Quelimane	1	Ditto.
»	»	»	18	Henrique J. M. Mendonça.
»	»	Mozambique	94	Companhia Ilha do Principe.
May 28	Africa	Quelimane	21	Sociedade d'Agricultura Colonial.
»	»	»	32	Henrique J. M. de Mendonça.
»	»	»	2	D. Claudina Chamiço.
»	»	Mozambique	20	Sociedade Agricola da Rozema.
»	»	»	4	Companhia Ilha do Principe.
»	»	»	5	Marquis de Valle Flor.
»	»	»	15	Lino & Ferreira.
»	»	»	13	Companhia Roça Alliança.
June 29	Portugal	»	166	Various.
July 28	Lusitania	Quelimane	2	Banco Nacional Ultramarino.
»	»	»	18	Nicolau José da Costa.
»	»	»	9	Sociedade Ió Grande.
»	»	»	103	Companhia da Ilha do Principe.
»	»	Mozambique	8	Companhia da Roça Alliança.
August 28	Africa	»	11	Ditto.
»	»	Quelimane	3	Nicolau José da Costa.
»	»	»	22	Januario José da Silva.
»	»	»	32	Sociedade Ió Grande.
»	»	»	9	Lima & Gama.
September 29	Portugal	»	4	Agencia da Empreza Nacional.
»	»	»	38	Marquis de Valle Flor.
»	»	»	25	Henrique J. M. de Mendonça.
»	»	»	8	Januario José da Silva.
»	»	»	41	D. Aurora de Macedo.
»	»	»	24	Companhia Ilha do Principe.
»	»	Mozambique	26	José Ferreira do Amaral.
October 29	Lusitania	Quelimane	26	Marquis de Valle Flor.
»	»	»	8	D. Aurora de Macedo.
November 28	Africa	»	58	Marquis de Valle Flor.
»	»	»	1	Henrique J. M. de Mendonça.
December 28	Portugal	»	58	Marquis Valle Flor.
»	»	»	102	Salvador Levy & C.ª
»	»	»	20	Silvestre Thomé D. da Silva.
»	»	»	26	Raymundo Jungla.
»	»	»	1	D. Aurora de Macedo.
1910				
January 30	Lusitania	»	97	Marquis de Valle Flor.
»	»	»	10	Henrique José Monteiro de Mendonça.
Total......................			2:373	

Labourers repatriated from S. Thomé to the Province of Mozambique

Dates of repatririation	Steamers	Ports of destination	Number of repatriated labourers
1909			
March 14	Lusitania	Mozambique	3
April 13	Africa	»	7
May 13	Portugal	»	1
June 14	Lusitania	»	6
»	»	Quelimane	1
July 14	Africa	»	78
»	»	Mozambique	1
August 14	Portugal	Quelimane	25
September 13	Lusitania	»	4
»	»	Mozambique	156
October 14	Africa	»	115
»	»	Quelimane	2
November 13	Portugal	»	20
»	»	Mozambique	8
December 14	Lusitania	Quelimane	23
Total......................			450

Maritime movement in the port of the Island of Principe during the year 1908.

Quality and name of the ship	Nationality	Tonnage	Months
Steamer Anno Bom	Spanish	80	
» Cazengo	Portuguese	1:922	
» Malange	»	2:404	
» Corisco	Spanish	118	January
» Zaire	Portuguese	2:073	
» Ambaca	»	1:788	
» Anno Bom	Spanish	80	
» Malange	Portuguese	2:404	
» Loanda	»	2:087	February
» Corisco	Spanish	118	
» Ambaca	Portuguese	1:788	
» Cazengo	»	1:922	
» Loanda	»	2:087	
» Corisco	Spanish	118	
» Cabo Verde	Portuguese	1:259,9	March
» Malange	»	2:404	
» Cazengo	»	1:922	
» Corisco	Spanish	118	
» Anno Bom	»	80	
» Ambaca	Portuguese	1:788	
» Cabo Verde	»	1:239	April
» Corisco	Spanish	120	
» Loanda	Portuguese	2:087	
» Malange	»	2:404	
» Anno Bom	Spanish	58	
» Ambaca	Portuguese	1:788	
» Zaire	»	2:073	May
» Cazengo	»	1:922	
» Anno Bom	Spanish	127	
» Loanda	Portuguese	2:087	
» Anno Bom	Spanish	68,10	
» Cabo Verde	Portuguese	1:259	
» Ambaca	»	1:788	
» Anno Bom	Spanish	127	June
» » »	»	68,10	
» Zaire	Portuguese	2:073	
» Malange	»	2:404	
» Anno Bom	Spanish	58	
» Ambaca	Portuguese	1:788	
» Zaire	»	2:073	July
» Cazengo	»	1:922	
» Anno Bom	Spanish	127	
» Loanda	Portuguese	2:087	
» Corisco	Spanish	118	
» Ambaca	Portuguese	1:788	
» Cazengo	»	1:922	
» Dondo	»	2:902	
» Corisco	Spanish	118	August
» Anno Bom	»	68,10	
» Zaire	Portuguese	2:073	
» Loanda	»	2:087	
» Cazengo	»	1:922	
» Malange	»	3:404	
» Corisco	Spanish	118	
» ʌ	»	118	September
» Loanda	Portuguese	2:087	
y Ambaca	»	1:788	
» Corisco	Spanish	118	
» Malange	Portuguese	2:404	
» Zaire	»	2:073	October
» Ambaca	»	1:788	
» Cazengo	»	1:922	
» Corisco	Spanish	180	
» Zaire	Portuguese	2:073	
» Loanda	»	2:087	
» Corisco	Spanish	180	
» Cazengo	Portuguese	2:574	November
» Malange	»	2:404	
» Dondo	»	1:922	
» Corisco	Spanish	180	
» »	»	180	
» Loanda	Portuguese	2:087	
» Ambaca	»	1:788	December
» Corisco	Spanish	118	
» Malange	Portuguese	2:404	
» Zaire	»	2:073	
		105:376,20	

Table of Produce exported from the Island of S. Thomé, and Ports of destination, during the year 1909.

Produce	Ports of destination	Quantities — Kilos	Values — £. s. d.
Methylated spirits	Principe	20	1.12.0
Brandy	Lisbon	73,2	4. 0.0
Palm oil	»	152	3. 0.0
Cocoa	Funchal	1.148:545	62:318. 0.0
	Lisbon	28.058:142,5	1 571:260. 0.0
Cocoa capsules	Principe	150	0. 3 0
	Lisbon	2:560	2 11.0
	Cabinda	4:168	4. 4 0
	Loanda	350	0. 7.0
	Benguella	150	0. 3 0
	Mossamedes	340	0. 7.0
Coffee	Principe	147	4. 9.0
	Lisbon	1.277:362	38:320 0 0
	Cabinda	91	2.15 0
	Loanda	30	0.18 0
	Lobito	657	19.14 0
	Benguella	7:691	230 0.0
	Mossamedes	27:139	814. 0 0
	Port Alexander	927	27.18 0
Wax	Lisbon	46	6. 9 0
Cocoa-nut	Funchal	1:000	1. 0 0
	Lisbon	69:378	69 7 0
	Loanda	100	0. 2 0
Cocoa-nut fruit	Funchal	316:887	2:535 0 0
	Lisbon	337:944	2:703. 0 0
	Quelimane	196	1.11 0
Hides	Lisbon	11:301	226. 0 0
Confectionery	»	378,5	39 18 0
Manioc flour	Loanda	5	0.10 0
Kola	Lisbon	163	1 12 0
Timber	»	771	15. 8 0
	»	—	329 0 0
Cocoa-nut kernels	Loanda	—	7. 4 0
Cocoa-nut fruit kernels	Lisbon	3:489	20.18 0
Indian corn	»	13:275	26 11 0
Goods taken from consumption	»	—	0. 6 0
Medicines	Various	—	1:316. 0 0
Skins	Principe	—	1. 4.0
Sundry products	Lisbon	—	0 12 0
	»	—	516 0 0
Plants	Cabinda	—	3 14 0
	Mozambique	—	2. 0 0
	Inhambane	—	1 8 0
Peruvian bark	Principe	218	59.11 0
	Lisbon	73:819	2:953. 0 0
Soap	Benguella	17,5	0 14 0
	Cabinda	900	19.12 0
Cocoa seeds	Benguella	—	0 12 0
	Lourenço Marques	—	0. 4 0
	Inhambane	—	0. 2 0
Total			£ 1 685:869. 2.0

Administration of the S. Thomé Custom House. 25th January 1910.

The Manager
J. O. Toulson.

Recapitulation of cocoa and coffee exported from the two Islands in the year 1909.

Cocoa from S. Thomé	Kilogr.	29.206:687		
» from Principe	»	2.395:832	31.602:519	
Coffee from S. Thomé	»	1.314:044		
» from Principe	»	1:006	1.315:050	

N. B. — Between these figures and those of table on page 81 there are the following differences: Cocoa, kilos 1.341:519, coffee, kilos 241:880. These differences arise from the fact that the period to which the two statistics refer is not the same (the table on page 81 represents the imports into Lisbon and Funchal from 1st January to 31st December, this table represents the exports from S. Thomé and Principe on the same date), these statistics are organized with the exact weights given by the respective customs, and those of page 81 by the average calculations of 60 kilos per bag of cocoa, and 70 kilos per bag of coffee, and also due to the fact that the 36:535 kilos of coffee which S. Thomé exported to Angola and Principe were not included.

We do not know on what basis the customs of S. Thomé and Principe calculate the value of cocoa, no doubt there is afixed one, which is neither the occasional price, nor the average for the last decade.

Agricultural Companies in S. Thomé and Principe.

Names of the Companies	Names of the Estates	Where Situated	Names of the Directors	Capital Reis	Capital £
Companhia da Ilhã do Principe	Agua Izé / Infante D. Henrique	S. Thomé / Principe	Alfredo Mendes da Silva / Conselheiro Anselmo de Assis e Andrade / Francisco Mantero	3.600:000$000	720.000
Companhia Roça Porto Alegre	Porto Alegre	S. Thomé	Dr. Balthasar Cabral / Henry Burnay & C.°	2.000:000$000	400.000
Sociedade de Agricultura Colonial	Santa Margarida / Porto-Real	S. Thomé / Principe	General Alberto Ferreira da Silva Oliveira / Francisco Mantero / Henrique José Monteiro de Mendonça	1.800:000$000	360.000
Companhia Agricola das Neves	Ponta Figo — Generosa	S. Thomé	José da Costa Santos / Antonio Manoel de Moraes / José Mendes Leite	1.000:000$000	200.000
Empreza Agricola do Principe	Terreiro Velho / Novo Brazil	Principe / S. Thomé	Conselheiro Custodio Miguel de Borja / Dr. Annibal Salter Cid / Conselheiro Francisco Cabral Metello	840:000$000	168.000
Companhia Roça Vista Alegre	Vista Alegre — Florinda	S. Thomé	Conselheiro Custodio Miguel de Borja / Conselheiro Francisco Cabral Metello / Germano Arnaud Furtado	500:000$000	100.000
Companhia Agricola da Ilha de S. Thomé	S. Miguel	S. Thomé	Dr. Domingos Pinto Coelho / Edmond Plantier / Eduardo Ferreira Pinto Basto / Henrique José Monteiro de Mendonça / Henry Burnay & C.°	500:000$000	100.000
Companhia Roça Santa Adelaide	Santa Adelaide	S. Thomé	Augusto Cesar de Oliveira Gomes / Izidoro José de Freitas / José Rodrigues Simões	500:000$000	100.000
Companhia Agricola Praia Grande	Praia Grande	S. Thomé	Elias Azancot / F. M. Swart / Salvador Levy	311:100$000	62.200
Companhia Roça Santo Antonio	Santo Antonio	S. Thomé	Francisco Bacellar / Henry Burnay & C.° / Sousa Lara & C.°	300:000$000	60.000
Companhia Roça Alliança	Alliança	S. Thomé	Conselheiro Antonio Maria de Sousa Horta e Costa / Dr. Antonio Osorio Sarmento de Figueiredo / Dr. Sebastião Maria de Sousa Horta e Costa	300:000$000	60.000
Companhia Roça Ribeira Izé	Ribeira Izé	Principe	Antonio Silva / Luiz Gonçalves Santiago / Marianno Ferreira Marques	100:000$000	60.000
				11.751:100$000	2.350.220

World's production of cocoa (in kilos) during the years 1894 to 1908 inclusive

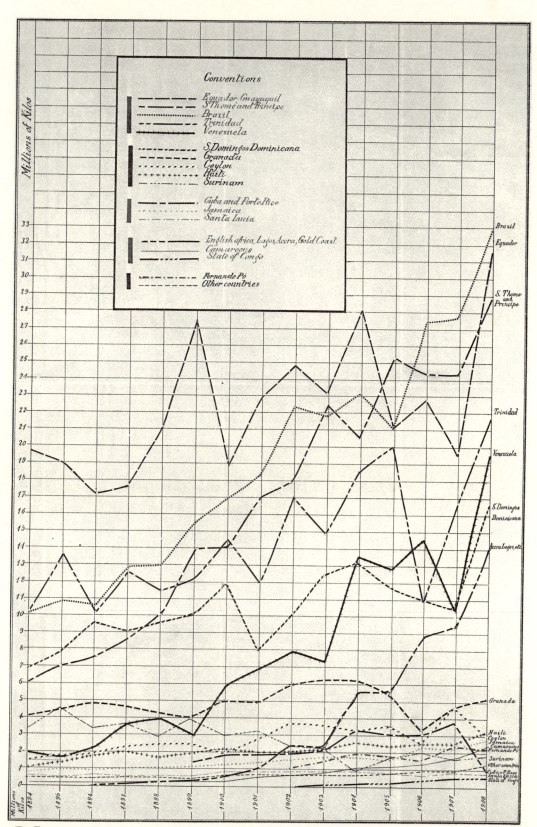

The French and Dutch Colonies are not mentioned, as their production is aproximately the same as that of Jamaica